A Farmer's Daughter

Bluma

A Farmer's Daughter: Bluma

Bluma Bayuk Rappoport Purmell

and

Felice Lewis Rovner

Alliance Heritage Center

2022

2nd Edition published in 2022.

Copyright © 1981 by Bluma Bayuk Rappoport Purmell and Felice Lewis Rovner.

Foreword in this edition Copyright © 2022 by Michele Rappoport.

Additional material Copyright © 2022 by the Alliance Heritage Center at Stockton University.

Frontispiece by Steven Zerby, used with permission.

All rights reserved. No part of this work may be reproduced or transmitted in any form by any means, electronic or mechanical including photocopying and recording or by any information storage or retrieval system without permission in writing from the publisher, except in the case of brief quotations embodied in reviews and certain other non-commercial uses permitted by copyright law.

ISBN: 978-1-947889-12-5

Manufactured in the United States of America by Signature Book Printing, Inc., of Gaithersburg, Maryland.

First published by:
Havenhurst Publishers

This edition published by:
The Alliance Heritage Center at Stockton University
101 Vera King Farris Drive
Galloway, NJ 08205

Dedicated to the memory of my dear parents,
J. Moses Bayuk and Annette G. Bayuk

Table of Contents

Foreword
ix

Preface
xiii

Acknowledgments
xv

In the Beginning
1

My Father—Moses Bayuk
3

My Mother—Annette Goroshofsky
9

Life on the Farm
17

The Seasons
19

Summer
21

Autumn
25

Winter
37

Spring
69

End of the Seasons
95

Looking Back
101

Philadelphia I Am Here
103

The Man in Our Bed
113

Summer Decisions
117

In Hospital
127

Private Duty
165

Early Marriage
189

Business World
199

Miles to Go
247

Full Circle
255

Illustrations

Memory Paintings by Bluma
265

Family Photographs
279

Index
291

Foreword

A Farmer's Daughter: Bluma

*

You're never old unless you want to be.

Bluma Bayuk Rappoport Purmell blew into her life on March 15, 1888, on the heels of the Great White Hurricane, the worst blizzard in American history. The vision I conjure of that blizzard, along with my own vivid memories of my driven, indomitable grandmother, mix in my mind until I am convinced some vestige of that mighty storm continued to swirl in Bluma, powering her through the challenges of a long and generative life.

Bluma was so many things that she could have chosen any one of them as inspiration for the title of her book. She was the daughter of immigrants who fled murderous Russian pogroms in the 1880s, a farm girl who could remember what it was like to break the ice in her wash basin in a house with no central heat, the daughter of a learned man who explored philosophical ideas with Tolstoy while the two played cards, a cigar packer in her half-brothers' factory, an early Red Cross nurse who cared for Civil War veterans attending their 50th reunion, the operator of a nursing home, the wife of a prison doctor, a celebrated artist and author, and a grandmother who loved the crunch of a grilled kosher hot dog at the Jewish deli where she stole a few moments from her busy life to have lunch with me when I was a child.

But Bluma's early years, spent in the Jewish farm colony her father helped to found in Alliance, New Jersey, in 1882, were so foundational that they served as a springboard for everything she would become. They were so memorable and sustaining that of all the Blumas she could identify with, she chose the farm girl to narrate her story.

As a farmer's daughter, Bluma soaked up lessons from every experience growing up on that hardscrabble land in the 1890s. The roots of thrift, resourcefulness and self-discipline that would serve her so well during the Great Depression, when her husband couldn't work and she had to put a child through college, were established much earlier when she toiled alongside her parents and sisters in the fields, picking strawberries and packing them off on the train to be sold in New York. No ripened berry was left unpicked, no precious moment squandered.

The seeds of courage and compassion, two strengths she would need to become a successful nurse, were sown early in Bluma's life, when she was forced to steady her mother during flashbacks of the pogrom in which a mob of Jew-hating peasants murdered her mother's parents and nearly took her mother's life as well.

A child who watched her parents prepare to chop up furniture and toss it in the fire during a three-day blizzard after the coal ran out, only to be saved by neighbors who trudged through the drifts with coal to revive them, surely learned something about the importance of friendship, community, and being a good neighbor. I saw her practice those lessons from the porch of her beach block house in Ventnor, New Jersey, where homes were so close together you could shake your neighbor's hand. I remember sitting with her on stifling summer evenings in the 1950s trying to catch the breath of a breeze while she chatted with those neighbors, listened to their troubles, and tried to support them through hard times.

Bluma died at 109, just three years shy of a new millennium. From 1888 to 1997, she witnessed a multitude of historical milestones—six U.S. wars, horse and buggies replaced by automobiles, women gaining the right to vote, Prohibition, the Great Depression, the Civil Rights Movement, a man on the moon, Women's Liberation, and the dawn of the Internet and social media, where people are still talking about her.

Foreword

I often wonder what she would think of our times, when technology dominates every aspect of our lives. I smile when I remember how she struggled with the simplest things. How she asked her son-in-law to "zero" her writing because she couldn't figure out how a Xerox machine worked. Or how she attempted to put her stories down on tape but gave up because mastering the "play" and "record" features was too much.

Yet Bluma knew how to reach others in ways that had nothing to do with today's ramped-up technology. After her book was published, she made the rounds of bookstores and talk shows to promote it. During one interview on the local PBS affiliate, Bluma sat demurely on set, waiting for her turn to talk. My husband turned to me, "What's that on her lap?" We didn't have to wait long to find out. When the interviewer expressed interest in reading her book, Bluma looked straight into the camera and flipped up the white cardboard she'd been holding upon which she had written the price of her book and a phone number to order it. Bluma had managed to sneak her own little commercial into the show—on ad-free public TV, no less! Who needs a blog, Twitter or Instagram when you've got that kind of gumption?

The world has changed dramatically since *A Farmer's Daughter: Bluma* was first published more than 40 years ago, but the stories in its pages are timeless. Children of immigrants continue to struggle to find their way in a new life that often demands they become the parent, serving as interpreters of the language, the customs, and the law. Women still fight for equal rights, still strive to support their families in a crisis, and still face sexual harassment in the workplace. Men and women still need to reinvent themselves constantly to find new jobs in a rapidly changing economy. Bluma's life—a life that spanned more than a century—can tell us much about how to meet the challenges of our own lives, and isn't that what we all want to know, regardless of our times?

Michele Rappoport
Tucson, 2022

Preface

I am ninety-two years old and possessed of all my faculties. To my surprise, I find that the lively curiosity and restless creative spirit that have always been a part of my make-up are still keen, urging me on to new goals.

Nine years ago, when I turned eighty-three, I decided to become a painter. Detailed scenes were projecting themselves in my mind, windows of the past, waiting to be opened. I have been a farm girl, a registered nurse, the wife of a prison doctor and a world traveler. I have lived through crucial and exciting eras of history. Moreover, I have retained vivid recollections of bygone days.

I thought, "What a gift to leave my family! Scenes of the past—the charming period of the late nineteenth century when I lived on the family farm in southern New Jersey."

Thus, I began to paint. Ideas seemed to tumble over themselves in my mind, anxious to be put on canvas. Soon the walls of my apartment were covered with bright paintings.

My work, classified as "Primitive Art," has won many local prizes. Friends and strangers buy up whatever pictures I can bear to part with. Recently, I was approached by representatives of the Dearborne Museum about including some of my works in their collection.

Last year, I won a prize for my oil "Cranberry Picking in Alliance, New Jersey." A librarian who viewed the painting asked me about my knowledge of Alliance. When I informed him that I am the oldest living survivor of that settlement and that my father was the original founder and leader, he exclaimed, "You know about the history, first hand, of the Alliance experiment! Your father was connected with the Baron de Hirsch Fund activities! You must write down all that you know about the history!"

The librarian touched a spark in my own spirit. Here was another challenge. For the first time, I realized that my detailed recollections were of interest, not only to my own family, but to all who cherish the past. My history is part of the history of the Jewish immigrants; my "roots" are of southern New Jersey; my farm experiences were a unique American way of life now.

And so, I set another goal for myself. In addition to my paintings, I have written this autobiography, with the help of a collaborator, Felice Lewis Rovner, the daughter of my old friend, Mollye Lewis. As I began to dictate my memoirs, each anecdote evoked a new picture in my mind. Whenever possible, I have transferred this memory to my canvas. As a result, my autobiography is a two dimensional work—the written work and the painted scene. Both are faithful to a strong memory. My past is so real that I can touch it. I can hear the voices of my parents, sisters, brothers and friends. The old farmhouse lives and throbs with the daily chores; Mother's good cooking spreads its pungent aroma from the wood burning stove; Father, Moses Bayuk, sits at the kitchen table, writing by the light of the oil lamp. The seasons of my yesterdays are here on parade brushing my heart as they pass in review.

Acknowledgments

To my dear friend, Felice Lewis Rovner, who absorbed my memories and faithfully edited my thoughts.

To my dear nephew, Marc Bayuk Franklin, who made the publication of this book possible in memory of his mother, Anna Fay Bayuk Franklin.

To my nephew, Judge Harry Levin, who owns and lives on the original Alliance farm, and has generously given me access to his collection of memorabilia dating from the day my father settled in Alliance, New Jersey, in 1882.

My thanks to my daughter Jackie and her husband, Herbert Siegel, for their continuous interest and help in every phase of this publication.

In the Beginning

Recorded history reveals that the past is not a rock on which to build a lasting structure. Rooted cultures rise and fall; governments peak and decline. At what point, then, can anyone truly fix the inception of his own life history? In their searching, Jewish children, especially, are perplexed.

They find that their roots extend from the earth's core to their fathers' knapsacks. Eternal scapegoats, we are a nation who carry our past in our pockets. Therefore, our wandering forebears allow us a choice of prefaces. From my father's bundle I choose this beginning.

My Father—Moses Bayuk

MY FATHER, Moses Bayuk, was married for the first time at the age of fourteen. He was born in Bialystok, Russia, in 1849, son of Rabbi Jacob and Chana Bayuk. Often, Jewish parents in Russia married off their children at a very young age. This was done to ensure that the children would marry within their faith. It also served another purpose: married men were not the first to be called up for military service.

Moses had never seen his bride, Minna, a cousin, before their wedding day. Although there was no real love between them, they speedily produced two children, Jacob and Chashaleigha. Because of the eminence of his family, and his own superior intelligence, Moses had been allowed to attend a Russian school. Even after he was married, he continued to study. He became an advocate and a tax collector for the Tsarist government.

In his position as tax collector, Moses was free to travel beyond the Pale, the restricted Jewish area, and to meet and mingle with high-placed government officials and political groups. At a social club, he became acquainted with *War and Peace* author Count Leo Tolstoy. The two men played cards together and found that they had much in common. Both had a strong interest in nature and in political reform. Moses often spoke to the Count about the plight of the Jews. Although Tsar Alexander II, a liberal ruler, was in power, persecution of the Jews had continued during his regime.

After four years of an unhappy marriage, Minna and Moses were divorced. Moses took their son Jacob; Minna kept their daughter Chashaleigha. In 1867, shortly after the divorce, Moses met and married a young woman named Fanya. With Fanya, he had three sons: Sam, Max and Meyer. The Bayuk family lived a happy and prosperous life until the fateful day when Alexander II was killed.

"TSAR ALEXANDER II ASSASSINATED!" These headlines shocked the world in 1881. The murdered ruler's successor, Alexander III, fearful of an imminent rebellion, immediately rounded up suspected revolutionaries for questioning. As a result, a friend of Count Tolstoy was arrested. The subsequent events led to the founding of a small community in southern New Jersey, a town which was destined to play a unique role in the history of American Jewish life.

My father was living in Bialystok at the time of the assassination. Being the Count's friend, Moses had often played cards with Tolstoy and the arrested man. When the suspect's rooms were searched, authorities found I.O.U.'s signed by Tolstoy and Bayuk. The two men were brought into headquarters for questioning. Finally, with the help of influential government friends, Bayuk and the Count were cleared of suspicion.

Meanwhile, Alexander III and his advisors launched a series of restrictions aimed at the Jews, using for an excuse the allegation that a Jewish woman had provided lodgings for the Christian assassins of the slain ruler. Moses soon realized that living in Russia under the new regime would be dangerous for him and his family.

Father joined with Michael Bacall, Sidney Bailey and Moses Herder to form a new group in the "Am Olam," a back-to-nature movement. The purpose of the group was to emigrate to the United States and to found an agricultural colony. The men wanted to live with nature as farmers, doing physical labor in their own fields.

After deciding to emigrate, the men turned to a unique organization for help. The Alliance Israélite Universelle, formed in 1860, was made up of wealthy members of the French-Jewish population. Based in Paris, the Alliance had been set up to help fellow Jews in other countries, wherever they were in need or in danger. Baron de Hirsch, a wealthy German Jew also contributed to the organization. The Alliance was able to set up an office in Russia during the terror-filled period of 1881 and 1882. Tactfully and unobtrusively, they supplied aid to pogrom survivors and to other Jews who wished to leave Russia.

Because of his government position, Moses knew that he would have to steal away secretly. In order to depart officially, one had to go through a series of procedures that were costly, time-consuming and dangerous. An easier method, widely used, was to proceed to the border and to bribe the guards. For five rubles, the guards would smuggle one person across to freedom. With the Alliance providing some of the funds, Moses and his family, his brother Shlomo and family, left for the border in the dead of night. After the guards were bribed, everything seemed to be going smoothly. However, the last person preparing to cross over was seized by Russian soldiers and shot. Shlomo was the victim.

Heartbroken, the families were forced to continue on. Shlomo's wife and children chose to emigrate to Palestine. Moses, his wife Fanya, and their sons Jacob, Sam, Max and Meyer, finally boarded a ship for New York. They landed with the forty-two other families with whom they were destined to live in the farm community.

Bayuk and Elias Stavitsky were chosen by the group to scout the countryside to find a suitable area for their agrarian life. After surveying several possible sites, the two scouts chose a territory in southern New Jersey. Ignorant of soil conditions, the men chose their location principally because it was adjacent to the Bradway Station, a stop in the New Jersey Central Railroad, fifty miles from Philadelphia and about one-hundred miles from New York City. Although the soil proved to be of poor quality, the men had chosen well because the railroad acted as the catalyst to keep their settlement together.

Before the group was ready to move, more tragedy struck the Bayuk family. Fanya became ill with "galloping consumption." Within a few weeks, the valiant wife and mother, weakened by the hardships of her voyage, died and was buried in a potter's field. With heavy hearts, Moses and the boys accompanied their friends on the New Jersey Central train to the Bradway Station to start their new lifestyle.

By authorization of the Secretary of War under House Resolution No. 230, the Army donated enough tents for sheltering the immigrants until more substantial quarters could be erected. In a short time, three large barracks were built to house the group. Each family was assigned to a cubical, eight by fourteen feet. The forty-three families lived together and ate their meals communally. Although living in close quarters is not normally conducive to harmony, the settlement survived its first crucial test. Strangely enough, in their communal living the group developed deeper ties in spite of the lack of privacy. Moreover, they received unexpected support from the old-time residents of the area. Because they were deeply religious Christians familiar with the Old Testament, the natives proved to be sympathetic to the newcomers. The Astles, Ackleys, Deas, Garrisons, Hanthorns, Leach brothers and Parvins provided aid and farm employment to the settlers, teaching them the rudiments of farming.

In the spring of 1882, the Hebrew Emigrant Aid Society in New York created a corporation which purchased 1,150 acres of land from the Leach Brothers of Vineland. One-hundred and fifty acres were reserved for common property: a school, cemetery, synagogues and factories. The remainder was divided into lots of fifteen acres each. After the lots were numbered, forty-three numbers were placed in a hat. The head of each family drew a number from the hat, which thereafter designated his site. The remaining lots were set aside for future immigrants. Each family then signed a mortgage contract with the Alliance Land Trust. The mortgage of $350.00 had to be paid back in ten years. It included $150.00 for a house and a well and $15.00 an acre for the land.

While their homes were being erected, the families continued to live together at the barracks, spending their time clearing the brush and tree stumps from their properties. All the houses were the same, built by the Leach brothers from lumber taken from trees on the land. The homes were only twelve by fourteen, consisting of one room on the ground floor and a garret above. Through the generosity of a group of charitable Jewish organizations based in Philadelphia and New York, each family was supplied with a stove, essential furniture and utensils. They were also given a small allowance each month plus money for tools, seeds and plants.

One of the sponsoring organizations sent a German-Jewish agricultural expert to the area to instruct the neophyte farmers. However, the teacher was not familiar with the special conditions of the stubborn soil he encountered. Except for the helpful advice of their Christian neighbors, the colonists were destined to learn the hard way, through trial and error. Fortunately, their mortgages were arranged so that they had to pay only the interest of 3% during their first four years of farming.

From the beginning, the odds seemed to be against the success of the experiment. The immigrants had arrived without funds. They had little prior knowledge or experience in growing crops. The soil was extremely poor and full of tree stumps which had to be cleared before cultivation could thrive. In addition to the regular hazards of farming—drought, too much rain, weeds—mosquitoes and bugs were present in epidemic proportions. Yet, the pioneers remained. Through the years they cultivated more and more of their land. Hard work and concentrated study helped the group to improve their yield each year until their fruit, berries, grain and vegetables became prized in the New York market. The Bradway Station became the town of Norma, shipping center for their crops.

The two-room Bayuk house served as the focal point of the community. Farmers came to Moses for help and for counseling. Bayuk was the acknowledged leader. Eventually, he was appointed Justice of the Peace, a post which he held for many years. Few of the farmers knew of Bayuk's renown as a philosopher and writer. The community considered him as friend, advisor and fellow toiler. So strong was the bond among the early settlers that the children born of these immigrants considered themselves as close as brothers and sisters. I remember many of my "brothers and sisters," for I was born in the Bayuk farmhouse in Alliance on March 15, 1888. I am Bluma—A Farmer's Daughter.

My Mother—Annette Goroshofsky

IT BEGAN in the middle of the night—the distant rumble of voices, loud laughter, hoarse oaths. Then came the screams, the terrified shrieks—and more laughter. Bluma Goroshofsky was awake instantly.

"Abe, Abe," she whispered, "They're coming! Our child, our child!"

Little Annette was awakened quickly and carried to the loft. Her parents rolled her in the featherbed and admonished her to be silent.

"Listen, my child," Abe begged, "and do as I say. When you hear them down here, no matter what they are doing, you must use their noise to make your escape. Drop out of the back window while they are busy down here—you must! Run across the fields to the tavern. Don't look back. Ask Mrs. Kowalski to hide you." He hugged his little nine-year-old for a second, tears streaming down his ravaged face, "Live, my child, Live! G-d Be With You."

This is the true story of Annette Goroshofsky. Until that horrible night, she lived with her parents, Abraham Isaac and Bluma, in a small two room hut in a village on the road to Odessa, Russia.

The featherbed was a plump soft quilt. It was the most treasured possession of the poor tailor and his redheaded wife Bluma. Their only child, Annette, was born in it in 1853. Abraham and Bluma rejoiced that their child was a female.

Oh, Abraham would have loved to have a son—what Jewish man did not dream of having a male descendant to say Kaddish for him after he was gone! However, in Russia, it was a heartbreak for a Jew to have a son; the Tsarist regime called for mandatory service for all male children. The vast majority of Jewish boys were forced into service at the age of 12, and their period of service was longer than 25 years. Often the boys were spirited away to an unknown location and their parents never heard from them again. No wonder that Jewish families went into mourning when their sons were forced into military service.

Having a female child also held perils for the Jew. The featherbed was not only a symbol of status in the Jewish settlement, but a grim necessity. When the first signs of unruly noises were heard in the village street, the parents hid their daughters in the featherbeds and admonished them to stay still, while the drink-crazed gangs of peasants or Cossaks raided the Jewish villages in the Pale. These "animals" looted, burned, tortured and raped indiscriminately. Jewish maidens were their special lust. These bestial forays known as "pogroms" were tolerated and even encouraged by the Tsarist regime; while the lower class were busy practicing their sadism on the "expendable" Jew, they did not cause trouble elsewhere.

The Goroshofskys had lived a perilous existence at best. Poor beyond description, they eked out the necessities of life by hard, hard work. Abraham's tailoring barely put bread on the table. Only once a week, on the Sabbath, was there a real meal in the house. By barter, traveling to nearby villages, barbering, selling trinkets, doing odd jobs, Abe managed to keep the roof over his family's head.

Bluma, too, worked whenever she could. On the outskirts of the town, a Polish couple, Wasyl and Mary Kowalski, ran a tavern on the road to Odessa. Here Bluma worked, often taking Annette with her to help in the kitchen. Mary loved the beautiful redheaded child and always managed to give her an extra ribbon or a sweetmeat to take home.

Abraham and Bluma could not take pleasure in the growing beauty of their only child. They devised ways of hiding Annette's shiny coppery hair. They smeared charcoal on her face when she ventured outside. She was taught to wear a babushka and to keep her head bent like an old lady when she left the hut. Both the parents believed in the "Evil Eye" and did not want Annette to be unduly admired.

Only when the family sat at the Sabbath table, with the shades drawn, did the parents dare to fill their hearts with the joy of gazing on their graceful gentle daughter, with her alabaster skin and deep blue eyes. Abraham used to whisper to Bluma that the sight of Annette, freshly scrubbed, dressed and beribboned at the table, with the light of the sacred candles caressing her face, was enough beauty to last a man for his lifetime. Annette was nine years old when Abraham's lifetime was brought to a violent end in the bloody pogrom.

Annette had done as she was told on that horrible night. When she heard the door burst open downstairs, and the ear-splitting shrieks that followed, she had run away, sobbing and dazed, through the fields away from the cobbled streets, and up to the back door of the tavern. Mary reached for the child as she stumbled into the kitchen. Then, Wasyl scooped the tiny child into his rough arms and ran up the stairs to a small closet. He thrust the child into the darkened space warning her to stay perfectly still. He bolted the door. The child was paralyzed with fright. Her loving little world had erupted into a bottomless nightmare! From downstairs in the tavern, she soon heard drunken voices, shouting and roaring. She began to tremble uncontrollably.

The ringleader was demanding more vodka, "We didn't finish the job. I want the girl, the redhead."

"Have some more vodka," Mary said, "You've worked hard enough for one night. Here, take my special store!"

The blood smeared group finally settled down to drinking and wild singing, recounting their exploits of the night. Finally, they took off to their own wretched hovels. Only after Wasyl had carefully bolted the doors, did they release the petrified child from her dark prison.

Mary hugged her and cried. "Don't worry child, you'll stay here with me. I'll take care of you. We'll cut off your hair and you will always wear a kerchief. But you must never forget your parents. They were good people. You must live for their sakes."

The next day Wasyl traveled to the burned out hut, retrieving nothing but a small piece of the charred featherbed. He arranged for the remains of Annette's parents to be buried in a Jewish cemetery. Then he returned to the tavern. He silently handed the piece of featherbed to Mary. Crossing herself, she bent her head in prayer. Then she straightened up, called Annette to her and said briskly, "Come Annette, there are potatoes to be peeled. It is almost time for the noon meal."

From that time on, Annette lived and worked at the tavern, always obedient and efficient. She never referred to her parents. No one in Russia ever saw her smile again.

When Annette was sixteen, Mary and Wasyl decided that the girl should marry a Jewish boy. The Jewish matchmaker, knowing there was no dowry, could produce only a stooped, skinny young tailor named Isaac Becker. He was not appealing, but Annette did not have much choice, being an orphan and so very quiet. Annette, ever dutiful, settled down to a loveless union with Isaac. In due time a son, Moishe, was born. Isaac's attitude toward his wife was intolerable. Finally, in spite of her child, Annette found it impossible to continue her miserable existence. She hated Isaac and Russia passionately. When she heard that many Jews were emigrating to America, her desire to leave became an obsession. Isaac eventually agreed to let her go. He divorced her on the condition that the child remain with him. Annette was forced to agree to his terms.

With the help and understanding of her foster parents, Annette was able to leave with a group of Jews who bribed border guards and escaped in March 1882. Through a series of aid, the group finally left port in steerage, landing in Castle Garden.

Annette had few belongings. The charred piece of her parents' featherbed was in her precious bundle. In New York, she was met by friends who arranged a place for her to stay. She found a job at a factory where the wages were low and the hours long.

My Mother

Although her living conditions were cramped, Annette did not complain. For the first time in her life, she was breathing free air. She thought often of her baby, and missed him; yet she knew that he was well taken care of and that she must make a new life for herself. Gradually, the tight feeling that had constricted her heart for so long began to loosen. She joined Jewish organizations, attended the Jewish theater, and met people of her own kind at dances and parties. Many young men eyed this spirited redhead, but she was a divorcee, without dowry or education, and she never smiled.

One day, a friend introduced her to Moses Bayuk, a recent widower, with four sons by two previous marriages. He was bearded, heavy set, older. His penetrating eyes seemed to read her history at a glance.

"Annette," he said at the end of their first evening together, "I am not much for small talk or dancing. I am a man of nature and philosophy."

Annette replied, "I never had any schooling. I'm afraid I don't know much about either subject."

"Good," Moses smiled. "Then you will be able to study all about nature at its source, on my good farm. And, as you learn about nature, you will evolve a philosophy to help you to come to terms with your environment."

"But, I don't understand," Annette said, bewildered. "When would I visit your farm?"

"When we marry," Moses answered. "I'm here in New York for a week. I intend to court you and to convince you to marry me. Then we can return to my country home in Alliance. The country-side is invigorating. The city, with its crowds and smells and noise, can't possibly compare with what real nature has to offer."

Annette was indignant. Who was this presumptuous man? Didn't he realize that she was a city girl? Yet, she felt the pull of his magnetic personality. Somehow, when she was with him, she always felt that the hint of a smile was about to coax her lips into an unaccustomed shape. In spite of her caution, the lonely woman found herself responding to Bayuk's compelling presence. For a week he escorted her each evening. They attended a concert, a dance and walked in the park. Annette enjoyed the displays in the beautiful stores in town. One evening as they strolled on Fifth Avenue, she gazed at the elegant gowns and hats in the windows.

"Oh, look, Moses," she breathed, "Look at the gorgeous bird-of-paradise hat in the corner."

"My dear," Moses said, "Those poor examples cannot compare with the beautiful plumage of the birds that decorate my farm with their colorful presence. At our home you shall see birds of paradise everywhere."

Moses painted wonderful pictures of life on the farm, with birds, trees and flowers. He also mentioned, in passing, his poor motherless sons, boys who needed a woman's firm but gentle hand. Annette considered her possibilities. She was alone in a crowded city, living in one room, working long hours in a factory. This absurd but lovable bear of a man was offering his four cherubic little sons and a warm, gracious farmhouse amid nature's abundance! A husband of education and stature! The lonely orphan was overwhelmed.

At the end of a week, Annette Goroshofsky became the bride of Moses Bayuk. As their friends crowded around them to wish them luck, Annette turned to look at her new husband, who gazed at her with tenderness.

Suddenly, a warm, beautiful smile transformed her face. From that moment on, Moses was completely devoted to the brave woman who had finally washed away her unbearable past and was ready to face the future as his wife.

The newlyweds left immediately by train for the farmhouse at Norma, New Jersey, where Moses had arranged for his horse and wagon to be waiting for them. As the wagon slowly bumped its way farther out into the desolate landscape, Annette became uneasy. Finally, they stopped in front of a two-story, two-room shack.

"This is it," said Moses proudly, as he jumped down to assist his bride from the vehicle.

"This is 'it'?" Annette cried.

"Well," Moses admitted, "the house needs a woman's touch and we do plan to build an addition in the spring. Eventually, of course, we shall build a larger farmhouse as our family expands. Then this building will become the barn. Our new house will be lovely," he assured his ashen wife. "We may eventually have indoor plumbing."

"Indoor plumbing," screeched the hapless city girl. "Then what—I mean how . . ."

"Chamber pots and an outhouse," Moses said matter-of-factly. "It's really quite easy to get used to."

Annette sat down on a large stone near the front door. Her husband tactfully busied himself with the horse and luggage. At last Annette arose and allowed herself to be led into the shack. Four surly young men sat in the one large room downstairs. The oldest, in his twenties; the youngest, about ten. The boys greeted their father solemnly, completely ignoring the stunned young woman. Moses finally introduced Annette to his sons as their "new mother." The boys gasped.

Jacob, the oldest cried, "She's not our Mother. We don't need her. Tell her to go away!"

The others nodded angrily. The youngest child, Meyer, took one look at Annette's fiery red hair and became terror stricken. He began to wail.

Annette, still wearing her best dress, stood in the middle of the crude shack amid the belligerent group. She was dismayed and heartsick. Suddenly she lifted up her head, and addressed the boys, "Have you eaten your supper?"

"Yes."

"All right then," she shouted in a firm voice, much louder than she had intended, "all of you! To Bed! Now!"

She stamped her small foot and shook her red curls.

"Now!" she repeated.

The four boys looked at her—their mouths open. She was like a bonfire in the middle of the floor. They slowly and silently made their way upstairs. Moses tried to hide a pleased grin.

"Now, husband," Annette glared at him, "Will you kindly show me where . . . where . . . ?"

Moses chuckled as he led Annette ceremoniously out through the back door to a small booth with a hole cut in the top of the door. He left Annette there. Reentering the house, he tidied up as well as he could.

When Annette returned, her head was held high. She quickly found an apron on a hook and put it on. She smoothed her bright locks tying them up with a kerchief.

"This—this—place will need a good scrubbing . . ." she said aloud. "And possibly a small rug near our bed. And—and, a curtain around the bathtub, if you can manage it."

Moses nodded, breathing a sigh of relief. The city girl would stay! Annette did stay. She became a true farmer's wife, working from dawn to dusk, performing her chores skillfully and willingly.

The beautiful birds of paradise never made their appearance. If they had, Annette would not have noticed. She was too busy chasing the predatory birds from the fields or rocking her babies. I was their second child.

Life on the Farm

AN OLD STURDY elm tree in front of our farm door spreads its branches in all directions, nursing buds, encouraging seedlings. It nods to the infinite sky, saluting the heavenly bodies. This woody plant has embraced the sun and the gentle rains. It has stood up to the buffeting storms and to the predatory spoilers. Age has marked deep lines upon its trunk; yet, the roots remain firm. New shoots appear, groping their way to the stars.

This tree is a symbol of my family. Long after my own branch is toppled to become again joined with the nourishing earth, my elm shall persevere. At its core is the strength of my forebears whose reverence for nature and man shaped our growth and assured our continuity.

My parents planted their roots in our farm, the scene of my earliest memories. Mother and Dad toiled through the path of the seasons, from dawn until midnight. Yet, their children were always their first consideration. No matter how busy they were, they paused to give us the attention we needed at the time we asked for it. The mutual respect that existed between parents and children benefited all of us.

My recollections begin at the age of three when I toddled into the fields to romp beside my beloved father as he hoed, planted or harvested. At five I was already a working member of the farm team. We children (Lena, the eldest, myself, and Bertha, one year younger) were given regular chores to do as soon as we were able to handle them.

I wonder what Freud would have thought about my childhood. Was I brought up in an emotionally healthy environment? We had little play time, shouldering responsibilities at an age when most children were still being waited upon. The whole family worked long and hard with few material rewards. We were poor, isolated from the urban centers of culture, lacking most of the conveniences of modern living; yet, we knew our place in the scheme of life. We functioned in an atmosphere of approval, secure in the knowledge that we were loved and needed. Our slightest contributions were valued. My childhood fostered the development of a quiet confidence and an independent spirit. In addition, I learned to cherish human values above material assets. These lessons have been the sustaining forces of my life. The shining moral fiber that has been my nourishment for almost a century grew in the stubborn soil of Alliance with our lifestyle on the farm.

The Seasons

My four-score-and-ten years have been nurtured by my childhood of joy in Alliance. I have absorbed, in my bones, the rhythm of spring plantings, growing periods, harvest, and, yes, bare, chilling times when growth hides underground. As I approach the threshold of completeness, time becomes universal. I am all ages simultaneously. All experiences live within the same framework. I open the splintering door and the seasons of the old farm are alive, waiting to be savored once more.

SUMMER

July—The Visitor

MOTHER NEVER seemed to mind receiving the well-dressed visitors who came to talk with Father and to inspect our farm area on many lovely Sunday afternoons. She welcomed them into our simple home and offered them her goodies graciously. We children, dressed in our best clothes, gradually overcame our shyness with the "uncles" who gave us sweetmeats and held us on their laps. Only one thing seemed to bother Mother about her guests.

"Suppose," she asked, fearfully, when Father announced the advent of a particularly important individual, "Suppose he has to—to—."

Father laughed. "Annette, no fancy bathroom in the city is cleaner or prettier than our outhouse. You certainly have made sure of that. I clean it thoroughly and spread the floor with lye, once a week, to discourage bugs; you and the children paint the booth every year. You plant flowers and beautiful bushes around the entire building. Our outhouse is so beautiful we may start a new fad for them in New York!"

Mother grimaced. As hardy as this city girl had become, she still could not get used to two phases of her life: pumping water from the outdoor well and going to the outside booth for her bathroom.

Whenever "Uncle" Jacob came to call, we girls were particularly delighted, because we knew that he always brought a whole chocolate bar for each of us. Afterwards, each bar, shared with our parents, was carefully rationed, square by square, often lasting for more than a week.

One Sunday in July, when "Uncle" Jacob arrived and had been greeted enthusiastically by Bertha and, demurely, by Lena and me, Mother noticed an unusual flaw in the attire of the well-dressed gentleman.

"Let me fix the rip in your coat," she offered. After the coat was removed, Mother brought her mending basket over to the window and began to sew.

"Mother," the gentleman asked, "don't you have a sewing machine?"

"Oh, no," she smiled, "but I manage quite well by hand."

Our distinguished visitor left. Several weeks later, a delivery wagon drove up to our gate. A large crate was unloaded and brought into the house. The package was addressed to "Mrs. Moses Bayuk." We all crowded around Mother as she opened the wrappings, trembling. Inside was a shiny new treadle sewing machine!

The note that came with the present was very simple: "Thank you for mending my coat. I hope that you will enjoy this token of my admiration for you and your lovely family. Your friend, Jacob Schiff."

Not until several years later did I realize that "Uncle" Jacob was the famous millionaire philanthropist who had been a trustee of the Baron de Hirsch Fund. The Fund had been a sponsor of the Alliance farm community's progress, hence his frequent visits to our home. The old treadle Singer Sewing Machine has been kept in our family as a beloved heirloom. We treasure this gift as we treasure the memory of my mother's bright head, bent over her sewing, by the light of the farmhouse window.

SUMMER

August—Storm

DO FARMS HAVE a special tendency to hold the heat in the summer? The stifling hot nights in Alliance sometimes immobilized the whole community. Even bees' and crickets' songs sounded limp and muffled in the paralyzing stillness of August. On one such evening, we three girls, unable to sleep, took our pillows downstairs to the parlor, the only room with a carpet and cross ventilation. Although the windows were opened wide, no friendly breeze wandered in. The quiet air seemed to hold a special menacing quality. We tossed and turned. Suddenly we were startled by an ear-splitting crash, followed by a spear of intense light.

Like the overture to a dramatic opera, the thunder and lightning of a summer storm began to crack and rumble. Then a bolt of lightning flashed through one window and out through the other. A tremendous roar filled the room! Mother came rushing down the stairs in her bare feet, her red braids flying.

"Are you all right, children?"

She hugged us thankfully. The atmosphere, no longer still, seemed to be charged with fury. We girls were feeling deliciously scared. Oh, thunder storms were so exciting!

Lena, Bertha and I jumped up to look out of the window. About a half a mile away we could see the barn belonging to Mr. Perskie. As we looked, lightning struck the small building. For a split second, a huge ball of fire sat on top of the barn. Then the whole roof turned into a blazing furnace. Suddenly, the barn door flew open. Out ran the horse, the cow and assorted fluttering chickens. We saw a dark object hurtle from the loft and, in rapid succession, two more objects.

By this time, Father was up and dressing.

"It's Perskie's barn!" We shouted, "Hurry, Father, hurry!"

Father was racing. We knew that Mr. Perskie often slept in the hayloft in the summer when it became too hot and crowded in the house with family and friends. Father and the other farmers quickly filled their buckets with water and drove their wagons over to the barn. They threw their precious water on the house to keep the fire from spreading. But alas, the barn was gone. Where was the owner? Relieved, they found him sprawled on the ground.

Lazar Perskie got up and dusted himself off, picking wisps of hay from his clothing, hair and face. He was unharmed. No bones were broken, thanks to the presence of mind of his helper who was also sleeping in the hayloft. The hired man, after throwing down a bale of hay, had pushed Mr. Perskie out of the open window, before jumping himself. Both jumpers, landing on the soft hay, had escaped injury. The hired man's quick thinking saved the life of his boss. Although I do not know the worker's name, his good deed had a far-reaching effect. Mr. Perskie continued to rear his happy family without interruption. His children and their offspring grew up to lead unusually useful and productive lives.

Lazar's son, Joseph, born in Alliance, became a judge and was the first Jew appointed to the New Jersey Supreme Court. Joseph's son David was a judge. David's son Stephen is a young and able senator in the New Jersey legislature. Jacob Perskie, brother of Joseph, became a well-known photographer and artist and was appointed official photographer for Franklin Delano Roosevelt. Marvin Perskie, David's brother, was a distinguished lawyer.

I wonder if the Perskie family living today ever knew how close their family came to tragedy one summer night eighty years ago.

AUTUMN

September—The Grape Harvest

I STAGED MY FIRST sit-down strike when I was seven years old. When grape harvest time came, I persuaded my younger sister Bertha to share a rebellion with me.

We faced Father bravely. "We don't want to harvest the grapes!"

"Why don't you want to pick those delicious dark blue beauties?" Father asked. "You always cram your mouths full while you work. And after the wine is made, you enjoy a few sips at the Shabbos table."

"It's those awful bugs," I pouted. "They get all over my hair and onto my clothes, I just can't stand those ugly things any more."

"The chameleons enjoy grapes too," Father said. "They don't mean any harm to you. And they really are interesting. Do you know how they protect themselves from their enemies?"

Father soon had us absorbed in the story of how the chameleons change color to reflect their resting place, so that they blend in with their surroundings and are not readily detected by their enemies.

"Now!" Father said, "If you want to prevent the bugs from getting all over you, simply shake the vines before you start picking. Most of the bugs will fall to the ground or scurry off."

As usual, I started to relent, ready to go back to work. Father never raised his voice to us. We were rarely punished, but his calm, logical way of dealing with us usually had the desired results. Bertha, however, was a spitfire who enjoyed a good battle and did not like to give up any chance to make a little excitement.

"I still don't want to pick," she announced.

Father's answer was mild. "Oh, really? That's too bad! Then I guess I won't be able to take you two with me to Philadelphia after the wine is made. That trip was supposed to be a reward for my best pickers. How disappointed your nieces will be!"

Bertha and I began to shout with joy—our rebellion completely forgotten. "Oh, Dad, can we really go to Philadelphia with you?"

Grabbing our baskets, we rushed to the grape arbor and began to shake the vines, picking and eating our way through the grape harvest. Although the bugs were as annoying as usual, the thought of our reward seemed to offset any discomfort.

After we finished stripping the vines, we brought the grapes down into the cellar, where we washed them carefully. Then we helped father put them into a wooden press to squeeze out the luscious purple juice. Next, washing my feet thoroughly, I joyfully squished my toes in the purple mash to squeeze out the last vestiges of the precious juice. My feet were stained a deep purple from grape season on. I did not mind this color, because many of my farm friends had the same purple feet as they too helped their fathers with the wine making process.

True to his promise, Father allowed us to come with him on his next trip to Philadelphia. Before we left, he had shipped up barrels of homemade wine to a friend's house in Philadelphia. From there, Father would distribute his wine to his customers. Because the wine was intended for ritual purposes on the High Holy Days, we were allowed to make and sell it without a government license.

What excitement in our little household when Bertha and I prepared for our first train trip! All the way to Philadelphia! Mother had made us lovely outfits for the trip. For me she had a special gift—a beautiful sailor hat, bright red with black leather trim. It was my first new hat, bought from a store and not homemade. How I posed and preened! I was ecstatic! Mother packed our nightshirts and cautioned us to behave.

We rode off in a wagon with a neighbor who took us to the train station in Norma, a few miles away. There, clutching our bundles, we boarded the panting train that made the trip once a day to the big city. On board, we peered out of the window, enjoying the scenery. Finally, we arrived at Camden.

More adventure awaited us. To get into Philadelphia, we had to take a boat the rest of the way across a wide river. We walked down to the huge docks at the waterfront where an immense ferry boat was just pulling in. On docking, the ferry knocked against the wooden pilings, first to one side, then the other. At last the boat was docked and tied to the wharf. The crewman unhooked a huge chain with a loud clanking and allowed us to rush aboard. Knowing that the best seats would be in the open area at the front of the boat, we rushed to perch ourselves on the long wooden bench outside and leaned over to watch the movement of the water as the other boats plowed their way past us.

"Look at that child," I heard a woman say, "I don't know which is redder, her hat or her hair!" She was talking about me.

As I turned away, self-consciously, a gust of wind caught my sailor hat and sent it overboard into the river. The beautiful creation, true to its name, bobbed merrily, quite at home in the water. Screaming, I started to climb over the railing, intent on retrieving my hat at any cost. Fortunately, my father was nearby. Grabbing me just in time, he took a deep breath.

"Bluma, what a foolish thing to do! The Delaware River is not like our Maurice River. This water is deep, way over your head. If you had jumped in, you would have drowned. Never, never be so fond of a piece of cloth again! We can always buy another red hat, but where could we ever find another redhead just like you?"

He hugged me with relief and joy. I never forgot his words. Material things can be replaced but human beings are precious and unique. We must treasure ourselves and our loved ones, not our possessions.

What joy and excitement awaited us when we left the trolley to enter the home at Tenth and Walnut Street in the heart of the city! Here my oldest brother, Jacob, lived with his wife Rose and their three daughters, Mamie, six, Etta, five and Anna, four. We five little girls, near in age, about the same size, looked very much alike, except of course, for my blazing hair. We immediately began to play together, jabbering for all we were worth. That evening, when all five of us were in bed in the same room, Father came in to hand a dollar bill to Mamie.

"Tomorrow you can treat all of the girls to whatever they want!"

A whole dollar bill! We began to make plans. Of course there was only one place to spend such an enormous sum of money. The candy store!

The most opulent department store today can never compare with the richly endowed corner candy store of bygone days. Did "Mom" and "Pop" who ran the store ever realize what they were selling? "Such stuff as dreams are made of!" Oh the agonizing decisions to make—the anticipation—the air of self-importance that each child exuded as he stood, deciding, with his precious pennies clutched in his grubby little hand. Oh, the penny toys! The wax containers, the celluloid dolls, the balls, the games, little books and colorful picture cards! One could even gamble two "chances" for a penny, pushing a rolled up piece of paper out of a hole on a punch board. There were marbles and noisemakers, tin "crickers" and fat crayons. And marvelous smells: pungent cinnamon, deep chocolate, grape, banana, licorice! The colors rioted together in the glass showcase! There were round balls that changed color as one sucked them; little black boys made of licorice; chewy, gooey, taffy, that pulled and tore at one's teeth and made the dentists rich; long strings of licorice, black and red, that colored our saliva; balls so sour they puckered up one's mouth for hours; colored sugary candies on a small tin plate, eaten with a tin spoon that always bent and broke; strips of paper with rows of colored sugary dots that looked like pills and were fun to pick off, one by one. The candy was more than a sweet taste. It had character and shape and a special feeling in one's mouth. The corner store was a complete sensory experience: sound, sight, smell, touch, taste—an "Art Form" all in itself! Where today can one find the equal of a trip to the old-time candy store!

The anticipation of our adventure kept us awake and giggling until very late. The next morning, we all awoke with the first streak of light in the sky. We crept quietly down the stairs. Everyone else would be sleeping for hours yet. In our night dress, we slipped out to the porch and looked down the street. The lamplighter was making his lonely way up one street and down another, snuffing out the gas flames with his long stick. No one else was in sight.

Mamie whispered, "The candy store is just at the corner. Let's go now."

We flew from the porch steps, feet bare, flimsy petticoats flying. Five little girls scrambled through the dawn-gray street toward the magic store at the corner.

Of course our trip down the empty street was in vain. The candy store was not open so early. In the bleak morning light, the closed store looked shoddy—just like any old store.

"Come on," Mamie said, "this old store's no good anyway. I know where there's a better one!"

We followed, wandering through one street after another, but no stores were open. Soon, as the sun began to get a bit stronger and a few people appeared on the streets, we started to notice our surroundings. The neighborhood was entirely different from the area where we had started. There were pushcarts emerging onto the streets; the garbage was carelessly strewn all around; ragged children came out on the steps, staring and pointing at us, shouting strange words in throaty voices. The whole area exuded a heavy, dirty odor. Little Etta began to cry.

"I want my Mommy."

"Hush," Mamie told her, "We'll be home soon."

But of course, we were hopelessly lost. Some nasty little boys jeered and threw garbage at us. Frightened, we all began to cry. A plump woman ran out of a grocery store, chasing the boys. Then she took a look at us—the motley, barefoot crew.

"Where do you children come from?" she asked. We sobbed louder.

"Are you lost?" We nodded our heads, still sobbing.

The kindly woman led us to the next corner where a young policeman stood, twirling his stick.

"Mr. Callahan," the woman called, "Look what I found!"

The officer took one look at five bedraggled waifs and began to whistle.

"Saints alive! What is it?"

"They're lost." She told him, and proceeded back to her store, leaving us with a very perplexed cop. Telling us to "stay put" while he called the station house, he went to a box on a post and opened it. I heard him say to the box, "I swear it, sergeant, and I'm not a drinkin' man. One of them has fiery red hair and purple feet!"

"The sergeant would like to meet yez," he told us. "So kindly walk with me to the station house."

Bertha had stopped crying. She stared at the policeman with interest.

"Are you going to arrest us," she asked.

"Not unless you have broken any laws," he replied.

"Oh," Bertha confided importantly, "I break laws all of the time. Last week I drew a picture on the Sabbath. And Bluma . . ."

"Never mind," the cop interrupted, "We'll have no squealing. The sergeant will find out all he needs to know about you. Just march along there now and tell the others to stop their cryin!"

The desk sergeant at the station house treated us very kindly. He and his men gave us toys to play with and spicy hard candies. We began to crawl all over the indulgent policemen, playing with their sticks and their badges. Soon we were making a shambles out of the station house. The poor desk sergeant didn't know what to do.

"Where do you live?" he asked us again.

"With Mama and Daddy," Bertha, the bold one, replied.

"Oh, and where is that?"

"At home, naturally," Bertha retorted.

The poor man shrugged his shoulders and turned to Mamie. "What is your address?" he asked.

"I don't think I have one of them," Mamie replied, sobbing.

Our interrogator sighed. "Tell me your names. Do you know that?"

"Bertha Bayuk," "Mamie Bayuk," "Bluma Bayuk," "Anna Bayuk," "Etta Bayuk." The policeman swallowed hard. Were these girls quintuplets?

Meanwhile, at Walnut Street, Father had awakened and had gone into our bedroom to rouse us. The room was empty.

"Where are the children?" he asked Rose, who was in the kitchen making breakfast.

"Sleeping in their beds," she replied.

Father looked at her in alarm. "Rose, they're gone, all of them!"

The frantic parents searched the neighborhood for about an hour, but no little girls had been seen. At last, Father decided to contact the police. He asked them to call the stations in the area to find out if there had been any reports of found children. Finally, the South Philadelphia precinct, around 5th and Bainbridge had happily admitted that five little ragamuffins were in their protective custody.

Father hurried down to where we were being held. When he walked into the station house, we all began to jump and scream with delight, "Father!" Bertha and I shouted.

"Grandpop!" shouted Mamie, Annie and Ettie.

The sergeant scratched his head again. Father had to pay a fee to have us released. Finally we were allowed to leave.

Five skimpily clad young culprits marched along the street, herded by an embarrassed man who flinched at the amused stares of the passersby. We did not dare to speak or to raise our eyes from the pavement. The jibes of the neighborhood children followed us as we filed by in our petticoats and dirty bare feet. When we returned to Walnut Street, we did not get our candy treats. Father took back his dollar. He made us stay in the house for the rest of our visit. It was a disastrous outing for the rebellious grape pickers and their nieces.

AUTUMN

October—The Country School

FARM CHILDREN did not start school until late in the fall. We were too busy picking and canning at harvest time. The school house was a two-room building with a blackboard, wooden seats, a potbellied stove, and, of course, an outhouse. Children of all ages studied and worked in the same room with the same teacher. We all progressed at our own speed. This educational method has great merit and is considered a valid teaching concept today.

Often, we had wonderful teachers. At other times, we were forced to endure grouchy, frustrated pedagogues who taught out of necessity and made us quite aware of their distaste for their profession. Nevertheless, we really loved school days because we spent time in the company of other children.

For me, the headiest excitement of learning was our introduction into the world of books. What a smorgasbord of literary feasts awaited the accomplished reader! My love affair with the written word was so intense that I often ran home after school, breathless, anxious to share with my mother the wondrous tales of Snow White, Cinderella or Black Beauty. Mother listened with rapt attention and delight. Soon, Lena and I were regularly sharing our knowledge with our mother. Whenever we studied our lessons, Mother tried to sit with us, absorbing hungrily, although she could neither read nor write in English. Father had started to teach her to read and write in Yiddish so that she could follow the tales that appeared in the Jewish newspaper *The Forward*. This Yiddish paper was the "bible" of information for the Russian Jewish immigrants.

Mother's hunger for learning was transferred to me; throughout my life, my fierce desire to learn has been a dominant characteristic. Even today, when I see something, I want to know about it. Always there are new questions I must ask, new knowledge that I desire to acquire. This trait, from childhood on, has been a driving force. To me, going to school was the reward that awaited us after a back-breaking harvesting season.

Israel Kraftzow used to call for Bertha and me when we went to class. My sister Lena went ahead with the older children. Every day Israel carried my books. Bertha and I brought our lunchboxes; school was an all day commitment. On the way, we picked up some other children—the Bailey girls and the Seldes boys. Gilbert and George lived with their grandparents who were in charge of the local post office. Later, of course, they became very famous. Israel, too, became successful in the motion picture business.

Together we children crossed an open field to take a short cut. In the winter, we often stopped to play in the snow before arriving at school. Once in class, we all took our seats according to height, and said "Good Morning" to our current teacher.

In the fall of 1898, our teacher was Mr. Wordsworth, a portly, red-faced, humorless man. Poor Mr. Wordsworth tried to insist on strict quiet in the classroom. However, a group of healthy, active, bright farm children of all ages, in the one room for the entire school day, could not logically be expected to remain absolutely still. Although we really tried to suppress our natural instincts, we could not succeed altogether. The irrepressible Bertha, my younger sister, found any restraints untenable. She was Mr. Wordsworth's most serious problem.

"Bertha, keep quiet!" growled Mr. Wordsworth one rainy afternoon.

"Yes, Sir," she answered with an impudent inflection.

A few minutes later, Bertha was gabbing again. Mr. Wordsworth became furious. "All right, Bertha," he shouted, "just for your fresh answer, you can write 'yes sir' one thousand times, and stay after school until you finish!"

Autumn   35

We were all dismayed! Such an unreasonable punishment could keep Bertha there until evening! Our parents would worry. Our teacher was really acting unreasonably. We all exchanged glances. Then the whole class began to write, secretly, on little scraps of paper. Whenever the teacher's back was turned, we slipped our "yes sirs" to Bertha. She was making quite a collection until Mr. Wordsworth turned around unexpectedly and caught us.

"Now, you will all stay in after school," he screeched, his face getting redder than before.

Bertha was not afraid of her enemy. She pranced up to his desk and dumped a load of small scraps of "yes sir" papers on his desk.

"Here," she said, "you take these. I haven't any more room on my desk."

Our teacher took the scraps and walked over to the potbellied stove. He thrust the papers into the flames. As he bent down to pick up an errant scrap from the floor, we all heard a loud rip! Mr. Wordsworth's long-suffering trousers had finally split, revealing a bright red flannel rump area.

We could not contain ourselves. The laughter exploded! Clutching his split, the poor man ran to the cloakroom to don his overcoat. He spent the remainder of the day, coat on, perspiring and sullen. He did not keep us in after school.

We rushed home in great glee. What a story to tell! Father and Mother listened appreciatively to our tale. Mother nodded to Father wordlessly. Soon Father left the house carrying a package. Later, he returned with another package which he handed to Mother.

The next day, Mr. Wordsworth appeared in class wearing another pair of pants. They were baggy and ill-fitting and, to me, vaguely familiar. When we returned home that day, Mother was mending. She handed the finished article to Father and said, "Here, I've done as well as I can, but I don't know if it will hold."

Father left to return Mr. Wordsworth's mended trousers and to retrieve his own. I believe that Mr. Wordsworth's patience had given out about the same time as his pants. A few weeks later, we met a new teacher. Mr. Larkins, a realistic educator, gave us more freedom in class. We responded by behaving well with our new teacher. Our learning experience continued, both inside and outside of our one room school.

WINTER

November—The Sacredness of Life

AS THE NOVEMBER night deepened, the glow from the oil lamps sent a cozy signal to our windows. All seemed to be well inside our red and white brick farmhouse, set back on Gershal Road, a few yards from the Jewish cemetery in Alliance, New Jersey.

When winter approached and the outside work diminished, Father and Mother began to do their winter chores. At his workbench, Father was repairing our shoes. From early spring, no self-respecting farm child would think of wearing shoes. First of all, we could not afford to waste valuable shoe leather; second, our winter-tortured feet demanded to be freed from their strait jackets to wiggle freely in the air. However, as the leaves turned, our feet had to be confined once more, to carry us to school.

We could afford only one pair of shoes each for the entire year; therefore, Dad did his best to keep our oxfords repaired so that they would last as long as possible. He had set up a large wooden shoe that he used as a holder, and brought over a rack of scrap leather. After cutting the leather into usable pieces, he pounded the patches into the worn parts with short, thin nails. Sometimes, the nails came loose while we were hiking to school. If this happened, we picked up a stone and pounded the nails back into place again. The shoe leather sent a wonderful odor into the house, mingling with Mama's chicken soup and sweet-sour cabbage.

Our infant twin sisters, Annie and Fannie, were wailing in their cradle. Mama was rushing back and forth from the stove to the crib, rocking the babies, tending the pot of soup on the stove, preparing a basin of water to sponge the little ones.

We three older sisters were sitting on the floor, near the black stove, keeping warm. Bertha, age seven, was playing with a tattered homemade paper doll, pretending to be a busy lady like Mama, with a baby of her own. Lena, the oldest, and I, Bluma, age eight, were playing "jacks" with a little ball—one of the few store-bought games that we owned. I had lost two of my metal "jacks" and had replaced them with stones, which were much harder to pick up. We played earnestly, intent on winning. Mother seemed busier than ever with the fretful babies. We could hear her sigh as she rushed about her work.

"Mama," Bertha whined, "this old doll is all torn and ugly. Why can't I have a pretty new one like Goldie has. Her papa bought it at Krassenstein's store."

Mother had finished sponging the twins who were quieting down at last. She looked over at us.

"You really have been wonderful helpers today, children—feeding my chicks, bringing in the kindling and carrying all that water from the well while I was busy with the babies. You deserve a special treat. I think I shall make you each a doll—more beautiful than Goldie's because . . ." her voice trailed off for a moment, but then she resumed, briskly, "because you deserve it."

Then we were watching, enthralled, as Mama took out a large piece of cardboard that she had stored in her cupboard. Stopping now and then to rock the babies, Mother began to draw on the blank sheet of cardboard at the kitchen table. Soon, a curvaceous lady, a bearded man and three girl dolls of different sizes took shape on the paper. We were delighted.

"It's a family," Lena announced.

"It's us!" Bertha squealed.

"Make the middle-sized one a redhead," I begged.

Mama used our school crayons to color the hair. As soon as the forms were cut out, we grabbed them.

"Wait," Mother said, "I am not finished yet."

She went over to the cradle, bending to examine the twins for a moment. When she returned to the table, her eyes looked tired.

"Rest a while, Mama," I said. "We can play with the dolls just the way they are."

"No, your 'family' must be dressed."

Mother reached into her sewing box for scraps of material. Cutting slowly, she fashioned a lovely outfit for each doll. She sewed each piece of clothing deftly. The father doll wore dark pants and a black "yarmulkah" on his head. We kissed Mama and thanked her. Soon we became absorbed in playing "house" with our beautiful new dolls.

Our play was interrupted by a knock at the door. We opened to admit a neighbor and good friend, Mr. Zager. The Zagers, a healthy and numerous brood, lived directly across the street from us. Our families were very close. In the Zager family were six boys and one girl, Goldie, age seven. We considered the boys as brothers. Whenever Dad left for Philadelphia to sell his wine, young Harry and Joe Zager would stay at our home every night so that we would have male protection and help. Joe and Harry piled into bed with us on those sleepover occasions. Our bed was large enough to hold their entire family. Father had built the huge bed himself. This comfortable monstrosity served as the family guest room. All children visitors of either sex shared this sleeping arrangement with us. Ours was such a natural way of life that with perfect innocence, we accepted all company in our bed.

Mr. Zager addressed Mama. "Annette," he said, "you are the best nurse in this area. I think I need your help. Our little Goldie is acting very strange. I'm afraid she may be coming down with that terrible fever that has been going around."

Mama replied sharply, "Don't worry, Zager, the fever is affecting only the babies. Goldie is safe that way."

"Perhaps," Father suggested, with a twinkle in his eye, "Perhaps Goldie needs Annette's famous 'cocktail.'"

We girls began to scream. Mama's "cocktail" was a famous concoction that was horrible to take. How we hated to hear any mention of that infamous remedy!

"No," Mama said, "Goldie's trouble is not in her stomach."

Mama turned her back and walked over to rock the cradle. She returned to face us girls, sitting open-mouthed at the table, listening to every word, the dolls forgotten.

"Children, take your dolls upstairs. You do not have to know everything that goes on."

"But I know what happened, I was there," I reminded her.

"You are right, Bluma, you may stay here. Lena and Bertha, go upstairs." The girls complied.

Mama returned to her chair, rocking the cradle slowly, wearily.

"Zager," Mama said, "my chicks start out as trusting little feathery balls. I love to take care of them from the time they break their shells, trembling and wobbly. I feed them and watch them grow. Sometimes, I think they recognize me. Each one has a different way of feeding and walking around. They are my pets. I feed them with crumbs soaked in milk. They know me because I care for them."

"I know all about that," Zager interrupted. "Everyone says that your chickens are the healthiest in town."

"It really hurts me when the chicks grow and some of them have to be killed for our Sabbath dinners. But I have learned to accept this. I know that it is their destiny. When their allotted time comes, they serve their purpose. All things have their special fate. Moses has taught me that much about life and death. I revere life and the sacredness of all living things. My husband's philosophy has made it easier for me to bear some of my memories and to accept what must be. I have learned that one must accept death as one accepts life. The most important thing is to respect and to preserve life—all life at all times."

"Agreed, agreed," Zager replied impatiently. "We men discuss these ideas at the synagogue very often. But why do you, a woman, speak to me on this subject. I came to you with a problem about my Goldie and you talk philosophy and chickens."

"To help you with Goldie, first, I must be sure that you understand about my chicks. Moses tells me that our religion stresses the sacredness of life. We believe that even a snake or spider has a purpose on this earth, and has a right to live out his allotted time. We have no right to kill a living thing unless it is necessary for our protection or for our sustenance."

Mr. Zager did not want to hear any more of this talk from Mother.

"Moses, do you allow a mere woman to talk of such matters? It is men who are supposed to deal with philosophy and theology. Women must cook and clean and sew and take care of children. It is written!"

Father laughed. "Where is it written, Zager? You are like an old horse with blinders who can only see the narrow path in front of his nose. Where is it written that women cannot think and express themselves equally with men? Look at the women in this community. What a strength they are! They labor with us in the fields and nurture our home and children as well. Why should they be barred from our ideas and our ideals? The Jewish religion has always exalted their women. Look at the Bible. Think of Deborah, Naomi, Queen Esther. My daughters work with me just as your sons work with you on the farm. I have taught my girls that they can do anything in this world that their brains and bodies are capable of. Their sex should not hinder them from any accomplishment, any dream. Perhaps if you raised your Goldie as I raise my daughters, she would not be a problem now."

"Moses," Mama interrupted, "I know what's wrong with Goldie. She is troubled because I sent her home in disgrace. She is no longer welcome here until Zager gives her the moral teachings that he has denied her. Goldie does not understand about the sacredness of life. You see, Zager, today I was very occupied with my babies, so I asked Bluma to feed my chicks for me. Goldie was here playing with Bluma at the time. Bluma loves the chicks as much as I do. She was happy to help me. Goldie went with Bluma into the hen house. Then, your daughter did a terrible thing. She picked up a helpless baby chick and squeezed its neck. She had no reason—just a whim—to snuff out the life of a living thing. Bluma was beside herself. So, you see why Goldie was sent home. She cannot play here any more until she understands the seriousness of what she has done."

Zager turned pale. His hands trembled. "I am sorry, Annette. I did not know about this. I shall pay you for the chicken, of course."

"Oh, no, Zager," Mama said. "If you think that a money payment takes care of the damage, then you are not a truly devout Jew and the lofty thoughts you repeat to your fellow men in the synagogue are just words and do not reflect themselves in your deeds."

Zager was silent for a long time. Then he cleared his throat.

"Reb Bayuk, you are indeed a fortunate man. You, a learned and pious philosopher, have married a woman of equal merit. I shall be leaving now. I thank you for your wisdom, Annette."

I did not fully understand what was going on, but I felt chilled by the icy wind that seemed to leap through the door as Mr. Zager left. The wind seemed to remain in our house, waking the twins who became more restless and fretful than before. Once again, Mama rocked and sponged them.

Their crying became more intense. Bertha and Lena rushed down the stairs.

"What is the matter with the babies," Bertha asked. Mama's expression frightened me.

"They are very ill. They will not take nourishment and their little bodies are very hot."

Father came over to the cradle, frowning. "How long have they been like this?"

"Since early this morning. They seem to be getting worse. I didn't want to upset you before, Moses, but they are very ill. I have tried all of the remedies that I know. Nothing seems to help. It is the same fever that took the Rosen baby last week. We can only pray."

Winter

I felt the cold chill in my stomach. Bertha ran to the cradle to look at the wailing babies.

"Let us hold them," Bertha begged. "Annie always loves it when I hold her."

"Sit down, Bertha," Mama said, "I will put Annie on your lap. Lena, you take Fannie."

The feverish infants were deposited into two loving pairs of arms. I ran from one to the other, making absurd faces and silly sounds, but the babies did not respond. Fannie's eyes were glassy and her skin was yellow. Finally, Mama returned Fannie to the cradle. Bertha refused to give up Annie. She kept rocking the infant in her arms, whispering tender words. The baby quieted down as we watched. It was strange to see bubbly, irrepressible Bertha, sitting so still, as she gentled her baby sister.

Later, after we all went to bed, I found that I could not sleep. Hearing unaccustomed noises downstairs, I crept to the landing and looked down. My mother and father were standing together. In her arms, Mother held a white bundle. Someone knocked at the door. The cold wind whistled before I heard the voice of Mr. Zager.

"Don't worry, my dear friends, I will see that all will be taken care of. Mr. Lentz is waiting outside. Moses, don't come. Stay with Annette."

Father took the bundle from Mama and handed it to Mr. Zager. A low moan came from my mother. Dad put his arms around her. They stood together for a long time after the door closed once again. Mama's foot had never left the cradle. All during the time, her left foot was on the rung of the cradle, rocking the whimpering baby.

The next morning, we saw the empty space in the crib. Mama and Dad explained that our little Fannie had been called back to God. Lena accepted the tragedy with her usual sturdy sensibility. I already knew what had happened and felt numb. Bertha became hysterical.

"Why, Mama, why?" she sobbed. "Is he going to take my Annie too? Oh, Mama, he can't take them both. It's not fair! Keep Annie here with us, Papa, don't let God take her."

Bertha hovered around the cradle all day, watching Annie and rocking her. The baby hardly moved. Bertha, however, kept giving us hopeful bulletins. "She just moved a little."

"Her color looks better."

"She opened her eyes for a minute."

Dad could not get Bertha away from Annie even for meals. She refused to leave her post. Suddenly, a strange gurgling sound brought my parents swiftly to the infant. Dad reached into the cradle and felt Annie's heart. He lifted the baby and examined her limp body carefully. Mama took the lifeless form into her arms, listening for some breath. She bowed her head.

My weary parents slowly put the baby down on the kitchen table. Mama went to the cupboard, drawing out another small clean white sheet. Papa called to our dog, Fido, taking him outside and pointing him toward the road. "Get Zager!"

My parents washed the tiny body and lovingly wrapped the doll-like figure in the sheet, winding round and round. We watched, hardly breathing. They carried the bundle to the door and waited in silence.

When Mr. Zager opened the door, the chill intensified. I caught a glimpse of Mr. Lentz, the caretaker from the cemetery next door. He was waiting outside. Mr. Zager lifted the bundle from Mother's arms and walked toward the open door. Mr. Lentz, a burly man, reached for the bundle and began to walk away. Suddenly, Bertha in her flimsy pinafore, without shoes, lunged out of the house and hurled herself at Mr. Lentz. She ran after him and started beating and tearing at his arms.

"Give me back my baby! You can't have her! Give her back!"

The dogged man kept walking toward the cemetery, dragging Bertha, who clung to his legs, screaming.

We all ran after Bertha. Father pulled her away, and bore her, flailing hysterically, back into the house.

"He can't take her! Annie! Annie!"

In the house, Dad held Bertha for a long time, rocking her in his arms by the warm fire, letting her sob and rage for all of us.

Lena and I were quiet. We held tightly to each of Mama's hands. Mama said not a word. She did not cry. But with her foot, she was rocking—rocking the empty cradle as hard as she could.

WINTER

December—The Family Bath

THE PAGES OF MY MEMORY turn to a cold, bleak Friday afternoon in December. My sister Lena and I had been put to work polishing the silver. We used the ashes from the wood-burning stove as our polish, rubbing and rubbing until we could see our faces in the pots, and distorted in the gleaming brass candlesticks. Everything had to be shiny and sparkling for the advent of Shabbos. Little sister Bertha, as usual, was more of a hindrance than a help. She always seemed to be doing more spilling and interfering than helping, but she was just five years old. Lena and I, at the ages of ten and six respectively, felt called upon to rebuke her often. Finally, Mother was satisfied with our polishing. She told us to put on our warm coats and wool hats for it was time for our next chore—pumping water for the bathtub.

"Oh dear," we groaned. What a chore! But we were not too sad, for the marvelous aroma of chicken soup, onions, freshly-baked bread and cake was enough to keep anyone in good spirits. We knew that at the end of the day, Mother's Friday evening meal would compensate us handsomely for our work. And naturally, one had to be perfectly clean before sundown. We took large pots out to the pump and laboriously filled them with the icy water. Then we toted the pots of water into the kitchen. We poured the liquid into the large kettles that were heating on the wood stove. Pump, pump, tote, tote, empty out, and then start all over again. We traveled endlessly up and back between the pump and the kitchen. Our legs ached and our arms grew numb. Our faces alternately froze outside of the house, and burned as we approached the stove. Finally, the job was done. There was enough water in the kettles at last. Just in time too, for Father's footsteps were heard outside. In he walked, a huge bearded bear. Greeting us all affectionately, Father began to remove his coat. We rushed to test the water for his bath. Yes, it was warm enough.

Using rags to keep from burning his hands, Father lifted the immense kettle of boiling water from the stove. He walked to the corner of the room and placed the hot kettle on a stool. He removed the wooden cover from the tub, thus changing it magically from bench to bathtub. Then Father poured the hot water into the tin tub and closed the curtain. Mother rushed to bring him his newly ironed long underwear, shirt and pants. The clothing smelled as warm and fresh as baking bread. We soon heard Father splashing and humming a pious tune as he bathed behind the curtains. Occasionally, he called out questions to the family.

"Lena, what did you learn in school today?"

"Bluma, did you finish embroidering the challa cover yet?"

"Bertha, are you behaving yourself?"

The question to Bertha always remained the same, because our youngest sister was a "minx." She just could not sit still. Her lively nature seemed to get her into one scrape after another.

Soon Father could be heard rising from the tub and drying himself vigorously. When the curtain was thrust aside, a ruddy giant, cleanly dressed, emerged from the steamy corner, with jovial good humor.

"Next!" he shouted.

Mother smiled and gathered her clean clothing. Dad scooped up some fresh water in a pot to add to the soapy tub. Once again the curtain was drawn. Mother's soft ablutions could barely be heard. At this point, Lena and I were disrobing and gathering our own fresh clothing in preparation for our turns.

We bathed according to age—the oldest first. Poor hapless, impatient Bertha was last. Overactive, she always managed to be ready first. Then she pestered annoyingly until it was her turn. Before Lena had even closed the curtain, Bertha was prancing around, naked and impatient. As she heard Lena get out of the tub, Bertha decided to beat me to the next turn. She quickly brushed past me. Unfortunately, Bertha did not realize that she was too near the heat. Her bare buttocks touched the hot stove. She screamed.

    Bertha did not take a bath at all that night. Mother bathed her wound with oil to keep it from blistering. That night Bertha ate her Shabbos dinner standing up. The burn on her posterior faded in time, but the scene is branded forever in my memory.

WINTER

December—My Mother The Doctor

IT SEEMS THAT every Jewish mother dreams of having her son become a doctor. One can give many reasons for this. A doctor must have many years of education; Jewish people have always revered learning. The medical profession is dedicated to helping people; Jewish tradition is heavy with the joys of "mitzvoth" (good deeds). However, there is another reason. The Jewish mother thinks she is already a doctor herself. My mother was no exception. She seemed to know the secrets of curing illnesses, without a diploma. She also acted as midwife for her neighbors when their birthing time came. None of her patients ever had any complications and all of her deliveries were of healthy babies. In the modern world of drugs and super-drugs, Mother's prescriptions would seem simplistic and archaic—except for one important factor: they did the job.

When we children came down with croupy colds in winter, Mother would give us hot mustard baths, plenty of hot tea with homemade raspberry jelly and homemade whiskey to make us sweat. Whenever I developed a deep cough, Mother would carry me down to the kitchen to lean over a boiling kettle of water inhaling the steam. Today's expensive vaporizers achieve the same effect.

Some of Mother's "medicines" were extremely difficult to take, especially the one we delicately called "Mother's Cocktail."

The first time I had to take "Mother's Cocktail" was a memorable occasion. It came about because Mother feared the "Evil Eye," a superstitious belief held by many immigrant wives. The basic idea behind the superstition is that if too much praise is given to a child, the "Evil One" will become jealous and cast a "spell" on the little one. Therefore, one does not allow one's offspring to be overly-petted or admired.

One December afternoon, when my mother invited some of her farm friends to visit, the company began to exclaim over my abundant red hair and freckles. Although Mother was busy serving cakes, tea and homemade jellies, she did not relish this "invitation to disaster" for her little daughter. Therefore, she hurried me out of the room by loading my plate with goodies and sending me upstairs to eat. Being a clever child, and anxious to take advantage of an unusual situation, I kept returning for more praise and thus, more goodies. After overeating outrageously, I began to feel sick. As soon as the company left, I went crying to Mother.

"Mama, I feel sick."

"No wonder," she said. "All they talked about was you, Bluma, your red hair and your freckles."

"It's my stomach," I whimpered.

"It's the 'Evil Eye,'" she countered. "You and your freckles. They even tried to count them. No wonder you are sick." She sighed, "Come here, child, and do what I tell you."

Her suggestion horrified me! I tried to run away but there was no escape. This remedy was handed down to Mother from her mother and, unfortunately, it works well. For those who remember Ipecac and have been subjected to its horrible taste and effect, I have no pity. "Mother's Cocktail" is much worse!

Mother calmly forced me to urinate into a bowl. She then poured the hot urine into a glass for me to drink! In a second, I had vomited everything I had eaten for a week. Although this drink is the most effective purge imaginable, I am sure that no modern doctor would suggest such a remedy. However, it is always available and doesn't cost a cent.

Mama's method of purgation is one family tradition that I have happily broken. No child or grandchild of mine has ever been forced to drink "Grandmother's Cocktail." However, my grandchildren do enjoy hearing the story about my own discomfort the first time my mother, the "Doctor," prescribed this concoction for me.

WINTER

January—The Logical Conclusion

ONE SPARKLING WINTER day in January when I was twelve, Israel Kraftzow, my favorite playmate, called at our home to invite me to come out to play.

We children looked forward to wintertime; then our chores were curtailed, allowing us more time for fun. The cold weather did not deter us from inventing splendid hijinks. Crisp days, strong with sunshine and snow, were like sirens, luring us to the outdoors, bundled and booted. On weekends and sometimes after school, we romped and crunched our way through fields and hills, hand in hand with Jack Frost.

Without fancy toys or sports equipment, we relied on nature and our own ingenuity to make our winter world a rich playground. Our parents had no similar respite in the cold weather. Cold weather chores inside were as pressing as the outdoor work in the mild time. Mama and Dad did all of the necessary interior work themselves. Together they painted the woodwork and papered the walls. Father repaired shoes and farm equipment. He did the plumbing and the carpentering as well. Mother also mended, knitted and sewed all of our clothing in addition to her household chores.

On the Sunday afternoon when Israel called for me, Mama made sure that I was bundled properly, uttering all of the usual precautions that translate into "I love you" in Mama-language. Then we took off in great spirits. As soon as we crossed the fields, Israel broke into a run, shouting to me that we were heading for

Peterson's cranberry bog. The other boys and girls were already there skating on the icy surface.

I stopped abruptly, "Israel, my parents don't like me to skate at the bog. I'm sure they would say 'no' if they knew where we were going."

Israel replied, "But everyone will be there. This is one of the best skating days of the year. Besides, your parents didn't say that you couldn't go."

How could I resist? Ice-skating was so much fun! Of course, we didn't use ice skates. We would just slide around in our boots. But what a thrill! When we reached the Peterson farm, the other children were already dancing and gliding over the surface of the bog, Mrs. Peterson, a fat, affable woman, was watching the fun, laughing so hard that her mammoth body shook from side to side like a giant balloon in the wind.

We flew onto the rink, running and slipping with the others. Then Israel grabbed my arm and began to waltz me to the far side of the bog. Suddenly, we felt a crackling and realized that we had ventured out too far. The bottom was giving way! Frantically, we lunged for safer footing but it was too late. The flimsy ice broke under our feet, plunging us into an icy bath. We were rescued immediately and brought into Mrs. Peterson's cozy kitchen where a reassuring fire crackled on the hearth. I was soaked to the skin and miserable. It served me right for disobeying my parents. What would they think of me? Although my father never spanked us, his disappointment in me would be worse than any physical punishment.

After Israel dried himself, he left for home and fresh clothing. I sat by the fireplace, shivering and drinking Mrs. Peterson's cinnamon tea. My sopping clothes had been wrung out and placed in front of the stove to dry. However, it was evident that I could not wear them again that day. The afternoon was waning. I knew that I must get home before my parents started to worry about me.

"Don't worry child," Mrs. Peterson said. "I'll lend you some of my clothing to wear home."

I looked at the woman, a female version of Santa Claus, with the same belly measurements. Then I looked at my own slender form. How could I possibly wear this lady's clothes? Mrs. Peterson noticed my perplexed expression. She shook with mirth.

"Well, Bluma, we may have to wrap one of my dresses around you three times to make it fit, but we can put pins all over to keep it in place. I have a warm woolen sweater that we can wrap and pin around over the dress, and a hat that will work if I take a few tucks here and there."

With much spirit and giggling, Mrs. Peterson wrapped, pinned, and tucked me into her oversized garments. When she finished, I was a sight to behold! Her little kitten took one look at me and scampered off into the parlor.

After saying goodbye, I toddled off toward home in Mrs. Peterson's huge boots, hampered by my awkward raiment. I hoped that I would not meet any of my friends while I was dressed so outlandishly. I walked very slowly to keep from tripping. The shadows were deepening outside and the fields were deserted. I was all alone in the still, eerie twilight. Fortunately, I did not have to pass the cemetery which was situated on the other side of my home, for I had developed a great fear of the burial ground because of the tales that I had heard from the farm wives.

Almost every Friday night, after synagogue services across the street from our house, the farmers and their wives were accustomed to drop in to our home for Mama's cake and tea. The men sat in the parlor discussing farm problems and philosophy; the women settled in the kitchen to revel in their morbid fancies, rehashing spine-chilling ghost stories. Although I was supposed to be in bed upstairs, I often eavesdropped from the top of the stairway, drinking in the fearful tales. Fascinated and horrified, I could not tear myself away from my hidden perch. However, after the company left, I would leap into my bed trembling, terrified of the images of tombstones reflected in my bureau mirror from the cemetery next door. The women used to repeat that the unquiet dead arose at night and walked to the synagogue. I was terribly afraid that the restless spirits might take a notion to use our house as a short-cut. Often, when I had to use the chamber pot at night, I would arise with eyes tightly shut afraid to open them for fear of what I might see. I would grope my way around rather than take the chance of confronting a ghastly shade trafficking through my bedroom. My fear of the dead stayed with me for many years.

As I stumbled home in sight of the forbidding cemetery, irrational fears surfaced. I thought suppose a ghost were out walking! Thinking that I heard footsteps I looked around. Then I saw someone—a pale young man, thin, white-faced and frail. He had appeared so quickly and quietly that I was sure he was an unearthly being.

"Go away," I cried, "Go back to the cemetery! I'm a real person. Go back where you belong!"

The gaunt creature kept on walking toward me. "Don't be afraid. I just want to ask you a question."

As I tried to run away, my awkward wrappings became caught in my floppy boots. Down I fell, rolling over and over in the snow.

He drew nearer, standing over me. "Don't run away. I just want to ask you a question. Do you know the Golder family? I am looking for them. I went to their farm, but it is deserted. Are Mr. and Mrs. Golder still living here?"

"Who are you," I asked, "What do you want?"

"I'm Frank Golder. I'm looking for my family."

At this point I became absolutely hysterical. Now I knew that the figure was really a ghost! I had heard the sad story about Frank Golder's fate many times from the farm ladies. Desperately, I tried to fend off the apparition.

"Go back, Frank Golder, go back! Your parents aren't here any more. They live in Philadelphia. Go back to sleep!"

He turned away. "Poor kid. I didn't realize. All right, I'll go. Don't be afraid."

After he turned to leave, I summoned all of my strength to get up and to run away in the direction of our house, not daring

Winter 59

to look back. When I reached our steps, I banged on the door in a frenzy. As my parents let me in to the house, I was babbling incoherently. They were aghast at the sight of their sturdy, dependable redhead, wrapped in outlandish garments, screaming about "ghosts and Golders." My father's arm went around me. Mother held my hand.

"I saw him, Mama, I saw a real live ghost," I sobbed. "It's true, it's really true what your ladies say, Mama. Ghosts do walk. I saw him. I saw Frank Golder. He talked to me. He asked me about his parents, Mama. Why is he up walking? Is it because he never got a stone for his grave?"

My father was excited, "Do you mean to say that you just saw Frank Golder?"

"I saw his ghost," I moaned.

Dad ran to the door and looked down the road in time to see a horse and buggy disappearing in the distance. He came back.

"I'm sorry I couldn't catch him. I would like to see that boy again. He is a fine youngster. Let's see, He must be about twenty now."

"But Papa, didn't you know? Frank is dead. Everybody knows he's dead. All the ladies say so."

Dad turned to Mother. "Annette, is this true? Do all of your lady friends say that Frank Golder is dead?"

Mama replied. "Yes, Moses, didn't you know the story? Bluma is right. We ladies have talked about it many times. It all happened about eight years ago. Bluma was just a small child then. It was a terrible tragedy. Poor Frank, such a pale, sickly child. After he passed on, the Golders never even spoke about him. It was a terrible thing. They acted just as if he had never lived. And right away, they moved to Philadelphia."

"But why did you think that Frank was dead? Did you go to the funeral?"

"There was no funeral. You know how poor the Golders were. About the time that Frank disappeared, Mrs. Perskie heard some weeping and sobbing in the Golder house. Then later, Mamie told us that she remembered seeing Mr. Golder walking toward the cemetery at night, with a bundle. We knew what must have happened. Poor little Frank died and the Golders couldn't afford a burial, so they took his body into the cemetery at night, secretly, and buried him so nobody would know. He doesn't have a proper grave or a headstone. That's why his ghost is walking around."

Dad's mouth began to twitch. "You women with your morbid ideas. You got together and decided that Frank's family sneaked him into the cemetery at night! What an imagination!"

Mama was indignant. "It was a logical conclusion."

"I can just imagine how you women have sat and embroidered on that story all of these years. The sad tale of poor little Frank Golder is now a part of your folk lore—or is it idle gossip? No wonder Bluma thinks she really saw a ghost!"

"Moses, are you telling me that Frank Golder is still alive?"

Dad nodded, "Yes, as far as I know. I never realized that people assumed that he had died. Poor Bluma, rest easy, child, you were not talking to a ghost."

It took me a few minutes to absorb Dad's information. Of course, I was relieved and happy to know that I had encountered a real live person. Then, as I remembered how I had behaved toward the poor man, I was mortified. "Oh, my, the things I said to him! I wonder what he thinks of me."

Father laughed. "I can just imagine what he thought, listening to your screams and seeing your get-up. I hope he doesn't find out who you are."

Mother became aware of my outlandish wraps. "Bluma, where are your clothes? What are you doing in those 'schmatas'?"

I tried to change the subject. "Mama, if Frank Golder is—"

"Never mind Frank Golder, young lady. Explain. What are you doing in these rags?"

I confessed to my parents about the spill in the bog. They were upset. I was forced to promise that I would never go ice-skating there again. I did not mind making that promise. To be honest, it had not been my most enjoyable day. Later, Mother and Dad returned Mrs. Peterson's clothing, after each piece was washed and ironed. Mama also baked a special honey cake for our jovial kind-hearted neighbor.

I remained curious about the Golder's oldest son, begging Dad to tell me why Frank had disappeared. However, Dad refused to speak. Although he knew the real story, he had given his word to the family and he would not break it. Not until years later did I learn the curious circumstances of Frank's disappearance. No one with a logical mind could have imagined the unusual situation that had changed the life of a poor young peddler who had dropped out of school to help support his family. I learned the story from a stranger. Father, a man of integrity, never divulged what he knew.

My fear of ghosts did not lessen even though the young man had proved to be of flesh and blood. Living next door to a cemetery was a precarious situation for an imaginative child. I believe that many children have devastating fears that they cannot reveal. Even with loving parents like mine, I never fully expressed the extent of my terror. The best childhood, with all of its innocent joys, is not spared a dark side.

Years after my days on the farm were over, I opened a nursing home in Ventnor, N.J. One of my first patients was a Miss Moore, who was recuperating from an operation. When the woman learned that I was originally from Alliance, she remarked that her brother was born there.

Being curious, I asked Miss Moore to tell me about her brother. This is the story she told:

"When I was a little girl, we lived in a South Jersey community. My father was in the glass business there and we had a lovely home. One very cold January day, someone knocked at our door. Mother answered to admit a shivering young boy, ragged, carrying a peddler's pack. Mother gave the child a warm drink and asked him why he was out in such bad weather. The boy replied that he was walking from town to town trying to make a few pennies for his family. His father was very ill and there were many other younger children at home. The boy himself was only twelve years old! He had been forced to quit school in order to help his family.

"Mother was heartsick to see the condition of this youngster. As she talked to him, she realized that the child was exceptionally bright. He confessed that his greatest dream in life was to be able to continue his education. Mother made the boy stay at our house until my father came home. Then we all got into our buggy and rode to Alliance to the farm where the boy's family lived. Along the way my parents spoke to young Frank, telling him that they always wanted a son. They wished to adopt him and to see to it that he got the finest education available. The boy was overwhelmed. When we arrived at the farmhouse, my parents convinced Mr. and Mrs. Golder that they owed their son his chance in the world. After much weeping and hugging, Frank was instructed to pack his few belongings and to come with us. From that time on, Frank became my brother. My parents and I loved him and provided for his education. He proved to be brilliant. He went to Harvard where he received his doctorate. Later, Frank taught mathematics in England. He served on President Wilson's board at Versailles. Now Frank is with President Hoover's post-war European Relief Board."

It was a heartwarming story, although it must have been heartbreaking to the parents to give up their oldest son. Frank Golder got his chance and the parents' sacrifice proved to be a worthy one. However, there is an ironic addition that I must make to this story.

The Golders felt obligated to give up their child in order for him to fulfill his potential. Meanwhile, the other children stayed at home suffering the privations of illness and poverty which plagued the hapless family. When they moved to Philadelphia, Mr. Golder left the family to live in the hills of North Carolina because of his tuberculosis. Thereafter, Mrs. Golder managed to eke out an existence while maintaining a happy boisterous home life with her brood. Each child worked to put himself through school and college. How did the children at home turn out, without a "fairy godmother" to ease their way? The two Golder daughters owned their own businesses and became extremely successful. Mandis Golder and his brother Sam became engineers and built the first subway system in Philadelphia. At age 33, Benjamin, a lawyer, became the youngest congressman ever elected to the State of Pennsylvania legislature.

There must be a moral to the story of the Golders.

WINTER

February—The Blizzard

THE DELICIOUS DINNER was over. Sabbath candles had been blessed and the gray February day had quietly succumbed to the chilly blast of evening. Our kitchen stove, glowing with the coal fire, was valiantly trying to spread its heat through the registers to the two bedrooms on the second floor. We children had already warmed some bricks and wrapped them with rags, delivering them upstairs to our chilly bedding in the hopes that the icy wind would not penetrate our blankets, warmed by this method. My sister Lena, eleven, was reading a story to her rapt audience: Mother, me, and Bertha. Father seemed preoccupied and restless.

Suddenly, we heard a knock at the door. Two old friends of Father's stamped into the room, red-faced and chilled. They removed their heavy coats and strode to the warm stove. Mother rushed to offer them some wine and cookies.

The men had just attended synagogue services across the road and had decided to drop in. The three farmers talked about the signs of bad weather.

Father remarked worriedly, "I hope the storm holds off. I'm almost out of coal. I placed my order in Vineland several days ago, but they haven't delivered it yet. I doubt if I have enough coal to last more than a day."

The men left as the first slow snowflakes began to fall. The next morning we awoke to a strange world, white and mysterious. Familiar objects outside had become ghostly sculptures, with unfamiliar shapes and meaning. The wind howled, threatening to pull our small house from its foundation. We remembered Father's fears and rushed to the kitchen. Father and Mother had already gathered all of the remaining wood in the house to add to the fire. It was lucky that our stove burned either wood or coal, because there was only a very small amount of coal left. Father had already tried to get out of the door to reach the woodpile, but the large drifts made venturing outdoors impossible. We did not even have a shovel in the house.

Father spoke calmly, "If we are careful, this coal could last us until Sunday."

"And then?" Mother asked.

"Then we have the crates from the sweet potatoes in the house. We can start breaking them up. Meanwhile, we will take our blankets and pillows and sleep together in the kitchen tonight."

It was Shabbat. Father tried to make it seem as usual. Shabbat was the Sabbath, that wonderful time when neither Father or Mother did any work, so that the whole family had an opportunity to sit down together to talk and to enjoy each other's company. We sang songs and told stories as usual. We took turns reading to each other. But a worrisome thread ran through our afternoon. Father kept getting up to tend to the greedy fire. Mother conveyed her worried questions in her eyes.

Father knew that the horse and the cow in the barn had enough food from the hayloft to keep them alive for quite a while. The snow, covering the whole structure, would even act as insulation. The little chicks had plenty of cover to snuggle in on the floor and on the roof. We, too, had enough food and water in the house. If only the Vineland company had delivered the coal!

Soon the time came for us to break up the crates of sweet potatoes to feed the fire. Although two days had passed, the blizzard had not abated. The entire house was layered in snow. Never had we experienced anything so devastating as this storm. It was almost impossible to see out of the windows; the front door opened only a crack. The chamber pots, in use daily, presented a sanitary problem. However, Father managed to force open the back door enough for us to throw the refuse outside where it froze quickly.

On the third day, the last few wooden bins were about to go into the fire. Father looked at Mother.

"What has to be done has to be done. It is only furniture."

Mother looked back at Father and began to weep silently. He held her hand, with tears streaming down his worn cheeks. We children did not understand why they were so unhappy. It was "only furniture."

Now I do understand. In those days one saved for years to buy a good piece of family furniture. It was intended to last and to be handed down to future generations. Furniture was a symbol of family solidarity and belonging. A bureau was like a member of the family. To chop it up for firewood!

Mother went to the window. She started to scrape off the ice from the inside. As she peered out of the window, trying to see, she became extremely excited.

"Moses, I see something moving out there. I really do, I think there's a man out there, shoveling toward the house."

"Impossible," Father cried, "It's wishful thinking. No one could possibly . . ."

But then we heard . . . something! A scraping. A muffled shout. We rushed to the door, all straining together to open it a crack, unmindful of the icy chunks that fell inside. Outside, thick drifts of snow seemed to be in motion. Finally, miraculously, two snowy giants shouted our names. Two men, each carrying a shovel and a large bag of coal over their shoulders, struggled into the doorway. Out of breath, covered with snow, coughing and jabbering, the two men stomped and laughed and cried all at once. We all began to cry, shouting and hugging each other.

Mr. Goldman and his friend were the same farmers who had visited us on Friday. They were the only ones who knew that we were out of coal. For the last three days they had tried to shovel their way to our home. Each time they had started out, they had been forced back by the elements; but at last, they had made it.

As they approached our home and saw how we were boxed in, they feared that they would find us frozen to death. Their joy on seeing us alive and well was immeasurable. To have them bring us the life-giving coal under such circumstances was a miracle!

Mother prepared a little feast, fortifying the men with "Schnapps." Afterwards, they insisted on going home again before the snow covered their path. The storm had weakened a trifle and they went with our prayers. That night we were warm and cozy. The precious furniture was spared.

We celebrated—not because of the furniture, but because of the great bond that exists among men of deep faith. Knowing that there are human beings who would risk their lives to save each other—is to know that Man is truly made in God's image. Such committed men existed in those early days in Alliance.

SPRING

March—The Eclipse

ON A LOVELY DAY in early spring, Dad was preparing the land for plowing. I was helping him with a hoe to turn the vines to the middle of the pile so that the land could be cultivated. In this manner the vegetables seem to grow better. Suddenly the sky darkened. My father, a little distance away from me, was looking up into a glass. Although I couldn't see what he was staring at, I took off my sunbonnet and looked up at the sky. The sight was very strange. After a while I heard my father calling to me. "Bluma why don't you finish the row of vines?"

"I'm waiting for the light to come back," I said. "It's too dark to see a thing."

Father ran over to me immediately. He led me from the field and brought me back to the farmhouse. I couldn't see! He and Mother rushed me off to a Vineland doctor, who told my parents that my eyesight had been seriously affected. For a week my eyes had to remain bandaged while I stayed in a dark room. The doctor suggested that I visit an eye specialist. Dad took me to Jefferson Hospital in Philadelphia where an ophthalmologist examined me. In a dark room, he sat me in front of a little gas jet burner. As the specialist studied my eyes with his reflecting glass, I began to smell something burning. The gas burner was too close to my curls!

"Doctor, my hair is on fire."

"Oh," he smiled, thinking I was joking, "I didn't know that, I just thought it was fiery red."

Too shy to say another word, I was beginning to smell like a singed chicken. Finally the doctor realized what was happening. He moved my head and discovered the charred hairs. He laughed, patted me and said, "Don't worry, child, you'll still have your red hair—and your eyesight; but never, never look straight into the sky during an eclipse!"

Although my eyesight finally did return, the muscles had been damaged. I had some difficulty in reading after the accident. My eyelids had a tendency to droop. For many years I practiced special muscle techniques with prisms to strengthen my sight. Refusing to allow this handicap to affect my life, I continued to read, to study and to pursue all of my activities, unchanged. My red hair, singed in the flame, grew back in all of its glory. Perhaps the burning contributed an extra glowing quality of its own.

At the age of seventy-five, I went through an operation to remove my cataracts. Strangely enough, after the operation, I had twenty-twenty vision! A new, clear world opened up to me. I reveled in a reborn landscape of heightened colors, shapes and vistas. No wonder I felt compelled to become a painter at the age of eighty-three!

The regeneration of my eyesight provides the theme for my whole history: rebirth and renewal are constant and ageless processes. When spring returns, young and old are reawakened and refreshed.

If I were to depict my lifetime abstractly, it would not be a linear representation of successive years. My life would be shown as a circle with the Vital Force at center. Each time period on the curve is of equal and essential value to the whole. The life cycle has no beginning or ending. In some form, it continues and renews itself eternally like the seasons.

SPRING

April—Laundry Day

THE SNOW had melted and the brilliant sunshine spilled into the fields, urging brave little springs of green to poke up through the softening soil.

"See, Bertha," I said, "the winds have lost their icy breath and they are blowing the seeds around. Passover will be here soon!"

My little sister clapped her hands. "It will be soon!"

At this time of year we prayed that the earth would hurry to become warm enough for that "Special Day." Without fail, before the Passover Holidays, there was always one perfect day. At this time, the obliging Weather Maker sent down a sample of summertime. The wind died down; the sun put on extra power. Mother somehow was in league with nature, because she was always prepared when that wonderful day arrived. Early in the morning she would awaken us and announce, "Up, Young Ladies, we are off to the River today!"

Oh, what a joyous bustle ensued! There would be no tedious pumping of water at the well today! We dressed quickly and did our necessary chores. After eating breakfast, we helped our parents to gather the accumulation of soiled winter clothes. Mother brought out her galvanized tub, a wooden washboard and the supply of soap she had made during the long winter. My older sister, Lena aged twelve, felt very important to be left in charge of the farmhouse while we prepared to leave home. Little sister Bertha, seven, and I, Bluma, eight, clutched our treasured washboards which were miniature duplicates of our Mother's, and almost as useful. We all carefully packed the clothing and the equipment into the large old wooden wagon.

My Father hitched up our horse, Mary, and off we went for the half mile trip to the Maurice River. We stopped the wagon at the top of the hill where a well-worn path led down to the water. Old Mary could not be expected to make the trip down the hill with the cumbersome wagon. Cheerfully, we unloaded the laundry and carried it down to the water's edge. How we feasted our eyes on the sparkling sight! Although the cedar water seemed reddish and muddy, we knew it was crystal-clean, shallow and inviting. On the other side of the narrow river, the clustered trees seemed to be whispering among themselves.

"Hooray, the Bayuk girls are back!"

We made several trips up and down the hill to unload all of the clothing and equipment. Bertha and I could hardly wait to finish. At last, off came the shoes and socks. Tucking up our skirts into our bloomers, we squirmed while Mother fished out some of the smaller articles of clothing for us, usually handkerchiefs and socks. Grabbing the small pieces and taking our soap and washboards, we raced into the water. Oh! For the first few minutes it was cold, but so refreshing! Soon we were delightedly wriggling our toes and squishing up and down. As we became more free, we began to splash around with uncontrolled delight. Mother really didn't mind how wet we got. Our joyous peals of laughter convinced her that the soaking was good for our souls as well as for our sturdy bodies.

We did not forget our main duties. Copying Mother's actions, we washed each small piece diligently and rinsed them thoroughly. After wringing well, we draped each clean article on a bush to dry in the sun. As the bushes nearby became filled up, we wandered farther up the bank to use more and more bushes for dryers. Finally, the work was all done and the clothing was all stretched out for sunning.

The day was still warm; birds were hopping up and down the tree branches, chirping their encouragement as we splashed and played. Mother, enjoying a short rest, sat down on a grassy knoll, her face in the sun, eyes on her frolicking daughters.

Father's voice at the top of the hill brought our merry capers to a halt. As the sun was setting, we hurried to gather the dried laundry from the bushes. On my way up the bank to retrieve the farthest pieces, I saw a skinny hand reach out to grab a colorful article from one of the bushes. I yelled. The crashing of the underbrush told me that the thief was getting away. Realizing that it would not be prudent to run after the culprit, I gathered the rest of the clothing and returned to the wagon to tell my family what had happened.

Mother's favorite apron was missing! We couldn't imagine who would do such a thing. All of the neighbors in Alliance were like one big family. Strangers rarely came to this area. We were all sorely troubled, not so much by the loss of the apron, but by the question of whose skinny arm had taken it . . . and why!

Father told us to pile all of the clothing into the wagon. Selecting one of his clean work shirts, he said, "Sit here on the buckboard until I come back." He then strode off toward the far end of the river, to the area that we called the "Men's Section." (In the summer the men bathed upstream and the women downstream, right at the place where we had washed our clothing.) Our customs did not permit the males and females to bathe in the same area. Besides, one of the more daring girls had told us that many of the men and boys did not use bathing suits at all when they swam in the river! Father soon strode back, chuckling to himself. He held the missing apron in his hand.

"Just as I thought," he laughed. "The thief was a poor shivering young lad, whose friends had taken away his clothing for a joke while he took a bare swim in the river. He would have given the apron back eventually, but the poor lad was desperate. I gave him my shirt to wear. Father began to laugh heartily. "If you could have seen him, Annette. This skinny scared little fellow, shivering, and wearing nothing but your skimpy pink apron!"

"Who was it?" I asked.

"Never mind," Father smiled. "We men have to stick together. If you knew who he was, you would make life miserable for him with your teasing. His secret is safe with me."

Feeling too tired and contented to think of making anyone's life miserable, we hopped onto the wagon again. Our old mare flicked her ears and carted us slowly back to the house. Refreshed and happy, Bertha and I chattered excitedly to Lena about the day's adventures.

We knew now that summer would really come again, and that the sluggish pulse of the winter farm would quicken soon with spring-time vigor. Our barren land and our spirits were renewed as the winter "blues" slipped away into the friendly, healing ripples of the Maurice River.

SPRING

May—The Far Away Look

YONKEL, the fish peddler, was a most welcome visitor at our farmhouse. As soon as we heard his horse and wagon clip-clopping along Gershal Road near our house, Mama's face would brighten and she would get that "far-away look" in her eyes.

Although Mama was always busy, she welcomed the opportunity to stop and to exchange a few words with Yonkel every Friday morning. While she carefully examined each fish, choosing only the best and the freshest, she carried on a long and earnest conversation with the little man, all of it in Yiddish.

It was certainly not his smell or his scraggly beard that endeared the peddler to Mama, it was his relationship. Yonkel was a "lantzman," an immigrant from Mother's birthplace in Russia. He occasionally received letters from his brother Jacob, who still lived in that small village near Odessa where Mama had spent her traumatic childhood. Jacob's letters were Mama's link to her past.

Nostalgia for that small piece of Hell where Mama had lost her parents in a bloody "pogrom" was not the reason for Mama's "far-away look." She brooded because she had left a part of herself in Russia—a little child, her first-born. No matter how occupied my mother was in present time, something seemed always to be pulling at her heart, calling to her from the tiny "shtetl." Her lost son was the reason for Mama's "far-away look."

After Yonkel departed, our activity would again start in earnest. Friday was our busiest day. Immediately Mama looked over the fish she had bought, deciding how she would prepare them. There were herrings, small trout, carp and butterfish (the prices ranged from ten to twelve cents a dozen). Of course, my sisters and I, from the time that we were quite small, would help with the cleaning of the fish, scales, heads and skins. Although the advance preparation was a messy, smelly job, the results were well worth the effort.

After the fish were cleaned, washed and dried, Mother usually boiled them with a little salt and onion for about ten minutes, making sure that they remained firm. Then the fluid was poured off into another pot. Vinegar and sugar were added to the juice with bay leaf and cloves for seasoning. Then the liquid was boiled down, cooled and poured in a crock to mix with the fish and onions. Within a few days, the fish would be ready to eat and it was delicious! During the week, we used the sweet and sour fish for our dinner almost every night. It was tasty, healthful, inexpensive and easy to serve.

When the fish had been made and put away, we began preparations for our ritual Friday night dinner. On the Sabbath eve, we had chicken. Enough fowl was cooked to serve on Saturday, Shabbot, the day of rest. Finally, early in the afternoon, after the beautiful Sabbath table was set with its gleaming napery and silver, Mama would walk to a special drawer in her kitchen. From under a pile of crisp white "company" linen, she would count out the crumpled dollar bills inside, fingering the change and sighing. We respected Mama's horde, knowing that it represented a sacred dream, a fund for "Moishe's passage."

Moishe Becker was the name of that mysterious relative whose "passage" we were all so anxious to arrange. You see, Moishe was our brother, the boy who still lived in Russia—the year-old baby that Mama was forced to leave when she emigrated to America in 1882.

In 1880 Mother had been wedded to Isaac Becker, a tailor in Russia. As touched upon earlier, her first husband turned out to be a cruel man who had married the orphan solely to obtain a free servant. From morning to night the bride was expected to work: sewing, scrubbing and obeying her husband's orders.

He scolded and criticized her continuously, reminding her of her good fortune in becoming the wife of such a fine man. In a year's time, a baby was born of this union. Starved for affection, Mama poured out all of her love and warmth on her beautiful curly-headed son, Moishe. Isaac did not approve of coddling babies. He ordered Annette to get back to work and to stop pampering the child.

The longer Mama stayed with Isaac, the more miserable she became. At last she could take no more. In the middle of the night, she bundled her baby in his blanket and ran away from her husband, seeking refuge at the inn of her Polish foster parents. Isaac followed her and caused a frightful scene. He threatened to beat her. The Kowalskis finally were able to talk Isaac into a divorce by offering him a bribe.

Unfortunately, Mother had to agree to let Isaac keep Moishe, who was then one year old. It was decided that Mother would emigrate to America. Isaac assured her that after she made her fortune, she could send for her child, if she would reimburse him for the baby's care. The tailor really believed that the streets of America were paved with gold and that Mama would make him rich when she redeemed her baby. The Kowalskis loaned their Annette the money for passage to New York.

Although Mama was heartbroken that she had to leave her "golden boy" she felt that their separation would be for only a short time. After all, wasn't everyone in America rich? Unfortunately, after she arrived in New York, she could find employment only in a shop where the wages were meager and the hours long. Mother found that she made barely enough to keep herself alive and to save a few pennies a week to reimburse her foster parents for their loan.

Later, after Mama married Dad and came to live on the farm, there was scarcely enough money for her ready-made family. Sending for the baby in Russia was out of the question. By the time my older brothers left, a new farmhouse had been built and new babies were arriving. First Lena was born; four years later, I appeared on the scene; and next, Bertha. After Bertha, there was the set of twins, who died of fever when they were eight months old. Another boy also died in infancy. Lastly, my brother Eddie was born when my mother was forty-five years old.

My earliest recollections of Mama were connected with the big old-fashioned cradle that sat in the kitchen by the stove. It seemed to me that Mama's feet were busy always rocking baby in the cradle while she worked with her hands, sewing, cooking or polishing. As she worked and rocked, Mama sang "Rozhinkins and Mondelin," a song about raisins and almonds. And of course, as she rocked her successive infants, her "faraway look" revealed that she was also thinking about another baby whom she could not rock—her firstborn—the "golden boy."

At sundown every Friday, when Mama lit the Sabbath candles, she always said a special prayer for Moishe. All through our childhood we were encouraged to include our absent brother in our prayers and thoughts. How we longed to meet him! It was not easy for my parents to obtain information about Moishe through the years. Neither he nor his father could read or write. The only meager news that Mama gleaned was from Yonkel's brother's letters.

"He was such a good baby," Mama would tell us, "so good natured, so happy!"

In our mind's eye we saw him, Mama's zindelle chuckling and gurgling. Time passed; we girls grew up, but somehow, our curly-headed, adorable Russian brother remained in our thoughts as the happy baby of my mother's memory.

Each time that Mama seemed to be within her goal with the money for Moishe's passage, a new emergency would crop up in our immediate family, and poor Moishe's journey was postponed. In due time we girls left the farm: Lena to marry a neighboring farmer; I to Philadelphia to become a nurse; Bertha to work in Philadelphia. Still, our brother had not arrived.

After we girls left home to seek our fortunes away from the farm, Mama began to increase her outside activities as a practical nurse. This extra source of income was the only way she had of speeding up the long-delayed arrival of her Russian son. For many years my mother had often been called upon to act as midwife for the neighboring women. Our small town did not boast of a doctor. If there had been one, he would have received very few patients. Most of the farmers considered medical care a luxury. Because the women viewed childbirth as a natural activity, they did not create a fuss when their birthing time came. Sometimes they called Mama, laboring with her help. Then after resting for a few hours, they arose to take care of their regular duties. Mother had a good reputation for delivering normal, healthy babies. Not once did any of her patients develop any complications. All of her babies lived and were healthy.

After I entered nursing training and learned of the complications that could happen during childbirth, I became panicky about my mother's involvement. The first time I returned home, I begged Mama to give up her midwifery. At first she would not listen to me. The extra money was earmarked for such a longed-for goal!

"Mama, you don't realize how foolhardy and risky your actions are. If anything goes wrong in a delivery, you could be held responsible. Mama, please, I'll go barefoot and send you my shoe money. I'll wear rags and send you my clothing money —I'll stop eating . . ."

"Enough, Blumella," she interrupted. "If you are so upset, there must be a good reason. All right, I'll stop. God will have to help me find the rest of the money I need."

I was relieved when Mama stopped nursing, but her sighs became deeper and her look became more "far-away" than ever.

Finally, it happened! One Friday morning, in May of 1922, forty years after Mama had arrived in America, Yonkel the fish peddler appeared at our door, his face flushed and his words tumbling out excitedly. Mama listened, then ran to her precious purse, counting. At last she returned, asking Yonkel to sit down. Fido, our farm dog, was at Yonkel's heels, enjoying the redolence of the fishmonger's clothing. Mama patted Fido on the head, "Go tell Moses I want him!"

Fido was our link between the farmhouse and the fields. Father never carried a watch as he worked. When it was time for lunch or dinner, Mama just sent Fido out to find Dad and tug at his pants, letting him know that he was wanted at the house. No telephone or telegraph was as dependable as Mama's canine messenger.

As soon as Father came back to the house, Mother told him of Yonkel's message. The old man had brought the news that Moishe, now a tailor, had been saving some money for his emigration too. Perhaps now, between the three funds, Moishe's, Mama's and Father's, perhaps there would be enough for our brother to make the long-awaited journey. Dad immediately consulted his little red bank book. After calculating carefully, he nodded, beaming. "Yes, Annette, now we can make it. I give you this money with a full heart."

Such hugging and kissing! Moishe was contacted through Yonkel's brother and all arrangements were made for his passage. We later received word that Moishe was to arrive before the High Holy Days in September.

I have often marveled at my parents' depth and endurance. Long before the experts on child care set up rules for successful parenting, Moses and Annette Bayuk were doing the right thing naturally. No matter how pressured my parents were, they always had time to stop and to show their special love and concern for each child's physical and emotional well being. At the beautiful holiday season, our parents seem to reveal the ultimate expression of their love for us, and we responded. It was most fitting that our beloved brother Moishe should make his appearance to his eager family during the High Holy Days.

Mother's Holiday meals were always magnificent feasts. No one had ever surpassed her baking of breads and cakes. She always managed to make each child his or her favorite goody and to set a splendid table. On the eve of Moishe's arrival, she outdid herself.

Spring

Our kitchen was magically transformed into a palace, with its holiday silver, polished to a superfine glow, and the cloths, dazzling white and crisp. Our entire home glowed with cleanliness, and more important, with the warmth of loving welcome.

When the memorable day arrived, Father departed to meet Moishe at the Norma train station. Bertha, Lena and I had returned home to be with Mama as the welcoming committee. Mother waited with us at home, in a state of agitated excitement, alternately beaming and crying as she stood by the door, straining for the sound of horse and wagon. When we finally heard them coming, we girls wanted to cheer, but we restrained ourselves for the sake of our white-faced mother.

When the men arrived, Father pushed open the door and shoved in a reluctant figure. The man who stood before us was stooped and greying. His lips were thin and his glasses were thick. He smelled of herring and unwashed skin. Was this Moishe Becker, our "golden" brother?

Mama stood and stared for a moment, bewildered. Then she embraced the exhausted stranger. Moishe began to speak haltingly in a deep gutteral Yiddish. Mama just kept holding on to his arm and looking up at him. Although we tried awkwardly to make conversation, at first there seemed little to say. The man answered every question with a monosyllable. Mama kept staring at him, searching, searching for one trace of the past.

Soon, our guest was settled, washed and refreshed. Mother had recovered enough to serve the holiday meal. We subdued our usual hilarity in the presence of this stranger. Eventually, Moishe began to relax a little, speaking about his life in Russia, and about the wife and four small children he had left behind. As he spoke, he proceeded to wolf his food greedily, belching and gulping as he put away Mama's goodies. Mama piled him with more and more food, as if she had to make up for the forty years of not feeding him, all at one time.

Our new brother stayed on at the farm for several months, enjoying the lavish attention and the delicious meals that Mama made for him. During that time he had made no attempt to help with the chores on the farm. Early in November, Father decided to speak to Moishe.

"What are your plans now?"

"I would like to bring my family over here from Russia," my brother answered. "If you think you can manage it."

Father looked at the man in surprise.

"Moishe, you are the head of your own family. It is up to you to work and to arrange for their arrival. It was very difficult for your mother and me to get you a passage with our funds. Now you must work to bring over your family."

My brother finally realized that he was not to be pampered and taken care of for the rest of his life. He then asked Father to find him a job as a tailor. Father wrote to his son, Sam Bayuk in Philadelphia. Sam sent a reply that he would arrange for a job for Moishe on South Street. Dad rented a room for Moishe with a Jewish family in South Philadelphia. By this time, it was December. I returned to the farm to be with Mother when she said "Goodbye" once again to her son. Although Moishe was going only as far as Philadelphia, it was unlikely that he would be able to visit the farm very often, once he began to work. I feared that this new separation would be a traumatic experience for Mama. When Dad appeared to drive Moishe to the Norma station, Mama embraced her son fervently. Then once more, he was gone.

Slowly, Mama closed the door. She sighed and walked to her favorite rocking chair. She sat down heavily putting her head down, hands covering her face. A soft moan escaped her lips as she rocked back and forth.

"Mama!" I embraced her, chair and all. "Please, please don't cry! Philadelphia is only a few miles away. Moishe is in this country now."

My mother lifted her head. She looked at me, "I don't understand, Bluma, I don't understand. All these years I worked, prayed, and saved, and waited to see my beautiful 'zindell' again. Now, he is finally here. I waited and he came. But who is this man—my 'zindell?' My little baby that I left so many years ago turns out to be—his father! My son is just like the man I ran away from forty years ago. Oh Bluma, Moishe is his father all over again!"

I tried to comfort her. "Mama, it happens. It is not your fault. At least you got him over here. You did the right thing."

"All those years when he needed me I wasn't there. Maybe if I had brought him over sooner! Oh, how can I make it up to him, all those years without his mother?"

"Mama, don't you see, it probably wouldn't have made any difference. He might have turned out just the same even if he had been with you. He takes after his father. Lots of children do. They call it heredity and there's nothing that you can do to change it. Just think, Mama, how awful it would have been to have an Isaac Becker living with us all these years!"

I did a clumsy imitation of my half-brother, coaxing a little smile from Mama. Then a strange thing happened. The "faraway look" came back into my mother's eyes. Watching her face, somehow, I knew that Mama's little first-born was back in Russia once again—a happy, gurgling one-year-old.

"Such a good baby."

This "Moishe" person who had just left, what did he have to do with Mama's "Golden Boy"?

SPRING

June—Sermons in Stone

THE YOUNG MAN at the Norma train station was wearing shoes in the middle of the warm spring day! My sister Bertha, fourteen, and just beginning to notice boys, was intrigued by this well-dressed stranger. Bare-foot, berry-stained, she stood gawking at him on the station platform. I, being fifteen, and more sedate, peeked from behind our old horse, Mary, as I helped Dad with the crates of strawberries we were shipping on the New York train.

Although it was only eleven o'clock in the morning, Bertha, Dad and I had already put in a full day's work before riding to the depot.

Mother had awakened us at five o'clock so that we could pick the berries before the heat of the day made such work impossible. Our harvest system was effectively simple. Father would set himself up under a wooden covered stand in the field. Shaded from the sun, he kept himself and the berries cool while he sorted and repacked them in crates for shipping. Bertha and I, in our pinafores and sunbonnets, bare-foot, of course, worked our way through the berry patch, picking the ripe fruit and placing them in quart containers. Our carriers held six quarts. As soon as we had filled a carrier, we took it over to Dad for processing. Then we returned to continue harvesting. In this manner, by 10:30 a.m., we had finished picking the day's bounty and were ready to hop aboard the wagon with Dad for the Norma station, to load the berries on the train for market.

The station was filled with farmers and their helpers, sending this day's produce to the city on the noon train. A stranger in city clothes was an unusual sight. Who was he? What did he want?

Most of us were too busy to ask questions. However, Bertha could not contain her curiosity. She boldly approached the young man and said, "Hello, are you arriving or leaving?"

The stranger took a look at Bertha, a grimy sight, and replied in an icy tone, "I'm looking for the livery stable. I should like to hire a carriage."

"Ho, ho," laughed Bertha, "I thought so! You got off at the wrong station. The livery stable is in Vineland. This is the Norma station."

"I am quite aware of where I am," he said, annoyed. "But I thought I could hire a carriage here in Norma."

"Do you want a ride?" Bertha said, "We'll be glad to take you where you want to go."

Overhearing the conversation, I was horrified. How could we carry this dandy in our splintery old farm-stained wagon! Since we were finished with the loading, I walked over to ask the stranger where he wanted to go.

"Well, I guess I should try the post office," he said, uncertainly. "I'm looking for the address of a very important personage."

I was impressed. "I didn't know we had any of them in this area. Well, we could give you a ride to the Post Office. Mr. Coltun the postmaster must know if there are any important personages living around here."

"Thank you," the young man replied. "Where is your carriage?"

Embarrassed, I pointed to the rickety wagon, where our old mare waited, chasing the flies off her leathery rump with a discouraged tail. The young man paled.

"Father," I called as our parent returned to the wagon, "Can we give this gentleman a lift to the Post Office?"

"Of course, hop aboard!"

Our hesitating guest climbed up into the wagon.

"He's going to see an important personage," Bertha explained to Father.

"Really," Father smiled. "I'm sure the personage will be delighted to see such a fine young man."

After a short ride, Father stopped in front of Krassenstein's grocery store. We girls shrieked with delight, knowing we were in for a treat. Father bought us a chocolate bar marked off in little squares. This bar was our reward—our wages for the day's labor. Of course we saved half of it for Mother and Eddie, our young brother. We offered the young man a chocolate square. He declined quickly and remained silent until Father brought the wagon to a halt in front of the Norma Post Office.

"Here you are," he said heartily. "Enjoy your personage."

The young man thanked us and left.

We continued on our way, voicing our opinions of the snobbish person who had just left our wagon.

"He looked at us as if we are dirt," Bertha fumed.

"What's so bad about us?" I asked, through lips stained with berry juice, as I contemplated my grimy toes and purple feet.

"Perhaps he has never seen a young girl with so many freckles before," Dad teased. "City girls don't get freckles."

"Yes, I know," I sighed, "and city girls don't dress in pinafores and sunbonnets either. They don't have feet stained purple from squeezing grape juice for wine."

"You are right, Bluma," Father said slowly. "City girls wear fashionable dresses and shoes every day. They buy fancy hats with bird feathers on them. And they go to school to learn how to make a good living." He was watching me carefully.

I sighed again, "Oh, how I would love to live like that!"

Deep in our own thoughts, we continued home without another word. As we approached our home, we saw a group of farmers standing in the yard waiting for us. It was time for a court session. In addition to his other duties, Father was the Justice of the Peace for the Alliance community. He held court in our kitchen settling all of the minor disputes that cropped up in our area. So respected was his judgment that the litigants accepted without question whatever disposition he made. Today two neighbors were in dispute. Father listened. Then he handed down his decision: "Ben," he directed, "you get your son to help you repair the damages that your cow did to Sam's field. Then, compensate him for his losses by giving him five carriers of your own berries. Sam, your wife makes a delicious berry pie. Ask her to bake one and invite Ben and his family over for tea and pie."

The two men shook hands and left. In a few months they would have another dispute. After father judged again, they would go away as friends once more, their differences settled.

The next case was that of a hired man and his wife. The woman complained that her husband had beaten her.

"I don't see any bruises," Father said.

Quick as a flash, the woman picked up her skirts and turned her ample rear in the direction of the Bench. Father reached out a hand to cover my little nephew Harry's eyes. In the midst of the laughter and commotion that followed, the young stranger appeared at the open door. He looked around him in surprise.

Father smiled a greeting, "What can I do for you this time, young man."

"I—I was told that I would find him here, the Great Philosopher, Rabbi Moses Bayuk."

"The great philosopher!" Bertha, Eddie and I began to hoot. This "meshuggina" person was talking about Father—our dad, the farmer!

Father motioned the visitor to a seat while he disposed of the last case and adjourned court.

"Young man, I am Moses Bayuk," he said, "What can I do for you?"

The man looked at Father in dismay.

"You, you are the great teacher?"

"I am only a student," Father said. "I write of what I have learned by the grace of the Almighty who has revealed certain truths to me."

"Forgive me," the young man stammered. "I—I—I just did not expect . . ."

Father interrupted, "You did not expect an old farmer in coveralls. Well, that's what I am."

"But you are a great writer and philosopher. I didn't expect that you would act like an ordinary person. I thought you would be spending your time at the synagogue or in your study, writing, reading, lecturing. You are a personage!"

I could hardly understand the conversation, but I knew that something amazing was being disclosed. It seemed that our Father was not just a "Dad," he was a "personage!" I was astonished at the revelation.

Father continued, "Young man, my greatest work is in the fields, providing hungry people with nature's bounty. My other work is done in my spare time, late at night, by the oil lamp. My 'Study' is this same kitchen table. I ease the body's hunger by day in the fields and the soul's by night."

"Rabbi Bayuk," the stranger replied, "There are others too whose souls are hungry for wisdom. I was sent here by men from Philadelphia who will pay you well for your teaching services. I am to offer you a position—a chance to spend your time with eager pupils. A group of devout Jews would like you to come to inspire and lead their sons so that they will keep up our traditions. They need you to kindle interest and feeling for the Torah. The fathers will pay you well. We have already spoken to your son Sam. He is willing to provide you with a home in the city with all of the comforts. You will be able to spend your days teaching and writing."

Even Bertha was speechless at this offer. I let out a squeal of joy! "Mama," I shouted, "No more pumping water."

Mother was laughing and crying at the same time. Her eyes were shining. "Hooray!" we shouted—"No more outhouses!"

Father looked at us and sighed. "Well, I suppose the time has come. The farm has served its purpose. My loved ones are ready to move on and I must accept what is."

The visitor was delighted, "Then you will come, Rabbi Bayuk?"

"Yes," Dad said, "we will come, God willing. Tell your kind friends that I shall accept their offer, and I shall write to my son Sam about the lodgings."

Joseph Karp was the name of the young man from Philadelphia. He stayed at our home that night. Bertha and I hurried upstairs to our bedroom before dinner. We washed up carefully, brushed out our matted tresses, put on fresh pinafores and our precious shoes. As we entered the kitchen, Joseph stared at us, suddenly becoming shy and tongue tied. The "hoodlums" had become girls!

Later, after dinner, Father sat on his favorite stone outdoors. Gradually, our friends and neighbors began to wander over to our front lawn as they usually did in the warm evenings, to discuss their ideas or to listen to Father's marvelous stories. We girls were kept busy, swatting flies away as he spoke.

That night the discussion was about the Cosmos. Father's flights of fancy took us with him on wings to the far reaches of the skies.

"Someday," he said, "Someday in the future, we shall be able to communicate with the heavens!"

Although I could not really understand Father's deep philosophy then, his words remained with me. Now I still hear his voice and recall his predictions as the newest marvels of the twentieth century unfold in front of me. Recently on that memorable Christmas day when the first Astronaut sent his message of "peace on earth" down from the moon, I sat stunned, remembering my Father's words of long ago. Surely, we have now "communicated with the heavens," just as Father predicted on that spring night in 1903.

At the end of the evening, Father informed his neighbors about Joseph's offer and his acceptance. The farmers were taken by surprise.

The next morning, we arose at 5:00 a.m. as usual to pick our berries, proceeding to the station at 10:30 a.m. to ship the crop.

Joseph went with us to the station to leave for Philadelphia, much to Bertha's despair. At the depot, the other farmers and their helpers seemed strangely quiet. Their usual good-natured bantering was missing.

We stayed to wave goodbye to our friend Joseph, promising to see him when we moved to Philadelphia. On our return home, we found a large group of farmers and their families waiting outside of our door. Their spokesman, Mr. Coltun, asked that Father set up his court session for a special hearing. Once again the kitchen table was cleared to become the judge's bench, Dad banged his gavel.

"Well, what is the dispute?" Father asked.

"No dispute, your honor, just a hearing. May I present the case?"

Father nodded.

"Well, Moses, er—your honor," Aaron Coltun began, "there are people in the city who wish to take our friend and leader away from us. I think that we should have a chance to express our feelings in this matter. Moses, they say you are a great Rabbi, and that they need you to teach rich people's sons about the Bible. We say that you are our leader and we need you to keep this community of poor people together.

We never knew that you have been writing great works. We are proud of you. But those great works were written here, inspired by the soil and your own labors. Your revelations have come from your farm experiences. Why should you leave the source of your inspirations? I am not a wise man like you, but I know that in the city a man like you would dry up. You are a part of the seasons of growing things, like the rest of us. The outside world is for our children. They have experienced our seasons; now they will go on to other challenges. But we, the pioneers, must maintain what we have built here. These are our roots.

You have always led us. With you we have held on and learned to live in dignity without fear. We can battle the elements on equal terms—not like the days of the pogroms. Besides, Moses, in a city one stifles; enemies can reach you; soft living can corrupt you. The meaning of life is in a seed—not in a flushing toilet. Moses, without you we are lost. Don't desert us. Stay here. Continue to write, but do it from here where you belong."

One by one the solemn men walked up to him and shook his hand, each adding a special plea. Dad's eyes were filled with tears. He shook hands with each man and embraced him emotionally. The men filed silently out to their waiting wagons. We children looked at Mother. She was busy cooking and did not turn around.

The next day was Shabbos. Father and Mother, unusually silent, sat outdoors in the warm sunshine. Towards late afternoon, Dad asked me to walk with him to the berry patch. As we approached, we were surprised to see a man furtively picking the ripe berries. A stranger was helping himself to the fruits of our labor!

Father motioned to me to stay behind the cluster of trees. "Stay here, hidden, and start making a lot of noise when I signal to you."

He then grabbed a carrier and began to walk slowly toward the field. Pretending to pick, Father bent behind the man and said, "So you're wise to the farmers' habits too!"

The man laughed, "Yep they never pick their stuff on Saturday."

"But sometimes they walk down to look at their fields," Dad warned.

"Well, so far I'm lucky," the man replied, popping a large red berry into his mouth. His carrier was almost full. When he was about finished, Father signaled to me. I began to stamp around and shake the branches of the tree.

"Quick," Dad shouted, "the Boss is coming!"

The stranger dropped his carrier and fled. Father laughed heartily. He lifted the filled carrier and brought it into my hiding place.

"See," he said, "Now we have a nice carrier of berries for our dinner tonight. And we did no work to get it."

Dad brought the berries to Mother who was still sitting outside watching the sunset.

"Annette," he said, taking her hand in his, "we must talk about what is on our minds. I know how it has been here for you all these years. You were a city girl when I met you. Yet, you came here to struggle with me without complaint. I don't know how you managed to accomplish all that you do. But now I realize how you feel. Enough is enough, we're getting older. You really want to go back to the city, don't you?"

"And you," Mother countered, "Do you want to go too?"

Father answered, "You have stayed with me, now it is my turn to go with you. You deserve to have an easier life. Lena is married and has a home of her own. Bluma is ready for new horizons and Bertha will take to the city like a native. And Eddie, too, perhaps the city schools will be better for Eddie. Here he is always playing truant and getting into trouble."

Mother turned toward Dad. Suddenly she became again the spitfire of her younger days. She stood up and stamped her feet angrily.

"Moses," she scolded, "you are not going to blame me for taking you away from this farm. This is where your heart is. These are your roots. I could never come between you and your roots. For a while I was tempted. You see, husband, ever since I left the city, I have missed one thing terribly, running water. Oh, I dream about turning a spigot on and getting water without having to pump and pump and carry and pour! And how I would love to have a toilet, indoors, one that flushes! But that is no reason for leaving. I came here to be your wife. I belong where you are. You know that you will always belong here. So here we stay!"

Dad bent his head and kissed Mama's calloused hand. "Thank you my dear wife. I would have gone away for your sake, but it is true. I need this land and it needs me. I belong, like this large stone, this rock on our grass. Here I sit in the evening to think, to count the stars and to tell my stories. This rock is like me. We are anchored to the soil.

"Someday, when I am called, I will be uprooted only for a short distance to be set again in the cemetery next door. And this stone I sit on now will go with me. Both of us will stay forever, a few yards from the farm where we have given and received our strength."

The next day, Father dispatched a letter to his son Sam, my half-brother, and to Joseph, telling them of his change in plans.

The whole town of Alliance was overjoyed with the news. Bertha mooned about for a few days, thinking no doubt about the handsome Joseph. Soon, she got over her disappointment, becoming her own pert self, barefoot and sassy as ever.

However, the situation was different for me. At fifteen, about to be graduated from the country schoolhouse, I was feeling bewildered and lost, aching for new horizons. Although I dearly loved my family, I knew that the hunger for knowledge and experience that I possessed would lead me away from the farm. My answers lay in a wider environment. It was time to tell my parents that soon I must leave them.

Time is an ambivalent master. While the circle of years chained my father to his fields, my fifteenth spring set me free to challenge the world outside.

End of the Seasons

OUR SCHOOLMASTER read the list of names of those who were graduating from our two-room public schoolhouse. Dressed in my best frock, I sat waiting to be called to the front to receive my diploma. I was fifteen and had completed the eighth grade. To each of us our teacher Mr. Randolph gave a personal speech.

"Bluma, you are a special person. During the school year, you were absent more times than you were present. I know that you often skipped class to take care of your friends when they were ill. I am not scolding you for missing so much class time. You kept up with all of your assignments. I do want to talk to you about your future plans. You are a girl with a sharp, inquiring mind. Continue with your schooling if you can. If you were a boy, I would suggest that you become a doctor. You love science and you have a gift for helping the sick. However, since you are a girl, and since your parents are struggling farmers, I can only advise you to do your best to find a way to continue your education."

I thanked the teacher and took my precious diploma. At the conclusion of the ceremonies, we graduates embraced each other. Israel Kraftzow shyly handed me a poem. "Roses are red; violets are blue. Redheaded Bluma—it always was you!" I blushed with pleasure. Israel was my first romantic admirer. What a surprise! I had always considered him a buddy. Gratefully, I kissed my old pal and told him how much I appreciated his friendship. We said goodbye at the classroom door. Shortly after graduation, Israel left to join his brothers in New York. He sought and found fame and fortune. I never saw him again.

After graduation day, my mind was in a constant turmoil. Where was I to go from here? I loved my family and felt as much a part of the farm as Dad's rock on our lawn. Yet, I knew that the time had come for me to seek wider landscapes because I wanted to become a doctor. My parents had taught me to feel that my sex was not a deterrent to any goal that I was capable of obtaining. Now, in order to pursue my dream, I would have to go to the city for my education. Philadelphia was the logical choice. There, I could find work and go to school at night. Yet, as I looked at the dear faces of my loved ones, I could not bear the thought of parting from them.

As I worried about my future, my parents shared my concern. They knew that their Bluma was different. Lena had married at an early age. She had married William Levin, son of a pioneer family, and was content to be housekeeper and farmer's wife like Mama. The Levins lived across the road from us, happily ensconced on their own farm. Bertha, unhurried, took life as it came. I was the restless one, with an overwhelming thirst for knowledge and adventure. Although my parents had always encouraged us to be independent, they were reluctant to let me go off to the city completely on my own. Fortunately, a new door opened up for me at the right time.

Many years ago, when I was a baby, my three half-brothers, Sam, Max and Meyer, had left home for New York City. Eventually, they had made their way to Philadelphia and to great success. Although my brothers came to visit us, they had never attempted to make life easier for their father, his wife or their half-siblings.

Shortly after my graduation, I was rather surprised to see a letter from my half-brother Sam. "Dear Father, (he wrote) I am coming down to see you this weekend to talk to you about Bluma's future. I would like to take her back with me and give her a job in our plant. She can stay with Edith and me at our home."

My parents and I decided quickly that this offer should be acted upon. On that milestone day when my wealthy brother Sam came from Philadelphia on the train, my farm days ended.

A few hours after his arrival, I took my battered suitcase, climbed aboard our old farm wagon, kissed my family goodbye and started off. I drove with Dad and Sam to the Norma station and to a new life.

I am grateful that my parents were realists. They loved me too much to make our first parting a sad occasion. They treated my leave-taking as a natural, inevitable part of growth, and their wish for my success was sincere, given with a full heart.

While I sat on the train, headed in a new direction, I reviewed a parade of memories.

Bertha and I had shared our lives like twins. Although there was little time for fun, we had managed to make good use of our leisure. Our favorite pastime was shopping. I remembered how we used to save up our pennies until we each had twenty-five cents. Then we would plan an outing to the big town of Vineland.

First, we would hitchhike for a mile and a half to the Norma station. There we started by foot on the seven-mile trip to Vineland. Usually a passing farmer would offer us a ride in his wagon. We had no fears about accepting rides because we knew most of the farmers in the vicinity. Once in Vineland, we headed for the store that sold ribbons and lace. There we often bought a piece of gingham or cotton to make a special present. After we got home, we would cross-stitch a design on the material, cut it out, sew it and present a homemade apron to our Mother. Mama cherished our efforts. She would don our gift and then put other aprons on top of it so that our special apron would not get dirty.

Next, my mind floated to our summer fun. Swimming was our great diversion in the hot weather. Our village was surrounded by beautiful lakes. The Maurice River, used for irrigation and washing clothes, was also the place where we enjoyed our summer swimming. The men and the women were segregated in different sections of the beach. The men swam nude in their isolated section upriver. The girls wore petticoats to swim in. The ladies wore aprons in the front, with nothing underneath, and nothing in the back. I laughed as I recalled the occasions when daring boys would swim down to our section. The modest mamas would scream and throw their aprons over their faces, thus exposing the rest of their ample, unclad bodies.

The river was shallow and extremely clear. Little black snakes used to share our swimming area with us. I always carried a tree branch when I bathed, to chase the snakes away without hurting them. Father had warned us never to kill another living thing unless it was trying to harm us. He said that every living creature has a right and a reason to live.

Summer vacationers were also a part of our lives. In our small house we "took in" city boarders for the entire summer. It seems that Philadelphians considered the South Jersey air beneficial to their health.

Many city families enjoyed annual vacations all over the area. Parvin's was the most famous hotel. Mrs. Parvin ran a lovely resort near the lake. Her pleasant manner and wholesome food brought visitors back year after year. Centerton Park also offered good facilities for boating and picnicking.

In our house, the boarders were given our bedrooms. We all slept in cots in the kitchen and in the parlor. In addition to her regular work, Mother cooked delicious meals for the guests, managing the extra work with her usual grace and skill.

As the train rushed toward the city, my memories continued to jog along in my mind. I stamped them on my heart to carry with me forever. Although I carried little in material belongings, I was fortified by the moral fiber of my early seasons. This strength made me a truly liberated woman at the age of fifteen.

True I was going to stay with family, yet I was more free than many of today's women whose goals and morals have become so confused in our supposedly enlightened era. Seventy-five years ago, at the age of fifteen, I took complete responsibility for my own life. I knew that my future was in my own hands and that I was the mistress of my actions. My plans were simple and straightforward. I would learn as much as I could wherever and whenever I could. I would always take time to help others who needed me. I would earn my own way, keeping my honor and integrity in all situations.

Of course, I was a little apprehensive. What would my "fancy" sister-in-law, Edith, think of me? I was a homespun carrot-topped country girl; Edith was a sophisticated, convent educated German Jewess from New York. Did she know that Sam was bringing me to live in her fancy home?

I was puzzled about Sam, too. Why had my half-brother suddenly become so interested in my future? He had shown no such family feelings before. What kind of work would I be doing in his business? Although I was rather naive, my common sense told me that I was not going to get a "free lunch." I realized that Sam must have extended his invitation for a self-serving reason. This suited me because I wanted to pay my way. I was prepared to do what I could, willingly, in return for his hospitality and the opportunity to learn a trade. Even with this attitude, I was totally unprepared for the strange situation I found when I entered the Sam Bayuk household in North Philadelphia.

Sam sat beside me on the train, puffing his cigar, unaware of the torrents of thoughts and memories that were passing through my brain. He was the catalyst for a milestone in my young life. All my days, I would be the farmer's daughter; yet, never could I return to the farm. The ride to Philadelphia was a one-way trip to the rest of my life.

Looking Back

Many seasons have carved their mystic messages upon our sturdy elm since my childhood on the farm. Although the physical town is almost deserted, the spirit of Alliance has dispersed into a limitless domain—enriching the lives of countless descendants.

The concept of the experimental farm community created by Jewish philanthropists, including the Baron de Hirsch Fund, was successful, sustained by the valor and dedication of our pioneer families. After escaping from persecution, our people accepted a strange environment with determination. Toiling with dignity, they achieved their goal—a peaceful existence in a new and beloved land. Those who are fortunate in tracing their roots to this unique setting wear their memories as precious jewels. It is a noble heritage.

Philadelphia I Am Here

IN ADDITION TO SAM, I had three other half-brothers living in Philadelphia. Jake, the oldest, offspring of Dad's first marriage, had left for Philadelphia at the age of twenty-two, soon after my mother came to the farm as Dad's third wife. Sam, Max and Meyer were the sons of Dad's second wife, Fanya. Jake had established a small tobacco business.

After Lena was born, Sam, seventeen, and Max, fifteen, had decided that they too would leave the farm. Dad understood. The boys did not like farm work and were unhappy about having a stepmother. My father gave his sons his blessings. Unfortunately, he could give them no financial help. Penniless, the two boys walked and "hitched" their way to New York City where they found jobs as laborers in a cigar factory. The young men worked long hours, learning the business from the bottom rung. They lived together in a rooming house on the East Side.

Meanwhile, at home, little Meyer had become a problem. He missed his mother and refused to be consoled. Finally, when I was about two years old, Meyer, age twelve, ran away from home. He hiked to New York to join his brothers. Because there were no child labor laws then, Meyer too worked in a tobacco plant. Life was difficult for the brothers. They shared cramped quarters. Among the three, they owned only one decent suit. Because they were all nearly the same size, they took turns wearing it. If one of the boys had a social engagement, the other two stayed home.

Soon, the brothers were promoted at their jobs. They learned new aspects of the tobacco business. Meanwhile, they saved their money and made plans. Finally, ready to go into business for themselves, they opened a small cigar factory in Philadelphia. At first, they did all of the work: buying, curing, packing and selling. When the business expanded, they employed helpers.

Sam became president of the company, responsible for the buying and the overall management. Max became general manager, supervising plant and office. Meyer was in charge of processing the tobacco, an intricate phase of the operation. The brothers managed to produce a quality cigar at a reasonable price. Later, to provide outlets for their products, they opened two retail stores: one at Ninth and Chestnut, the other in Atlantic City on Atlantic Avenue. Eventually, they became the largest cigar and tobacco manufacturers in the United States.

I was proud to be starting my career at Bayuk Brothers Tobacco Company at Third and Market Streets, because I knew that they were supplying our country with a very essential commodity. Everyone was repeating the slogan, "What this country needs is a good five-cent cigar!" That famous "good five-cent cigar" was Bayuk's Phillies, a product that brought my brothers renown, respect and riches.

I knew Max better than the others. A lovable person, full of fun, he visited us often at the farm during my childhood. Once, he brought my mother a special gift—a stunning hat, insisting that she model it while cooking dinner. Chubby Mama, wearing several aprons, looked ridiculous wearing the fancy chapeau as Max waltzed her around the kitchen in high spirits. Later, Mama whispered to me that Max had probably intended the gift for one of his lady-friends who had "stood him up." My mother carefully put the hat on her shelf. She loved to look at it, but never wore it again.

Although Meyer was almost like a stranger to me, I had learned that he was intelligent and stubborn. Throughout his life, Meyer remained bitter about my father's remarriage. Because he had lost his own mother, he was prejudiced against Mama. He showed little interest in his younger siblings and rarely visited the farm.

Meyer's wife Julia had introduced her bachelor brother-in-law Sam to her friend Edith Adler. Although Sam was enjoying life as a "ladies' man," he fell in love with Edith and married her. They had two children, Anna Fay and Harry. When I became a member of the household, Anna Fay was three; Harry was nineteen-months old. Sam was already a wealthy man when he brought me to his home for the first time.

As Sam and I drew up to the home on Fifteenth and Clearfield Street, I was puzzled to find that it was just an ordinary row house on a modest street. When we entered the house, I was astonished! One could hardly imagine a more upsetting welcome. Edith, in disarray, opened the door for us. After a hurried greeting to me, she launched a tirade aimed at my brother. The two children, dirty and bedraggled, were screaming and racing around the vestibule. Like animals, they grabbed me and dragged me into the house. Once in, I looked around, amazed. Was this the home of a magnate of industry? The floors were bare. Cheap pieces of furniture were placed around in helter-skelter fashion. Clothing, papers and toys were strewn all over. What a mess!

Sam carried my suitcase upstairs into the spare room which lived up to its name. It was "spare" in every sense of the word.

"This is your room, Bluma," Sam said. "Now, I suppose I should explain about the house. You must be wondering why we live like this."

I nodded. Sam continued, "Ever since I married Edith, we have not had a decent home life. It seems that my 'fancy' convent-educated wife has never worked a day in her life. She just can't cope with ordinary routine. When we first got married, I brought her to a lovely home. In six months, the place was in shambles. Edith can't keep servants. We kept moving around, first to hotels then back to homes again. After the children were born, it became worse. Edith has no control over the children. She is hysterical most of the time. I stay away from home as much as possible, but I am worried about the children. What effect will all this have on them?

After our last stay at a hotel, Edith begged for another chance to live in a home. This time, I decided to test her before I invested in good furniture and an expensive address. I told Edith that she would have a trial period. If she can manage a plain home, furnished with the barest necessities, for one year, then I will buy her a real showplace. Edith promised to do well. We moved here a month ago. But—" he shook his head, "so far, I see no improvement. The servants won't stay. Edith meets me at the door every night, just like you see her today. Well, Bluma now that you are here can you teach my wife to manage a household and take care of her children? I know how well-organized and capable you are around the house. Since you will only be working for me six days a week, you will have plenty of time, nights and weekends, to help her."

Now I knew why my brother had brought me to the city. His "generous" act was for his own benefit. However, I was pleased to repay my host. Although I was disappointed in the appearance of the house, it was delightful to contemplate living in a place with indoor plumbing and running water. No more trips to the outhouse on a cold day. No more pumping at the well. What luxury!

After unpacking, I straightened the house, fed and calmed the children, made dinner and cleaned up the kitchen. Edith watched me in awe. She was pathetically grateful. During my stay with the family, Edith became a loving and appreciative friend. Although she was originally a sophisticated New Yorker, she did not patronize me because I was a country girl. She sincerely wanted a nice home, but her talents did not extend to domesticity. What a shame that social customs often forced women to assume a role for which they were not suited.

The next day, a Monday in July, Sam escorted me to the factory, introducing me to his bookkeeper, a fatherly man. Mr. Wilson soon taught me the office procedure. In a short time I was able to help with the payroll and to act as bank messenger. In a few weeks, I added typing duties. Although I used the "hunt and peck" system, I was quick and accurate. Eventually, I handled all of the correspondence for the business. Sam rarely came to our quarters. After I started to work there, we seldom met. I left the house before he did in the mornings, and returned home earlier.

In a very short period of time, I shouldered increased responsibilities at work; yet, I managed to complete the day's assignments early. When I finished my duties, I was free to come and go as I pleased. This arrangement was fortunate because, almost every day, I received a frantic call from Edith, begging me to come home early to cope with a crisis or to babysit. Naturally, I responded to my sister-in-law's cries for help.

Our secret arrangement produced good results. Staying in the background, I helped to get meals ready, to see that the house was straightened, and that the children were clean before their father arrived. On the weekends, after Sam left, I scrubbed the entire house from top to bottom. Also I did the laundry and planned the meals for the following week. Sam was delighted with the improvement in his home. He praised Edith, believing that his wife had learned to do the chores herself.

Meanwhile, I was having a difficult time financially. I was paid only $3.00 a week for my work at the office. Carfare of 84 cents, lunches and bare necessities cleaned me out each week. Often I had difficulty affording a postage stamp. Sam would not listen to any request for a raise. He acted as if he were giving me charity already. When I saw that my one pair of shoes was wearing out, a replacement pair seemed out of the question.

Edith never noticed my plight. Naturally, I was too proud to tell her. When I started to take stock of my situation, I realized that I was working harder than ever; yet, I had nothing to show for it. My future looked bleak.

I had been taught that whenever I encounter a problem, I must try to solve it myself. As I looked about for a solution, I noticed an interesting fact. When I made up the payroll, I saw that factory workers earned between $15.00 and $18.00 a week, working by the hour. In addition, they worked less hours than I did. After formulating a plan, I approached the foreman.

"Mr. Gartman, is it hard to learn to pack tobacco?"

"No, not really," he answered. "Why do you want to know, Bluma?"

"I want to learn factory work," I replied. "It pays better than my present job. Since the workers are paid by the hour, I thought I could spend lunch time and a few spare hours in the plant, earning extra money.

The foreman agreed to teach me the packing procedure. We decided not to mention our activities to my brother, fearing that Sam might object to my working in the plant. Fortunately, he rarely visited the packing room, knowing that Mr. Gartman was efficient and reliable.

The most difficult aspect of packing was shading the tobacco leaves. When I had become proficient, I spent lunch hours upstairs, packing tobacco at the plant. Whenever I could spare an hour during the day, I ran up to pack again. Each packer wore a heavy black leather apron to protect her clothing from the juices. None of my co-workers knew that I was the boss' sister. I kept quiet at my table, working swiftly. Listening to the earthy talk around me was a learning experience for a farm girl. With the added income from packing, I soon was earning $12.00 a week. At last, I could buy a pair of shoes. Later, my office salary was raised to $5.00 a week. Now medical school seemed a little nearer.

When I had lived with Sam and Edith for almost a year, Edith began to remind Sam of his promise. My brother, believing that his wife had learned to cope, was delighted to arrange for more suitable surroundings. He bought a magnificent mini-mansion at 32nd and Berks, next door to the Jacob Lit estate.

Edith soon became absorbed in buying furniture and decorating the new residence. When the house was finished, it was beautiful. There was an elegant drawing room, a library, formal dining room, gorgeous bedrooms and baths. Two maids and a porter were employed to maintain the ambience. After we moved in, we delighted in our new elegance. Edith was so happy that I felt that she would, at last, be motivated to take charge of her dream home.

A short time after we moved into Strawberry Mansion, Sam asked if I would like to accompany him to the farm on the next weekend. I was eager to go. When we arrived, I hugged my parents and gave them little gifts. However, my joy diminished when I overheard a conversation between my father and Sam.

"Well, Sam," Dad said, "how is Bluma doing at work?"

"I think it was a mistake to employ her," Sam said. "Just because Bluma is my sister, she thinks she can do as she pleases. Every time I look for her at the office they tell me she has left early. She takes advantage of me."

What a frustrating development. It was so unfair! I knew that I was doing a very good job at the office. Because I was so grossly underpaid, I was forced to spend my lunch hours and spare time at the packing table. In addition, I was leaving early only to help Sam's family. What a dilemma! I could not defend myself because of my loyalty to Edith. I had promised her that I would not reveal to Sam that I was the one who had been running the household. Evidently Sam had no idea of the truth and believed that I was no longer needed.

Hurt and indignant, I vowed, silently, that I would no longer leave work early to help Edith. She would be on her own. For her sake as well as mine, it was time to stop the dependence. Thereafter, I began to refuse to rush home whenever my sister-in-law called. I explained to her that I could no longer continue the deception.

Three servants and a beautiful home were not enough incentives for Edith. She could not manage. Once again, when Sam arrived home, her shrieking and complaining assailed his ears. The situation became worse. This time, I knew that the family was falling apart. Within a year, Sam and Edith separated for good. Sam obtained a divorce, taking custody of the children. He placed Anna Fay and Harry in a boarding school run by nuns, so that they would be educated and disciplined. Actually, I believe that Edith was relieved to gain her freedom.

When the household broke up, I decided to leave my job at the factory office. My brother Jake offered me a room with his family at 10th and Walnut Street. Accepting, I immediately moved and went to work at Wanamaker's as a contingent sales girl, later changing to Lits where I sold jewelry. Meanwhile, with my savings, I decided to take a semester of classes at Temple Business School at night. I studied English, spelling, history and touch typing. After using up all of my savings on the first semester's tuition, I stopped school, figuring that I had learned enough to merit a good office job. Next, I applied at a lawyer's office near Jake's small factory at 6th and Walnut. The attorney, whom I shall call Mr. Ross, was a pompous dandy. He looked me over from head to toe before hiring me at the salary of $15.00 a week.

On the first day of my new job, I dressed demurely in a starched white blouse and black skirt. My curls were tamed under a black velvet ribbon. Mr. Ross kept me busy with dictation and typing. At the end of the first day, my employer asked me to have dinner with him. I refused, pleading another engagement. The second day's activities were much like the first. Again, Mr. Ross asked me to go out with him. I declined. When he asked me on the third day, I told my employer that I made it a rule never to date the boss.

On the last day of the week, Mr. Ross called me in to take dictation. I prepared my notebook, rising from my desk, pencil poised, intending to enter his office. Suddenly, Mr. Ross bounded out of his room, grabbing me in a violent embrace. Since he was very short, his head just reached to my neck. I was completely taken by surprise, as the little man started to rub his body passionately against mine. I struggled to get free. Finally, Mr. Ross released me. Almost hysterical with outraged feelings, I screamed at him.

"How dare you treat me like this! I ought to have you arrested. Wait till I tell my brother. He'll tear you to pieces!"

The attorney was red-faced and panting, "Please, Miss Bayuk, I'm sorry! It won't happen again. I don't know what came over me. I just had to have you."

I grabbed my belongings and flew out of the room. At the door, I turned to face him. "You owe me for a week's work. Send the money to my brother's place."

Sobbing, I rushed into Jake's. I blushed as I stammered out my story. Jake, to my surprise, took a rather calm view of the situation.

"What's in a kiss?" he said. "All men try those tricks on their secretaries, Bluma. If the girls won't play ball, they stop. He won't try it again. Why don't you go back?"

I was indignant at his attitude. Jake had daughters my age. How could he treat such harassment lightly? "Only a kiss" did not adequately describe the offense. I wondered how many women were subject to such indignities. I vowed that I would never again work as a private secretary. My next position would be in a large office with many coworkers for protection. I had learned a valuable piece of information: male sexuality does not take a holiday during business hours.

My next job was at an office in Center City. The Magic Curler Company, my employer, conducted a thriving business. Fashionable young women were regularly using their rolled leather curlers. There, I was just one of many office workers doing routine assignments. Although I was paid well, the work was boring. I met the boss' private secretary, a stunning, curvaceous blond. When I found myself wondering what her "private" duties entailed, I realized that my naive country outlook had given way to urban reality.

The Man in Our Bed

AS SPRING APPROACHED, my sister Bertha, who was now living in the city, suggested that we spend a weekend in Alliance during the approaching Easter holidays. I wrote to my parents asking if we might come home, bringing a guest, Clara Golder, whose family had moved to Philadelphia from the farm several years before. Dad replied that, although there was a boarder at the house, we were welcome. A doctor who planned to practice in Norma was staying at our home temporarily while waiting for his quarters to be completed. The doctor, who had been sleeping in our bedroom, graciously offered to move to a cot in the parlor for the weekend so that we could reclaim our big bed. I remember thinking how kind the old man was to give up his comfort for us. I was sure that the doctor was old; no young physician would want to settle in the country, far from modern hospitals and technology.

Bertha, Clara and I arrived on a Friday afternoon. In the evening, after the Shabbos table was set, Mother told us to leave a place between me and Bertha for the guest. We waited dinner until we heard a buggy stop outside. Then Mother began to serve the food. As the door opened our boarder entered. I looked up to encounter the stare of a young, handsome man, dark-haired, with piercing eyes. Without a word, he went over to the kitchen basin to wash up. Then, still silent, the good doctor jumped over the table to land expertly at his seat to my right. Bertha watched him with a startled expression. Clara giggled. I looked down at my plate, blushing. Before dinner was over, I managed to overcome my unaccustomed shyness, asking Dr. Rappoport question after question about his medical training, internship and experiences at the hospital. He answered each query fully. It was obvious that he was a dedicated medical man.

After dinner, the family decided to visit my sister Lena at her home across the road. Dad, Bertha, Clara and David took the lantern, preparing to leave. At the door David turned to me.

"Aren't you going to join us, Miss Bayuk?"

"Not just yet," I replied.

"Are you tired of my company?"

"Of course not. I enjoy talking to you about medicine. I'm just going to stay here with mother for a while, to help her with the dishes and the cleanup. We'll both be along later."

Dr. Rappoport smiled and murmured, "Of course, of course."

Later that evening I spent a great deal of time talking to David. Before we parted, he asked if I would like to accompany him on a call to a patient the next morning. I asked if he would mind taking my guest with us.

"If I had wanted to take Clara, I would have asked her."

"Then I suppose I should tell her what you said."

"Do that!" His answer was short and blunt. Abruptly he walked away to his cot in the parlor. I went upstairs.

When I repeated David's words to Clara, she pouted good-naturedly. "Just my luck, Bluma. That handsome stranger goes for you and not for me. Well, don't let me stand in your way. It will be good experience for you."

I was ready the next morning when David set up his horse and buggy to visit a sick farmer. Along the way, I spoke to the doctor about a plan that I had been formulating.

"I know that it will be a long time before I save enough money to enter medical school, so I'm seriously thinking about entering nursing training. At least nursing is in the same field. And the pay is good. I heard that nurses can make $25.00 a week!"

"I'm not so sure that it's a good idea at all," David said. "You don't look like the type to be a nurse, Miss Bayuk. It takes a lot of discipline. And nursing isn't exactly a romantic occupation. You have to empty bedpans and do a lot of nasty jobs."

"I'm not afraid of any kind of work," I declared.

"All right then," he said, "just pretend that you are my nurse today and help me with my patient."

"But—"

David steered me into the house. He washed up and started to examine the patient.

"Miss Bayuk," he ordered, "please take this thermometer and get the patient's temperature." He handed me a thin glass tube.

I looked at the thermometer in dismay. We had never owned such an instrument at home. Mother simply pressed her lips to our heads to see if we were feverish. Where did one put the thermometer to get the reading? I considered the possible areas open to insertion and narrowed my choice down to two places: "heads or tails." Understandably, I decided to bet on "heads." First, I carefully washed the tube before placing it into the patient's mouth. With great relief I saw that neither the doctor nor the patient objected to this action. So far so good. When the doctor ordered me to remove the glass from the patient's mouth and give him the reading, I was baffled. I did not know how to read the tiny numbers. In desperation, I held up the thermometer, examined it and then exclaimed, "Doctor, just look at this temperature!"

David took the thermometer and read it, scowling.

After we left the house, I lost my control, giving full vent to my anger. "How dare you put me in such a humiliating position!" I screamed, "I never held a thermometer in my hand before. All I know about medical instruments is that they must be cleaned before using. What a mean trick to play on me! Don't you ever do anything like that to me again!"

"Aha," David said triumphantly, "I knew it. You have a very nasty temper!"

"I only show my temper to people who deserve it."

The rest of our ride home was made in icy silence. Ignoring the boarder for the rest of the weekend, I was busy with my friends, encountering David only at meals.

On Monday we returned to the city. Later that week, I received a package in the mail. After unwrapping many layers of paper, I found a small thermometer in a box. The glass was intact. Inside were carefully worded instructions for its use and interpretation. The accompanying note read, "Feverishly, David."

I had to laugh. How could I stay angry with such a man? He was brusque, rude, and yet, strangely appealing. As the weeks went by, I found myself thinking about the young doctor more and more. I had written to him to thank him for his gift. David had replied and now we were corresponding regularly. I should have realized that I was foolish for continuing the relationship. I was eighteen, full of dreams for city activities. David was committed to a practice in the country. Our future plans were incompatible. So were our tempers. Yet, I found that I wanted to see him again; for my heart kept whispering his name.

Summer Decisions

DAVID'S QUARTERS were ready in June. He moved to his home and offices in Norma, determined to be a horse-and-buggy country doctor. Meanwhile, back at the city, my feet, bound in leather, hungered for the feel of the new-born grass. The prospect of continuing a boring job in a stifling city had little appeal. I knew that if I went home for the summer I could obtain seasonal employment at the Allivine Canning Factory. In my spare time, I could help with the chores, swim at the river and enjoy an active social life. I must admit that at the back of my mind was the desire to be nearer to a certain "cantankerous" ex-boarder. I left Magic Curler at the end of June, much to the delight of my parents who were pleased to have me at home again, even temporarily. Immediately, I applied for a job in the Allivine office. Finding no clerical vacancies, I went to work in the cannery, packing vegetables.

Allivine was a new industry for our area, erected and paid for primarily by Maurice Fels, owner of the Fels Naptha Soap Company. Mr. Fels was the special benefactor of our Jewish colonists. It was he who had proposed the idea of the local factory to our farmers so that they would have a convenient place to bring their vegetables to be canned. It was situated on the Central Railroad right of way in Norma. Members of the communities also benefited from the employment opportunities in the factory.

Although Mr. Fels was a bachelor, he had always shown a special interest in the children of our area. He had staffed and equipped a manual training building in Norma so that the boys could learn vocational skills. In addition, he established a domestic science school for girls in a lovely bungalow near the Norma school. He had also subsidized several young men and women with tuition for higher education in the teaching profession.

One day when I was packing in the factory, vegetable-stained and overheated, I heard footsteps approaching my bench. Looking up, I found Maurice Fels staring at me intently.

"Why, Miss Bayuk, is it really you? What are you doing here?"

"I needed a job," I answered, pushing a limp curl back under my cap. "There were no openings in the office."

Mr. Fels smiled and winked, "We'll see about that."

The next morning, I was transferred to the office, where I remained for the rest of the summer. My salary was $10.00 a week, a nice sum, especially since I had no board to pay at home.

Maurice Fels took a special interest in me. Sometimes he would invite me to accompany him on tours of inspection to the vocational schools, which were his pride and joy. When he called at our home, we often went for long walks in the evening. He loved to talk about the experimental farm which he had set up and turned over to the expert administration of Mr. Raymond Lipman. The farm tested new seed, fertilizer and modern methods of getting more yield from the southern New Jersey soil.

Whenever David was free, he too called on me. Our dates were usually expense-free, because he had little money to spare for entertainment. What a contrast between the two men! David was usually over-serious, blunt, humorless and quick to anger. Maurice was gentle, kindly and understanding. David was painfully poor; Maurice, extremely rich. Naturally, I found myself more interested in the wrong one. Although at times David acted as if he cared for me, he said nothing of his feelings. Truthfully, he could not afford the luxury of falling in love. The young doctor supported a sister and father. His practice was not a flourishing one. Farmers rarely called on the services of a doctor. Home remedies were used unless the case was extremely serious. Also, whenever my "grumpy" swain visited a poor family, he would not charge.

Gradually, as I found out more details of David's past, I began to understand why he was often bitter and thin-skinned. He was born in Russia of good, orthodox Jewish parents. Unfortunately, David's mother, Baila, had died when he was just a young child. His father, Mordecai, a highly respected and learned man, was heart-broken at his wife's death. He vowed never to remarry. The decision forced Mordecai to become both mother and father to his five small children. The family emigrated to this country, where they settled in Carmel, N.J. Here the hard-working father opened up a small sundry store to make a living. After coming to this country, David, fifteen, entered public school. Educated only in Hebrew, he learned English and completed his grammar school commitments in one year. He finished high school in two years and entered Medical College immediately. In those days there were no pre-med requirements. The entire family sacrificed their own needs to help David through medical training. His brother Lou, three years younger, shouldered the greatest part of the financial responsibility. Because David was exceptionally brilliant, his father, three sisters and brother never complained or resented their efforts on his behalf. David, too, suffered to achieve his education. He had started medical school in an inexpensive institution in Baltimore. However, fearing that his degree would not be accredited, he transferred to Philadelphia based "Medico Chi," a much more expensive medical school which was later absorbed by the University of Pennsylvania. Living conditions in the city were stark for the penniless student. He rented a fourth floor room, with no heat and a broken window pane. David had to stuff his threadbare overcoat into the window to keep from freezing while he studied.

 Sometimes, his hands became so numb that he had difficulty in turning the pages of his book. Eating was a luxury. He existed on a minimal diet. David's one obsession was to graduate to earn enough money to repay his family for their unselfish help. His father wanted David to practice in Norma so that the family would be near to each other. The oldest daughter, Rivka, was married to

Dr. Greenwood, who practiced medicine in Rosenhayn, a nearby farm community. When David was twenty-three, he started his practice, living with his father and sister.

Evidently, the years of privation and starvation had left their scars on David, for he was inclined to be melancholy and irascible. Yet, to me, his honesty and deep altruism were more indicative of his real character than were his passing moods. I came to respect his integrity and to understand his mercurial nature. However, the learning process was long and painful. On many occasions David and I had serious quarrels which caused us both great anguish.

On one occasion, a prank on my part caused a most unexpected retaliation. David tried to have me arrested. I suppose that my jealousy was to blame for the situation. In the summers when I worked at Allivine, David and I were not "going steady." I had other boyfriends and David was free to go out with other girls. Since we had no romantic relationship at that time, I felt free to confide in him about my dates. David always had a disparaging comment to make about each boy I went out with; however, he never mentioned any social engagements of his own. One day, when David came over to visit my sister and me, he began to boast about meeting some lovely girls from Philadelphia who were staying at a nearby boarding house.

Rather nettled, I said, "Why are you wasting your time here with us when you could be visiting such interesting girls?"

David did not take the hint. He stayed, mentioning the young ladies so often that I really became annoyed. After he left, I said to my sister, "I am going to play a trick on him."

Bertha, always willing to participate in a joke, went with me to Lena's home.

"Lena, I want you to help me play a trick on a conceited doctor," I said.

I directed her to write a note to Dr. David Rappoport, ostensibly from the two Philadelphians, whose names David had mentioned. Lena signed their names to the note which read: "Dear Dr. Rappoport, we were so delighted to meet such a charming man. Do come over to our boarding house tomorrow evening so that we may get to know you better. (signed) Betty and Rose."

I assured Lena that we really wouldn't let him go through with it. We would waylay him in time—tell him that it was just in fun. I didn't want to mail the letter myself. We waited for one of the farmers to pass by on his way to the post office. When Mr. Allen came along, I stopped him asking if he would post my letter in Norma. When Dr. Rappoport came to the Norma post office to pick up his mail, he received the note and immediately became suspicious, surmising that it was one of my pranks. He asked Mr. Coltun, the postmaster who had mailed the letter. The postmaster replied, "Mr. Allen." David went off to find Mr. Allen, asking him who had given him the letter to mail. Mr. Allen replied, "Bluma Bayuk."

David became enraged. He drove up to our home and asked for my father. Bertha wondered why he wanted to see Dad. David replied that he needed the Justice of Peace. Dad, of course, had been the Justice of Peace in our community for many years. David entered Dad's office, greeting him seriously.

"Mr. Bayuk," he said, "I want to swear out a warrant of arrest."

Dad, alarmed, asked David solicitously if someone had harmed him.

"Yes," said David. "Someone has committed a very serious offense against me and I want to see justice done."

"Who is the person?" Dad asked.

"Your daughter Bluma." Dad looked at David in astonishment, seeing that the doctor was in earnest.

"I don't know what is going on," Dad said, "but I know my daughter. Bluma would never do anything to warrant an arrest. You must be mistaken. If you insist on this charge, go to another justice of the peace. Perhaps he will take care of you."

David stalked out of the house in a fury. Although I was angry with myself for my own actions, I was furious with David for his unsportsmanlike reaction. Perhaps it was a foolish joke, but it was not a damaging one. Our friendship cooled for the rest of the summer. When I returned to Philadelphia, I received a note from David apologizing. He said, "What a poor sport I am. I often play tricks on you and you take it with humor and grace. But I blow up and make a fool of myself. Please forgive me." I forgave him, of course. After that incident, whenever we quarreled I would ask David if he knew a good justice of the peace.

The summer-winter employment pattern that I had established in 1906 continued for three years. In the cold months I returned to Philadelphia, taking temporary employment; in spring, I moved to the cannery office, living with my parents and continuing my tempestuous relationship with David. Although I continued to see Maurice and dated other boys, I found that no one meant as much to me as the impossible David. Finally, I decided that the time had come to resurrect my medical plans. Before I left Allivine in the fall of 1909, I confided my problem to Maurice Fels.

"I still have a great desire to be a doctor. Yet, I don't seem to be getting any nearer to my goal. I'm twenty-one and I think I had better get started."

Surprisingly, Maurice did not encourage my aspirations. He told me that I should be thinking about marriage, not a career. If I really had to do something, he suggested that I become a teacher or a social worker. I was disappointed in his advice.

Because Maurice believed so strongly in education, I thought he would be more sympathetic. I tried to convince him that a person's sex should not limit his or her vocational choices. Maurice did not agree.

"Surely, you do not object to women becoming nurses," I challenged. "I think that should be my next step. I would be advancing my medical knowledge while learning a profession. It would only take three years."

Again, I was surprised by his reaction. Maurice urged me to delay my decision.

"Wait, Bluma," he advised. "Three years is a long time. You will have to give up coming back here in the summer. Why not

Summer Decisions

try something first. Work with a physician for a year and see how you like it. I will get you a job with a doctor friend of mine in Vineland. Then I will be able to see you more often."

Against my better judgment, I agreed to take the Vineland job to please my friend. I felt that if I proved to him that I was in earnest, he might agree to lend me the tuition money for medical school. However, things changed when I returned to Philadelphia to buy uniforms and supplies. My city friends disapproved of my plans. Abe Berkowitz, especially, could not understand why I was leaving town.

"You aren't thinking straight, Bluma," he scolded. "Working for this doctor will get you nowhere. If you want to be a nurse, start now. Go to an accredited school. The Jewish Hospital has the finest training available. If they accept you, you won't have to pay tuition. In fact, they pay you. You get real hospital experience there, and you meet doctors who will employ you when you are in private duty. In three years you will be a professional."

I realized that Abe's advice was sound. Losing no time, I boarded the Willow Grove trolley which took me to York and Olney Roads. I applied for admission to the nursing school of the Jewish Hospital. After passing an oral and written examination, I was accepted for immediate placement in their incoming class.

Hastily, I gathered my belongings and reported to the student nurses' quarters at the hospital, entering a building which became my home for three years. I lived with nineteen hopeful young ladies with whom I shared the trials and joys of our training period.

After getting settled, I wrote immediately to Maurice Fels.

"Dear Friend, I have decided not to take your friend's kind offer of a job. I hope that you will forgive me for changing my plans. I am entering nursing training at Jewish Hospital. It makes more sense than working for a private doctor. Here we get hospital training in every field of medicine, besides our classes. When I finish after three years, I will be a professional. I don't have to pay any tuition, in fact, they pay me. The first year, we are paid

$6.00 a month; the second, $8.00, and during our senior year, we make $10.00 besides room and board and tuition. This is a good setup for me because I have no funds. Maurice, I am truly sorry that I will not be seeing very much of you for the next three years. I hope that you will understand and remain my dear and valued friend. Bluma."

I received no reply to the letter. Maurice Fels did not communicate with me in any way after that. I still cannot understand why this kindly gentleman reacted so strangely to my decision. Perhaps he felt that I was ungrateful. Perhaps he had other plans for me. I will never know. Whatever his reasons, my friendship with Mr. Fels ended on the day that I entered nursing school.

Maurice wasn't the only one who disapproved of my action. Everything had happened so quickly that I had not informed my parents of my whereabouts until after I was already launched into the new situation. I wrote a letter home to describe my new life. When Mother learned of what I had done, she became hysterical, afraid that her little girl would contract every disease that was brought into the hospital. Dad could not soothe her. In desperation, he wrote a letter to Bertha, asking her what he should do. Bertha, who was still living in Philadelphia, promptly brought Dad's letter to me at the hospital. Dumbfounded when I read his words, I began to cry. What should I do? Finally, I took the letter downstairs to the office of the Superintendent of Nurses, an austere woman.

"Miss James," I cried, "I have a serious problem. I don't know what to do. I know that I made the right decision in coming here. But unless I can convince Mother, I won't be able to continue with this course. Nothing is more important to me than my mother's peace of mind."

My superior advised me to go home for a few days to straighten out the matter. She gave me written permission to leave. I returned to the farm on the next train.

When I entered the house, Mother greeted me in surprise.

"Blumella, what are you doing here? Are you sick already?"

I embraced her. "Mama, I came home to talk to you. Listen to me, please. I really want to be a nurse, but I can't go on if it is going to upset you so much. But first, I want you to know that nurses are taught how to protect themselves against disease. It is important for us to stay well so that we can help others."

Staying with Mother all day, I described our training with great enthusiasm. I talked and talked. Mama kept watching my face.

At last, tears in her eyes, she hugged me and said, "Bluma, the way your eyes shine when you talk, I know that you are happy in your new work. Go back and do just what you want to do in life. Don't change your mind for anyone—not even me. I'll get used to it. And I know that you will accomplish whatever you want to do. It is your life."

With a grateful heart, I kissed my mother and returned to the hospital. In the fall of 1909, when I was 21 years old, I began in earnest my three years of training at Jewish Hospital, now known as Einstein Medical, Northern Division. I was a member of the Class of 1912.

In Hospital

My world expanded immeasurably during the three years of hospital training. In our science courses I learned about the intricate and precise engineering of our bodies. As I studied the methods used to mend and restore the human system to health, I developed great pride in my profession, feeling privileged to perform whatever tasks were necessary to heal my patients.

Education and experience convinced me that a master brain has fashioned this wonderful creature who walks upright on the earth and reproduces his kind. How brilliant of our Maker to give man the knowledge and skill to repair his own body. What a privilege to serve as a member of the repair team!

In Hospital

JUST AS David Rappoport had warned me, a nurse's life was not romantic. As novices we would start immediately to work in the wards when we were not attending classes, assigned to menial jobs: making beds, carrying urinals and feeding patients. For the first quarter of the year, we would be on a trial basis. At the end of three months, we would be either capped or dismissed. During those test months, we were rotated to different departments to get a wide range of experiences.

I was introduced to one piece of medical terminology and procedure in a rather strange fashion. On the first day of my stay at the school, we novices had breakfast with the upper classwomen who were interested in meeting us and learning about our backgrounds. We in turn, were eager to find out from them what was in store for us for the next three years. Naturally, the first questions directed to us concerned romantic attachments.

"I am free," I announced, "When I came here, I broke off my 'understanding' with someone. Now I intend to 'play the field.'"

My words were brave, but I was deeply hurt by my latest problem with David. Before I left Alliance in the fall, David and I had quarreled again. Once more I had resolved to banish him from my heart.

A few hours after I had unpacked my belongings, I was able to test my new freedom. An attractive doctor had asked me for a date for the following evening. I felt rather smug to realize that my new social life was beginning right away.

"As a matter of fact," I continued, at the breakfast table, "I already have a date tonight with a good-looking doctor whom I just met here. His name is Roger Blank.* Do you know him?"

---
* Not his real name.

The senior nurses looked at each other, exchanging glances that I could not fathom. Finally, Ilene Greene, a lovely second-year student, cleared her throat. "Bayuk, child, I'm afraid I have to warn you about Dr. Blank. You see, many nurses who have gone out with Dr. Blank have ended up having to get a D.&C." She waited; my reaction was one of bewilderment.

"A 'D.&C.'—what is that?"

The older women began to snicker. Greene silenced them with a look. "Bayuk, you are an innocent. A 'D.&C.' is a 'Dilation and Curettage.'"

"Oh?"

"You see," she continued, "This procedure is sometimes done to women to prevent bringing unwanted babies into the world, if a woman has been carried away on a date, especially with an amorous doctor. You understand what I mean?"

"I'm a farm girl, Greene, and I know how babies are made. I have gone out on many dates, but I have never had to learn what a 'D.&C.' is. I never behaved in a way that could bring an unwanted baby into my life."

Greene shook her head, sadly. "Bayuk, you are in another world now. You will find that some doctors put a lot of pressure on us sexually. Dr. Blank is one of the worst offenders. Everyone thinks that nurses are promiscuous because we 'know the score.' And, we are in a vulnerable position, both with patients and doctors. We tend to look on doctors as superior beings, so when they pay attention to us, we sometimes fall!"

"Not me," I said, proudly, "I have too much respect for myself. As far as a 'D.&C.' is concerned it is a medical procedure that I have just learned about. I will add it to my knowledge, but certainly not to my own experience."

"Please Bayuk, don't be too sure of yourself. Watch out for Dr. Blank."

"Oh, I can handle him," I said, "A man only does what a woman lets him do. I assure you, he will respect me."

Although Ilene remained perturbed, she did not pursue the

matter. In the early evening, as I prepared for my date, I felt a small twinge of apprehension. Why had I agreed to meet the physician at his offices downtown? The theater was close to Dr. Blank's headquarters. Since he maintained office hours until 7:00 p.m. it had seemed logical for my date to arrange to send a taxi for me, rather than to make the long trip himself. Stifling my misgivings, I dressed in the one truly sophisticated dress that I owned—a stunning peach-colored outfit, trimmed in black velvet. Stepping out of the building with head held high, I felt capable of handling any situation that might arise.

As Roger welcomed me to his office, he complimented me on my appearance. After his last patient left, he insisted on showing me through the elaborate suite. Because we were all alone, I braced myself for what might happen. However, the doctor's manners were impeccable. As I began to feel more relaxed, I examined my surroundings with interest. Then I received a shock! A picture on the wall of the inner office drew my attention. It was Dr. Blank's medical college graduation class. There, in the front row, staring out at me with angry, accusing eyes, was my ex-boyfriend, David.

"I didn't know that you graduated with David Rappoport," I said, wondering why I felt so guilty.

"Ah, yes, Rappoport, I remember him. An odd duck. He'll never amount to anything—too dedicated."

We took a cab to a theater on Broad Street. As the house lights dimmed in the theater, I told myself to relax and enjoy the show. When the curtain went up on the first act of *Rebecca of Sunnybrook Farm*, Dr. Blank gently reached for my hand. Since that gesture seemed harmless, I left my hand in his. Then, as I continued to watch the show, enthralled, I was vaguely aware that the doctor was guiding my hand to a new position. First to his knee and then, with a shock, I realized that he had placed my hand at his open fly, against his exposed penis. Quickly, I gave his private parts a vicious twist, and pulled back my hand. A moan escaped from his lips. I was so furious that I was almost hoping that he would cause a commotion so that I could shame him before the whole audience. However, Roger controlled himself and managed to sit through the rest of the performance. We said not one word to each other. I refused to let him see how upset I was inside. Evidently, he was trying to pretend that nothing had happened. I am sure that it was an heroic effort, for I had pinched him with all of my strength.

It was a curious standoff. After the show ended, my escort, pale but courteous, asked me if I wanted some refreshment. I said, "Yes," still trying to maintain the veneer of a lady of experience. When we entered the restaurant, I was in such a suspicious state of mind, that I feared the doctor might slip something into my drink. Throwing aside my pose, I ordered an unopened bottle of soda pop, hardly a sophisticated move. When we finished our refreshments, my mind was already racing to the next possible danger. What would he do on the long taxi ride to the hospital? After my escort hailed a cab, and helped me in, I quickly closed the door, calling to the driver to pull away at once. We drove off, leaving a bewildered doctor at the curb.

When I returned to the dormitory, Ilene was waiting up for me, like a big sister.

"There will be no 'D.&C.' for me, Greene," I told her. Then I started to laugh uncontrollably. When I finally calmed down, I continued, "This time I think that the doctor will need some treatment. I believe that he will have an 'S.P.' tomorrow."

"What in the world is an 'S.P.'?" Greene asked.

"Greene, you are an innocent," I said, airily. "Don't you know the score? When a nice nurse goes out with a 'fresh' doctor, she can give him an 'S.P.' It's an effective medical procedure done to men, to prevent bringing unwanted babies into the world."

Ilene was puzzled about this new medical procedure until I told her the full story of my evening's adventure. Then my friend roared with laughter.

"Well, Miss Redhead," she giggled. "I guess we don't have to worry about you!"

Soon the story spread through the nurses' quarters, and was overheard by some of the doctors. His colleagues did not let Dr. Blank forget his comeuppance. They teased him as he deserved. The older nurses were extremely cordial to me, for I had retaliated against an all-too-common form of male abuse.

Dr. Blank avoided me as much as possible. I was told that for a few months after our encounter, the medical Romeo was not quite so aggressive with the nurses he dated. I am sure that his amorous ideas were temporarily suspended, at least until his 'S.P.' (sore privates) had a chance to heal.

As our routine gained momentum, it was difficult for me, a free spirit, to accept the strict regimentation. The nurses' quarters were in a separate building on the hospital grounds. The Superintendent of Nurses maintained her offices on the first floor. Each floor above contained double rooms for the students, sparsely but adequately furnished. There was one common bathroom on each floor. In addition to monitoring our "comings and goings," the superintendent inspected our rooms daily. If our quarters were not perfectly kept, we found notes on our desks. Then we would have to visit her to explain our lapse and to receive punishment. Also, we were not allowed to leave the grounds without written permission. The superintendent (whom I shall call "Miss James") was a veritable Tartar. Only a few weeks after classes began, I received one of her dreaded notes. It seems that my pen had leaked onto my bureau scarf. Although I had attempted to remove the stain, a small spot remained. The "important" infraction had prompted our superior to send for me. She ordered me to clean the spot off completely—"or else." Returning to my room, I scrubbed so hard that I finally made a hole in the scarf. Furious at the whole incident, I brought the scarf down to Miss James, showing it to her. "Well, I did what you ordered. The spot is out!"

Miss James could not believe my bold manners. She raged and threatened. I stood my ground, telling her that her instructions had caused me to destroy property, rather than to preserve it. Although it was foolish to make an enemy of an authority figure, I felt that the issue was important. I would not follow stupid instructions simply because I was ordered to. Power is not a license to inflict mindless chores on underlings.

Although Miss James proceeded to watch me closely after our initial clash, I refused to be cowed by her surveillance. As I struggled to learn, Miss James was standing by, ready to pounce on my every infraction. Ironically, it was she, not I, who failed to make the grade.

Probationers obeyed superiors without question. Often the novices were asked by the superintendent to bring certain medical equipment or medicine. We blindly followed her orders. Since we had not yet studied *Materia Medica*, a nursing text, we had no idea what we were being asked to bring to our superior. However, I began to wonder about it. One day I asked Mary, my roommate, whether she had ever been ordered by the nurse to bring her a particular medicine.

"Oh, yes," Mary replied. "Often. I suppose she has a special patient who uses quite a bit of it."

"I wonder why it always seems to be the same medicine," I mused.

That night, on looking up the medication in the *Materia Medica*, I found it an odd choice to be using in quantity. On questioning my classmates, I learned that they too had been asked to bring the same medicine to Miss James.

The others advised me to forget it. "We have no right to ask questions of our superior."

Although my uneasiness remained, I took no action; however, someone else did. Before our own probationary period ended, Miss James had left, replaced by another woman, Miss Susan Frances. Our former superintendent did not say goodbye. No explanations were given to us for her leaving. Later we learned that Miss James was a dope addict. She had been using us to get her supplies, because, being novices, we did not realize the properties of the morphine she had so often asked us to procure. I hope that she was eventually cured. We never heard any more about her.

When the probationary period was over, I knew without a doubt that I had found my true vocation. After being capped,

I was assigned to regular shifts in various areas of the hospital. We spent three months at each department to become familiar with the specific procedures there. Our routine called for either day or night duty. Day shift started at 7:00 a.m., and lasted twelve hours. Night duty began at 7:00 p.m. Sometimes student nurses were forced to work more than twelve hours if a postoperative patient needed extra attention. It was not unusual for us to have an eighteen-hour day. Of course, if a class was scheduled during duty time, we were given a substitute for the duration of the class period.

Our new superintendent was a highly educated woman, kind, yet strict. She continued at her job for many years. I know that I was not always an angel of decorum; yet, Miss Frances was moderate in her punishments. I respected my superior and felt welcome to come to her with my problems, assured of her fairness and sincere interest in my welfare. Our superintendent rated us mainly on our ability and integrity as nurses, considering our occasional "high jinks" as minor faults.

Although I loved every part of my work, one phase of nursing terrified me—facing death, or to be more accurate—facing dead bodies. I knew that I must change my outlook if I were to be successful in my profession.

As referred to previously, my phobia had developed early in life when I lived at the farm, which was situated next door to the Alliance Cemetery. As a child I had often eavesdropped on my mother and her lady friends, late in the evenings. The wives, drinking tea by the fire, loved to recount macabre tales about ghosts. They said that the dead rose at midnight and walked to the synagogue to pray. No doubt, to the ladies, these occult conversations were merely titillating entertainment; to a little girl, they seemed factual. At night, when I awoke to use the chamber pot, I could see the neighboring tombstones reflected in my bureau mirror. Then the old wives' tales would possess my mind. I would imagine that the dead were walking around outside. Through the years I had retained these haunting images. Now, losing them became vital to my future.

My first trial arose immediately when I was on initial assignment to the Incurable and Tubercular Division of the hospital for three months' duty. In charge of the night shift, I had been called after midnight to do a chest cupping for a tubercular patient who lived in a cottage not far from my quarters. In order to reach the cottage, I had to pass the morgue. Petrified, I raced past the building, running so hard that I was completely out of breath when I reached the patient. By that time, my hands were shaking so violently that, when I attempted to put the flames in the cups, a flare dropped to the sheet, causing a fire. Fortunately, I did not panic. With the help of other patients, I was able to extinguish the flames before any real damage was done. I continued in my duties, promising myself that I would not allow my irrational fears to cause any more extra problems.

Later, as I prepared to return to my quarters, I steeled myself to walk calmly past the dreaded building. Everything was quiet. No ghosts followed me. At last, back in my room, I wrote to my father, telling him of my predicament. I reviewed some of my foolish childhood fears and how I had conquered each one. Sharing my thoughts with Dad gave me needed strength. I knew that other ordeals would come, for I was not completely cured. Yet, I knew that I must eventually overcome my problem. As a nurse, I would be forced into intimate contact with death, serving the moribund as well as the living. "Bluma," I told myself, "grit your teeth and meet the challenge!" I tried and improved; but not until my senior year was I finally able to lay my "ghosts" to rest. Meanwhile, other challenges awaited.

On the first day of my next assignment, I became a "prisoner," sentenced to a four week term. When I reported for duty at the Children's Ward, I found that I was in sole charge. None of the youngsters in my unit was critically ill; yet, they were unhappy in alien surroundings without their parents. My first aim was to put my patients at ease. Cheerfully, I talked to the children to win their confidence. Then I made a game out of looking into their mouths and taking their temperatures. To my surprise, several of the little ones were running high fevers and showing angry rashes.

"Aha," I said, remembering the text books. "This looks like measles."

Dr. Raab, who answered my call, confirmed the diagnosis. He arranged to send the sick ones to a small cottage on the hospital grounds.

"Miss Bayuk, you will stay with them. Under no circumstances are you to leave the premises!"

"But Doctor, I can't do that! What about my classes. My time off?"

"I'll have an orderly bring your books and lessons. You can keep up with your homework after the patients are asleep. No time off!"

What a situation! I was completely responsible for the care of five sick children, night and day. I would have to eat and sleep with them. No free time, either. It wasn't fair! Fair or not, I had to do what I was told. At first, I was extremely resentful. Gradually, my buoyant spirits returned. I gathered my charges and told them.

"We have to be here so let's make it a party!"

My patients responded to the upbeat atmosphere that I created. As each one felt better, he joined in the games and impromptu skits, singing and dancing. The little tots who were feeling very ill were given the best treatment available—lavish doses of affection, administered often. How responsive children are! They returned my loving tenfold. Soon we were all enjoying our enforced confinement, playing games, exchanging love and laughter.

When the quarantine was finally lifted, saying goodbye to the children was an emotional trauma. Being a mother to them had been a wonderful experience.

In my tours of duty during my freshman year, I was often appointed to supervisory functions. As charge nurse, I ranked above the junior and senior students on the same duty. Naturally, I encountered resentment from some of the older nurses. They did not relish taking orders from a mere freshman. Sensing their attitudes, I spoke to my supervisor.

"The older students resent me. I understand how they feel. I'm new; they've been here for a year or more. Why should I be placed over them?"

My supervisor replied, "Miss Bayuk, I have observed your work. It is my responsibility to put the best available nurse in charge. If the others had proved themselves better than you, they would have been at the top. It is your duty to accept the position that I assign you."

Although I continued as charge nurse on many of my tours, I still was unhappy with the cold attitude of some of my colleagues. Their enmity preyed on my mind; yet, I was powerless to change the situation. During one particularly uncomfortable night assignment, I became very depressed, and homesick for the warmth and approval of my family. . . . Whenever we completed a night duty, we received an extra day off before reporting for our next assignment. I decided to use my upcoming extra time to visit home. How I looked forward to the trip! Finally, the longed-for day arrived. I flew to my quarters to pack. Stopping off at the office for my permit, I found that no authorization had been made for a leave. . . . Every other student completing night duty had received her permission except me. I was bewildered. When the chief returned to her office, I was there waiting for her.

"Why, Miss Bayuk, what are you doing up?"

"There must be some mistake," I said, "I just finished night duty, but I can't find my permit. Now I've missed my train, and I'm planning to go home."

"I'm sorry. I haven't been able to find a suitable replacement for you. You will have to stay on duty for a few more nights."

I looked at my superior in utter disbelief. My need for home was so great that I could not cope with a delay. Miss Frances had turned away, expecting her orders to be obeyed. Suddenly, the realization became overwhelming. Like a child, I began to cry, becoming so hysterical that a doctor had to be brought in to

In Hospital

sedate me. He sent me to bed. When I had calmed down slightly, Miss Frances came up to my room.

"Miss Bayuk, you have to be realistic. Lonesomeness is part of this job. Your needs no longer come first. If personal desires conflict with duty, you must be prepared to postpone your own wishes. No matter how unfair it seems, you have to make sacrifices if you choose to stay in training."

Although I tried to understand and to be brave, I was too exhausted and drained to go on with my work. Miss Frances was obliged to find a substitute for me in the duty roster. I was incapacitated for two days, missing any time off until the next month. Taking stock, I realized that my free spirit was being forced into a restraining mold. Yet, all along the way, I had free choice to stay or leave. The "taming of Bluma" was self-imposed, necessary if I were to reach my goal of service to my fellow human beings.

In choosing my restrictions, I had no intention of forfeiting all of my normal instincts for fun and recreation. I just had to rearrange my priorities. Whenever an opportunity arose for pleasure, I tried to take advantage of it, providing that my work did not suffer. When I found out that my father would be visiting in Philadelphia, I knew that I had to see him. Dad wrote that he would be staying over night at a hotel at 9th and Chestnut, where my brothers' tobacco store was located. I worked out a plan to visit him in the morning after my night duty. Because of my schedule, I could spend little time with Dad; yet even a few minutes would be a treat. When the day arrived, I completed night duty at 7:00 a.m. and rushed to the superintendent's office to get a pass. Miss Frances was not in. Because there was so little time for my trip, I decided to leave without permission, hoping that I would not be missed before my return. I hopped the trolley and arrived downtown at the hotel. Greeting Dad with a loving hug, I sat on his bed, resting as we talked and talked. Suddenly, I felt someone shaking me.

"Bluma," Dad said, "It's twelve o'clock. When do you have to go back?"

I couldn't believe the time. Tired from my long night, I had dozed off in the hotel room. I had missed my 10:00 a.m. class. Now, my absence would have been discovered. I told Dad that I was in trouble.

"Well, daughter, what is, is. Don't worry about it now. Since you are in trouble anyway, let's enjoy a little more time together. I am going to take you out for a special lunch. We will forget everything but how good it is to be together."

We enjoyed a wonderful lunch. To be with Dad and to share his wisdom and love was the greatest tonic I knew. After we said our reluctant farewells, I returned to school with renewed vigor. Naturally, I found a note on my door.

When I confronted Miss Frances, she asked me to explain my absence. After hearing my story, the chief nurse imposed the penalty. I was to have no leaves for one extra month and was restricted to the hospital grounds. Not even this confinement could dim the glow of my father's visit. I must admit that sometimes the "crime" is worth the punishment. Certainly, it was so in this instance, for I am still warmed by the memory of the luncheon date I shared with Dad almost seventy years ago.

In all honesty, I must report that when we were restricted, we often found ways to sneak out. In order to do so, we had the connivance of two wonderful maids, both named Mary. They helped us to break some of the strict rules of our training. The burglar alarm on the fire escape was a needed protection. If anyone tried to break in, its siren would alert us. However, the fire escape was also a means of egress—to slip away on a date and to return without being caught. Whenever we left without official permission at night, we arranged with a "Mary" to disconnect the alarm until our return. Occasionally I took this route when the restrictions became too much to bear. I dated a few of the nicer doctors, friends from Philadelphia, and, yes, David Rappoport, who sometimes came to the city for a visit. In spite of myself, it was still David who held a special place in my heart, between fights.

David and I continued to battle our way through our long relationship. "True love never runs smooth" aptly described our romance. Although he still practiced in the farm communities, my "grumpy" swain managed to get to the city every few months while I was in training. On one occasion, David wrote to me saying that he was coming to the city and would like to visit me on my day off, but he thought I might not want to see him because of his haircut. I replied pertly that his haircut was a matter between him and his barber. I was interested in what was in his head, not on top! He wrote again, saying that he would arrive the following Thursday evening to take me out for dinner. When the day arrived, I was dressed, with permit obtained, eager to greet my beau. At 5:30, a young nurse came up the stairs, screaming.

"Bayuk, call the police. There is a convict downstairs and he is after you!"

"A convict? What are you talking about?"

I leaned over the railing, calling, "Who's there?"

"It's David," a voice answered.

I gave my colleague a quizzical look and proceeded down the staircase. When I saw David, I, too, began to scream. His hair had been completely shaved off. He looked like a "thug."

"How dare you?" I screamed. "How dare you come here looking like this?"

"But you said it was between me and my barber."

"Whoever did that was not a barber—he was a butcher!"

"Bluma, I had to do it. You know that I'm the school physician in Norma. Well, I discovered lice in some of the children, and I was afraid of getting it. After scrubbing and scrubbing, I still felt itchy. So I decided to shave it all off!"

"I refuse to be seen with you. You are just going to have to stop being so fussy. What if those children catch measles? Are you going to shave off your skin? You can just turn right around and go back again, David Rappoport. Our date is off!"

Today, David would have been right in style with the sexy male images of Kojak and Yul Brynner. Then, he just made me feel ashamed. Again, our quarrel led to a temporary estrangement. He went back to the country; I continued my studies in hospital.

Our most valuable learning experiences occurred during our tours of duty; text books and charts merely gave us the tools. Dealing with patients turned us into nurses. One night, after making rounds and doing my chores, I was collecting the trays that were left over from dinner, taking them to the deserted diet kitchen. As I passed the service elevator, the door opened, revealing an emaciated man, dressed only in a white nightshirt. Remembering the old wives' tales of ghosts, I panicked, dropping the pile of trays on the floor. The clatter echoed and reechoed through the empty corridor. Nobody else was in sight. The man tottered. Regaining my senses, I grabbed him out of the elevator and placed him in a wheel chair, covering his legs with a blanket. Then I phoned the men's ward.

"I found a patient riding in the service elevator. Check your beds and see if anyone is missing."

The charge nurse was brusque, "Look somewhere else. Nobody walks out of this ward. I'm sure he's not ours."

"Well," I said sarcastically, "Suppose I put him back in the elevator and let him ride up and down until somebody claims him. Or do you think you should check your beds?"

Quite angry, the nurse rang off. A few minutes later, she called me apologetically. "I'm sorry, Bayuk, my nurses slipped up. He is ours. I'll send someone down for Mr. Sander right away."

With great relief I returned Mr. Sander to an orderly. How long had he been riding up and down in that deserted elevator? Why hadn't they missed him? It was frightening to realize how vulnerable our patients were without proper supervision.

Nurses, too, were often vulnerable to their patients. Sometimes, unintentionally, a patient could pose a threat to our well-being. In another section of the hospital, I was tending to the semiprivate rooms. One night, a handsome young man was brought in, delirious and incoherent. He was suffering from pneumonia. I was ordered to give him a cold bath during the night if his temperature exceeded 102 degrees. After midnight, his temperature reached 103. Bringing in a basin of ice and sponges, I put my patient between blankets. The procedure was to place the iced sponge under each arm in succession, then on the groin and so on. The final step was an alcohol rubdown. The unconscious man was quiet as I prepared for the bath. When I placed the ice sponge under his first arm, he suddenly gave me a punch in the stomach with his other arm, sending me sliding under the bed, with ice spilling on top of me. Hearing the commotion, a nurse in the hallway rushed in. She rescued me, drenched and shivering, and sent me to my quarters to change clothes. When I returned to duty, the nurse said, "I called the doctor to examine the boy. He will get well without baths. Don't give him any more treatment tonight."

After the boy recovered, he called me to his room before leaving for home.

"Nurse, I want to thank you for all that you did."

I laughed. "I never told you what you did when I was trying to help you in your delirium."

After I told him, the young man put his arm around me and kissed me. "Will you forgive me?"

"Of course," I said. "Just promise me that the next time you serve 'punch,' you won't put quite so much ice in it."

A hazard of another kind occurred in the women's ward when I was preparing a young woman for an operation. Because the girl had contracted a severe case of gonorrhea, I was told to administer a prophylactic douche with a solution of permanganate. In the midst of the treatment, the young lady became agitated, angry with the world because of her infection. She suddenly grabbed the syringe, pulled it out, and poured the solution all over the bed. A passing doctor rushed in. Ignoring the patient, he took me over to the dispensary immediately for eye treatment, to make sure that I had not received any infection from the spill.

"You are very lucky," the doctor told me. "A splash in your eyes could have caused serious trouble."

In the men's ward, the next day, an epileptic took a bite out of my finger as I grabbed his tongue during a seizure. I still bear the scar.

Sometimes our abuse from a patient was emotional rather than physical. I tried to be tolerant, remembering that sick people had to be excused for their crankiness and ill-temper. However, sometimes the patients were just nasty people who carried their meanness around wherever they went. One such patient was petulant and resentful from the moment that she entered her room. As I made my rounds on night duty, I introduced myself to the middle-aged woman in 315 and asked how I could be of service to her.

She looked at me and whispered, "Come back after rounds. I want to talk to you." I returned, not knowing what to expect.

"Come closer to the bed," she advised in a conspiratorial manner.

"What is wrong?"

"I don't want *them* to hear me. I don't know why I was brought to this hospital, of all places."

"We have a very fine staff here. I'm sure your doctor was trying to do his best for you."

"But, don't you understand? It's a *Jewish* hospital. And you know what *they* are like. I want to get out of here. I hate them."

I realized what she meant by "them," but I tried to keep calm and to reason with the woman.

"These people are all trying to do their best for you. Why do you hate them?"

The woman sighed, "Can't you see? They're not like us. They're different. Can't you stay with me on day duty too? I feel safe with you. My day nurse has an accent."

"My assignment this month is for night duty. Why do you feel safe with me?"

She replied, "You're not one of *them*."

After this conversation I left to attend some of my duties, assuring my patient that I would return later.

Finally, on my return, I continued, "Now, explain to me about *them* and why I am not one of them."

"They're foreigners—they don't belong in our country. They're not real Americans like we are."

"Most of the doctors and nurses in this hospital are American citizens . . . Even people with accents can be Americans!"

"But they're *Jews*," she said, making the name sound like a dirty word.

"Jews have a different religion from yours but that doesn't make them foreigners. Can you imagine how you would feel if you were born in this country and loved it, but someone called you an outsider because your religion was different from hers?"

She looked at me in amazement. "Why are you defending them?"

"Because I am a Jew. I was born in this country and I am very proud to be an American and a Jew. Now do I suddenly seem changed to you? Did I grow horns?"

My patient's face turned red. "But, but—you looked so different—your hair, no accent . . . I—You just don't . . ."

I finished making her comfortable for the night. Leaving, I was shaking inside, but determined not to show my anger. The next night I wondered how this prejudiced woman would react when I entered her room. There was no need for apprehension. She had checked herself out early in the morning, unable to face another day with "them."

Prejudice was not usually a problem in our hospital; male sexuality was. Men who were patients sometimes gave us trouble because of the sexual tension that was aroused by our presence. Fortunately, hospital rules helped to lessen part of the problem. Female nurses were not allowed to perform certain functions for the male patients, unless our charges were unconscious. Orderlies were called in for duties such as enemas and other procedures that included handling of male genitalia. These rules did not completely prevent the men from becoming amorous. Experience soon taught us how to forestall or to turn aside any advances . . .

As a slim, attractive woman, I had many encounters with ardent patients. On one occasion, a well-known politician had checked into the hospital for a routine examination. On the first evening, I introduced myself to him as his night nurse. He asked me to come back to talk with him after rounds.

When my chores were done, I returned. Our conversation was enjoyable, about politics, theater and current events. On the second night when I came on duty, I found a beautiful bouquet of roses waiting for me at the office. The note said, "To a lovely nurse who is sweeter than any flower." (Signed) "your patient in 204." I decided to take the gift as a sincere and friendly gesture. However, to forestall any other ideas, I gave away all of the flowers to the other nursing stations, except for one red rose. Then I walked into N. 204 and said, "Thank you for the flowers. I have spread them around for all of the nurses to enjoy. But I kept one for fragrance. I shall put it in your room."

On the next night when I came into my office, I found a large package from Wanamaker's. Inside was a beautiful black chiffon nightgown and robe. The note said, "My compliments to the lovely redhead whom I would like to see when she wears this outfit." The gift was from the same man.

This time my patient had overstepped his friendliness. I thought carefully about how to deal with the situation. Then I packed the items back in the box and brought them to his room. With a friendly but business-like manner, I handed the box to the politician.

"Thank you so much for your lovely gift. I am sure that you were just being kind, but I cannot accept such a present from a man. I assure you that you will never see me in anything else but my nurse's uniform. I am here to do my job and for no other reason."

On the following night, there were no gifts. The patient asked to see me again when I was available. When I entered his room, he apologized, saying that he had misunderstood my natural friendliness. Thereafter, he treated me with great respect and courtesy.

In Hospital

Not long after my encounter with the well-known public figure, I faced another sexual dilemma. I was forced to figure out a way to discourage a doctor without rejecting him. A fine physician, much older than I, had lost his wife very suddenly. The poor man became emotionally and physically ill as a result. This doctor, whom I shall call Max Frank, had always shown courtesy toward me. After his wife's death, he often chose me to be his duty nurse. In addition, he seemed to seek out my company very often; yet, he had never asked me to go out with him. When the doctor entered the hospital as a patient for tests, he requested that I attend him. When I started my duties, Dr. Frank told me that he wanted me to perform every needed procedure by myself. However, when he needed an enema in order to take certain tests, I went out to call the orderly, which was standard hospital procedure.

"No," Dr. Frank stopped me, "I want no orderlies. You do it."

"But doctor," I replied, "hospital regulations forbid a nurse from doing certain jobs on a male patient unless he is unconscious. Would you like me to hit you on the head?"

He laughed, "Don't be funny, Bayuk, you can break regulations this once."

I did not answer. Continuing out of the room, I called the orderly, feeling rather uneasy about the doctor's attitude.

A few days later, when I entered his room, Dr. Frank was sitting up in bed. As I approached to straighten his covers he reached up, grabbed me, pulling me down on the bed. He locked me in a fierce embrace, kissing me hungrily. I struggled to free myself. Immediately, my anger welled up. As I was about to let him have a choice piece of my mind, I noticed his stricken look. It was more than I could bear. I controlled myself and spoke quietly.

"Dr. Frank, you are a fine man and a wonderful doctor. I truly like you. And I know how you are feeling right now. Please don't be upset. I am not rejecting you. Any woman could fall in love with you, but I just happen to be in love with someone else—someone whom I have been going with for three years. So please, don't take it personally. You are a very attractive man."

The grateful look he gave me was compensation for my restraint. It was unusual for this "firebrand" to be so gentle after being subjected to an uncalled for attack. Yet, I could not bring myself to hurt a bereaved man. He was my patient and my first duty was to think about his welfare. Until his wife passed away, Dr. Frank had never bothered another woman. His uncharacteristic behavior was a cry for help. He needed some sign that the future still held life and love for him. The warm response of a young, vital woman would be an affirmation—an act of renewal. Although I could not respond to him sexually, I tried to strengthen his ego with my words.

I was not so kind to other doctors whose behavior was out of line. During my second year, I was sent on a tour of duty to the Jewish Maternity Hospital at Sixth and Pine. This center was affiliated with our hospital. On my first night of duty, I found out why the nurses had nicknamed the dilapidated building "the rat hole." The nursery was upstairs; the mothers' ward downstairs. At each feeding time, the infants had to be carted down a squeaky staircase, then, carried up again. At the 2:00 a.m. feeding, I carried two babies at a time, one under each arm. As I descended the steps carefully, with two precious burdens, something darted right between my legs, scampering on down. Shaken, I managed to keep my balance in time to see a large rat disappearing into the darkened basement area. The babies, who had been screaming for their dinner, were joined by another screamer—me! After regaining control, I continued down to the mothers. On the next trip I took only one child, making as much noise as I could on each step to warn the rodents of my approach. I gradually became used to the four-legged rats, but the human variety continued to be most distasteful. One such "animal" spent a week as our chief, substituting for the regular Resident.

During most of my maternity duty, Dr. Sophie Ostrow was the Resident. A skilled obstetrician, Dr. Ostrow was an inspiration to me as a woman doctor. In spite of the hospital's physical deterioration, much good work was done there. I welcomed the chance to learn how to bring little citizens into the world. Before long, I had the thrill of delivering babies all by myself.

My first "solo" delivery occurred when our doctor had gone out on an emergency call, leaving me in charge. At midnight, a woman entered. She was already in hard labor. It was obvious that the patient could not even get upstairs to the delivery room. There was no time for panic. I grabbed a pad and blankets, and spread them on the floor, underneath the writhing woman. The baby was already on its way into the world. In no time at all, a little girl lay on her mother's stomach, placed there by my own proud hands. Then the mother began to heave once more. To my surprise, I was delivering a second baby, another girl! After the births, I called my assistant nurse who helped me to prepare the babies for their cribs. An orderly helped carry the mother to the ward. When our Resident returned, she was surprised to find two lusty additions to the nursery.

A week later, Dr. Ostrow left temporarily to sit for her State Board examinations. A young male, whom I shall call Martin Grey, became the substitute resident obstetrician. On his first night of duty with me in the delivery room, the doctor kept rubbing against me as we worked together. At first I thought that his movements were accidental. I kept trying to stay out of his way. Finally, I realized that his activity was intentional.

"Doctor," I said, "I think that you have been working too hard. You are neglecting your health. Why don't you see a dermatologist about your terrible itch?"

The young man smiled and continued his offensive behavior. Although I was seething, I did not know exactly how to handle the situation. The next day I asked the other night nurse whether she too had been suffering from the doctor's rude actions.

"Yes, Bayuk," Bridget Cannon admitted, "I sure have been annoyed. He keeps rubbing against me until I want to slap him down. But he's so clever at his game, that it's difficult to catch him."

"Be on the alert," I told her, "A man like that is liable to get aroused and go too far. Let's help each other in case of trouble."

A few nights later, the doorbell rang very late at night. A pregnant woman entered with her husband. I called the doctor to examine the woman in the downstairs office. After the examination, Dr. Grey told the woman, "You're not quite ready to deliver. Since you live nearby, go home, and come back in about six or seven hours."

After escorting the couple to the front door, I turned around, surprised to find that the glass doors leading to the vestibule were closed. I was sure that I had left them open. When I opened the doors to reenter the hallway, Dr. Grey jumped out from behind a door, and fell on top of me, bearing me to the floor. I struggled to get out of his clutches. Desperately, I managed to push my elbow into a door, breaking the pane. The sound of glass breaking alerted my colleague, Bridget, who was upstairs in the delivery room. Because of our previous conversation, my friend was ready to respond. In her haste to reach me, she bypassed the steps and slid down the side railing. From my helpless position, all I could see was a flash of white and blue, sliding down the banister. She landed and rushed to my side, screaming and clawing. Then, I was able to get free. Bridget and I turned on all of the lights downstairs and marched the disheveled man to our headquarters.

I spoke my mind: "You are the lowest form of animal I have ever met. If you ever dare to touch me or Bridget again, you will never recover from our revenge. Keep your dirty hands and everything else to yourself! If you're too sick to control yourself, you should be locked up with all the other sex maniacs. And I'll see to it that you are!"

Suppose I had been alone on duty with this creature? There was no doubt about his intentions. I was so lucky that Bridget was around and wide awake to my danger. Dr. Grey did not dare to come near us again that night. When it was necessary for him to call on the services of a nurse, Bridget and I responded together, showing by our actions that we were ready to fight back if he touched us.

The next morning, we reported Dr. Grey to the chief at the main hospital. The brash doctor was called into the office and seriously reprimanded. He was made to realize that his sexual advances were not to be tolerated. The offender was not allowed to make rounds with just one nurse. For the duration of his stay, at least one other person would accompany Bridget or me when we made rounds with the aggressive doctor.

Etched in my memory is the sight of my dignified colleague sliding down the post, like a fireman, to the rescue of her beleaguered friend.

After experiences with men like Dr. Grey, I appreciated David Rappoport more than ever. Whatever faults my beau had, he was the soul of honor and integrity, possessing a moral nature that was both an asset and a liability. He was so altruistic that it was difficult for him to make a living at his profession. Besides treating the poor for nothing, he was often short tempered with the idle rich. As a result, David's practice had not been flourishing. During my second year in training, my "country doctor" left Norma to begin again in Philadelphia on south Sixth Street, where he moved with his father and sister. By this time, David and I had an "understanding," although we were not in a position to marry.

On afternoons off, I usually went to the Rappoport home in town. I remained there until after dinner and office hours. Then David would accompany me back to my quarters. On our long trolley ride home, we had an opportunity to be alone together.

One evening, as we sat on the trolley, my boyfriend did not talk to me at all. David was probably mulling over some important problem; yet, I did not relish being ignored during our precious time together. When we reached our destination, the absent-minded doctor walked out of the trolley, still lost in thought. I motioned to the motorman, whom I knew, to let me out through the back door. Then I scooted off and hid behind some trees, just to see how far my escort would walk before he missed me. I peeked out as David proceeded up the path. Finally, he turned around realizing that I was not in sight. He searched, perplexed. Then, walking back, he stared at the disappearing trolley car, obviously wondering whether I had failed to get off. Seeing that the poor man was frantic, I came out of my hiding place and walked over to him.

David was furious. "I just don't understand you, Bluma. That wasn't funny at all. Why was it necessary to give me such a scare?"

I replied, "Sometimes it's necessary to give you a scare so that you'll remember that I'm around. Do you think it was right for you to sit with me for one hour on the trolley without saying a word?"

David shook his head. "I'll never be able to accept your humor."

"Why not, David? Why do you always have to be so serious? I like to have a little fun when I'm off duty. I want to let down my hair and laugh—enjoy some good times. What joy is there in being together if you just sit and stare into space? Next time, if you are so tired, stay home. I can ride back alone. As a matter of fact, I was alone today. You weren't really with me."

On our future rides together, David was careful to make conversation. Perhaps that silent trolley ride symbolized the difference in our natures. David was a deep thinker, often lost in another dimension. The real world was not so important to him as the world of ideas. In contrast, I have always been people-oriented. Although I love to learn, human relationships take precedence over thoughts in my orbit. How sad that David could not learn to enjoy a frivolous moment with a friend, instead of traveling the dark side of the road. My landscape had brighter vistas. I have always charted my way through paths of beauty and enlightenment, with plenty of time for joyous and humorous stopovers.

I approached my work with the same spirit of light, trying to impart happiness whenever possible. On one tour of duty, I was horrified to find that some of my patients had lived in a world of shadows for many years. During my senior year, I worked at the hospital's Home for Incurables. There I observed that some inmates never left their rooms. Either they had no relatives or their families neglected them, for many never received a visitor. My heart ached for those abandoned souls who vegetated in despair. While I was on duty there, I was determined to give each forgotten person a special treat.

Many of the neglected were stroke victims, completely bedridden and forced to stare at the same four walls every day. My plan was to take one patient out of bed every day until each one had experienced a change of routine and environment. It would take extra effort, but I felt that these victims deserved a "lift."

One particularly appealing lady was a Mrs. Solomon who had been in the institution for more than a decade. Although she could not move or speak, her eyes showed that she had some understanding of what was going on around her. I felt that with special attention, Mrs. Solomon might show some improvement. Even as a young woman I believed that old people should not be written off. As long as a person is alive he is valuable and has a right to live as fully as he can, and to be treated as a worthwhile improvable human being. My first step was to move my charge out into other surroundings, away from her four walls. On a lovely May afternoon, I entered Mrs. Solomon's room and worked with an orderly to put her on a stretcher. Then I wheeled her to the front of the hospital, explaining that I was going to give her a treat. The wide glass doors of the hospital afforded a vista of the blossoming grounds and the busy street beyond. As we approached the glass doors of the entranceway, I raised the head of the stretcher so that Mrs. Solomon could have a clear view of the outdoors. As she watched, instead of a smile, a look of sheer terror crossed her face. The patient, who had not spoken a word in years, made a noise like a whimpering animal. I ran to the front to see what was causing her agitation. Nothing unusual was out there. It was a normal day—the busy street was filled with traffic. A car was traveling up the driveway toward the building.

As my patient continued to shake with fright, making her agitated noises, I finally realized the object of her fear—the car!

Mrs. Solomon had been in the hospital all during an era of rapid change. When she entered her room, the automobile was in its infancy. Evidently she had never seen one. Now, in her first view of the modern world, she was confronted with a horrible two-eyed metal monstrosity that seemed to be bearing straight at her, with engines roaring. In addition, outside, hordes of these frightful monsters were zooming up and down the street, rumbling and honking ominously. What a nightmare it must have seemed to one who was unaware of a decade of progress!

After calming Mrs. Solomon and returning her to her accustomed shelter, I decided to temper my headlong enthusiasm thereafter. From that experience, I learned to prepare my charges gradually for their jaunts. Soon, the extra attention that I showed to the older people brought results both in raising their spirits and in improving their health. Mrs. Solomon, in particular, was thriving under my continued care. After I instituted a new regimen of exercises, she gradually regained some speech, enough for basic communication with others. Then, I found out that she had two children who had not visited her for many years. Having lost track of her family, the hospital was keeping her free of charge.

One day, to my surprise, I learned that Mrs. Solomon was receiving two visitors. As I entered her room, a couple greeted me effusively. The woman, Mrs. Granger, a daughter, had come from the South with her husband. The other patients had already told the visitors how much I had done for their mother. Mrs. Granger thanked me warmly. The last time that she had visited, Mrs. Solomon had been a "vegetable." It seemed miraculous to Mrs. Granger that her mother was able to communicate again. The visitors asked me to have dinner with them the following evening. During their week's stay, they insisted that I dine with them every night at their hotel. Before they left, we had become good friends.

Mr. Granger, who worked on the Merchant Marine line, offered to send me a ticket to visit them in Savannah, Georgia, during my vacation period. In September I received the ticket and traveled to my Southern friends. However, the stay was cut short. While I was there, Mrs. Solomon died. We all returned to the North to arrange for the funeral. The Grangers and I continued our warm friendship. Following the death of their mother, they would come to Philadelphia once a year, wining and dining me on every visit. A strange incident abruptly ended our relationship.

Several years after Mrs. Solomon's death, the Grangers telephoned me that they were once again in Philadelphia. I arranged to have dinner with them on the following Thursday, my day off. My friends were delighted to see me when we met at Stauffer's in Center City. We sat down at our table, talking, anxious to compare notes about our lives since the last time we had met. We ordered our dinner, sitting back in a relaxed and jovial mood. Suddenly, just as the platters arrived, Mr. Granger turned red and jumped up. Grabbing his hat and coat, he stalked angrily out of the restaurant without uttering a word. His wife followed him quickly. I was left at the table, bewildered. I examined the food, but could see nothing wrong with our orders. I looked around at our fellow diners. They all sat calmly, eating. To the right of us was a group of elderly women; to the left a black minister; in front, a young couple—all absorbed in their own business. I didn't know what to do. Rising from the table, I put on my wraps and headed for the cashier.

"I don't know what happened to my friends," I told her, "but they left without eating or paying their bill."

I took the check and paid it myself before leaving. My friends were several yards from the restaurant, in an agitated state.

I approached them in alarm, "What happened? What's wrong?" Mr. Granger sputtered, "Didn't you see? Can you believe it?"

"I didn't see anything. What did I miss? What went wrong?"

"At the table," he said. "Didn't you see—at the table next to us?"

"No, everyone seemed calm and normal to me." Mrs. Granger whispered in my ear. I looked at her in disbelief. Was that the cause of all this excitement?

"A minister, a colored minister, is that really why you left?"

"A Nigra," he screamed, "A Nigra, sitting right next to us in a restaurant. Did you ever hear of such a thing!"

"Of course," I replied, "it is an every day occurrence. We don't have any of those ridiculous segregation rules here in Philadelphia. Someday the South will know better too."

Mr. Granger became apoplectic at my reply. He turned away from me without a backward glance and went charging down the street. Mrs. Granger gave me a helpless look and took after her husband on the run. That is the last glimpse I ever had of my two erstwhile friends from Savannah, Georgia. I am sure that they never entered the North again.

After my tour of duty at the Home for the Incurables, I was on the home stretch toward graduation. Although I had previously done well in my studies, during my senior year, my marks had fallen below their normally high level. Miss Frances called me into her office.

"Miss Bayuk, we are getting closer to graduation. I have been especially pleased with the way you have been doing in school up to these past few months. You know all of the doctors have recommended you for our gold medal nurse. At graduation time, the best all-around graduate becomes the winner of the gold medal. This is a great honor and you well deserve it above all of your classmates. However, certain standards have to be maintained. At this point your class marks have changed radically, please tell me what happened?"

I answered her with tears in my eyes. "I have personal problems. They seem to get worse all of the time. You see, my fiancé and I have a serious difference of opinion. I can't budge him in his stubborn ideas, and I can't see the logic in doing things his way. We are at a terrible impasse, and I just can't concentrate on my studies."

Miss Frances advised me to think seriously before marrying someone whose ideas were so different from mine, especially since he refused to compromise.

"Marriage is difficult enough without such extra burdens," she advised.

"I know," I moaned. "David and I are so different. We are incompatible; yet, I know that this is the only man for me. I love him. I guess I can't live with him or without him. It is driving me crazy!"

Our latest arguments concerned marriage. After going together for six years, we seemed no closer to matrimony than we were at the beginning of our friendship. David's income was not sufficient to support two homes. This circumstance did not change my fiancé's insistence on being the sole support of wife, sister and father. He objected to my suggestion that I continue to work as a nurse after our marriage. David decreed that after we marry, I must come to live with his family, taking over the household chores and cooking. I objected. If I accepted his plan, all of my training years would be wasted. Besides, I loved David's father and sisters. I wanted them to love me. If we lived together, there was bound to be friction. His sister had been running the household. Understandably, she would be hurt if I were to take over. On the other hand, my employment would bring in an added income to benefit all of us. My sweetheart refused to listen to any suggestion of my working. I was frustrated and dejected. David and I once more became estranged. This turn of events preyed on my mind. My school marks did not improve.

Already in a low frame of mind, I was called upon to face my greatest challenge, one that I had avoided for three years. One evening, a young, beautiful woman was brought in, dead on arrival. Although I was charge nurse, there was no student available to prepare the body for the morgue . . . I was faced with doing the job alone, for the first time. A friend on another assignment passed by.

"Florence," I begged, "see if you can arrange to come back and stand by me. I just don't know how I am going to be able to prepare this corpse."

My friend paused, "Bayuk, I'd like to help you, but I won't. You have to conquer the fear by yourself. If you don't shoulder this responsibility now, you never will. And it will remain a hurdle all of the rest of your life. Do it alone now, and it will help you in the future."

She left. For the next half-hour, I struggled with my fears and my conscience. As a senior, I knew that I should be able to do the necessary work. Finally, I decided that even if I died alongside the patient, I had to try.

Alone, in tears, I set about my grim assignment, pulling every fiber of my being into a taut line of determination. It was a long, lonely task, but I carried it through. After I had sent the beautiful body to the morgue, I sat down, unable to move.

Later, my friend came back, "I had to return, I know how you must be feeling. I've gone through the same thing. Bayuk, I'll stand by you while you prepare the patient."

Sobbing, I told her, "Florence, I did it already—all by myself. The patient is in the morgue."

She sat by me, patting my hand, until I calmed down.

"I'm so relieved," she said. "I know that from now on it won't be so bad for you. You'll be able to handle the grief. No matter what you are called on to do, you'll be able to do it now."

Not long afterward, ironically, I was called on to prepare the body of a dear relative. When my brother Jake contracted pneumonia and died, I was able to care for him with loving hands, to send him to the funeral parlor. My ordeal with the lovely young corpse had set me free.

From that time on, my terror was gone. I have since attended many patients and loved ones in their last hours. Although the ultimate earthly experience remains a mystery, I have lost my fear of death because, without exception, all of the dying as they slip away attain an expression of peace and serenity. Since death is built into the pattern of our physical being, I accept it as I accept every other event in the life cycle. Along with acceptance, I have the certain knowledge that the mind does not die. In the course of a lifetime, we learn so much; our span includes so many significant experiences that it is impossible for vibrant beings to come to an abrupt and final end, merely because our bodies wear out. Something of us remains in the Universe, converted to another dimension.

My father often stated, "After my body crumbles, I shall still be. In some way, my vital force will continue, and I shall always be near when you need me."

I have felt Dad's presence so often that I know the truth of his words. Nothing so powerful as human thought can be destroyed. The soul, the sacred vessel of the mind, exists forever.

As graduation time approached, David and I continued to quarrel about my future. My fiancé still insisted that I give up nursing after we married. I refused to consider being "just a housewife," because I was embarking on a career that I loved. Our conflict became so bitter that I could scarcely concentrate on my studies. Meanwhile, I was offered a permanent position in the hospital as charge nurse of the Incurable and Tubercular Department, a section which I had enjoyed as an undergraduate. I accepted the job, much to David's chagrin. He was furious that I would defy his plans.

In spite of our troubles, I was looking forward with great excitement to the big day. My parents and my fiancé were invited to the graduation ceremonies. Afterwards, there would be a reception. In the evening, a dinner and a dance had been scheduled. I had bought a beautiful dress for the occasion, planning to enjoy the festivities with great gusto. The day before the affair, I received a telephone call from David.

"I won't be able to attend your graduation. My Dad is ill with pneumonia. I plan to visit him in Vineland in the afternoon."

I was so shocked that I could not answer him. After hanging up the telephone, I began to cry. How could David do such a cruel thing? His father, who had a trained nurse taking care of him, had already passed his crisis. David could have postponed his visit for one more day. There was no emergency.

Joyous anticipation turned to despair. My sweetheart had let me down again. He would not share a most memorable and important occasion in my life. In addition, I would miss the dance because I had no escort.

The next morning, as I sat in my office, despondent, one of the young doctors making rounds came into the room and looked at me in surprise.

"What's this? You look unhappy. Aren't you excited about graduating today?"

"Of course," I said slowly, "It's just that my escort can't be with me for the dance. His father is ill."

Dr. Meyerhoff smiled at me. "Well, perhaps fate has done me a good turn, Miss Bayuk. I realize that you are engaged. I know, because when I first came to the hospital, I asked about you. The other residents said 'hands off, she's engaged and she's true blue.' But I have always admired you and enjoyed your company. I would consider it an honor to escort you to the dance."

I was delighted, "Dr. Meyerhoff, you saved the day, I think it is very kind of you to offer. I'm happy to go with you."

In the afternoon, all of our loved ones watched and smiled as we sat on the podium, waiting to be called up to receive our diplomas. Some of the physicians with whom we had worked during the past three years also came to the ceremonies. For me, one face stood out among all others in the audience. A plump little lady, beaming from ear to ear, was broadcasting silent messages of approval and love. She was my own dear mother who had originally opposed my training. Now she sat, prouder than all of the rest, knowing that I had followed my heart and realized my dreams.

As the moment came for revealing the name of the Gold Medal Nurse, we all felt a ripple of excitement. Miss Frances stood up to make the announcement. Most of my colleagues

In Hospital

looked at me and nodded as Miss Frances read the requirements for the award. As she announced the winner, an audible gasp seemed to go through the room. The assembled doctors began murmuring to each other, scowling. As one of my classmates rose to receive the medal, I sat, stunned. The coveted award had gone to someone else!

After the end of the ceremonies, I joined my parents to receive their hugs and congratulations. Unaware of my disappointment, they were ecstatic over the day's events. Later, several doctors walked over to me asking that I accompany them to Miss Frances' office. I took leave of my parents and followed the physicians.

Several doctors were already in the office, talking with the superintendent. She looked at them calmly, drumming her fingers on the desk.

As I entered, she said, "Miss Bayuk, I have something to say to the doctors here—something that may interest you. I would like you to listen and to answer me honestly. These gentlemen have come here to protest. They say that you should have received the gold medal. I happen to agree with them. You certainly are the best nurse that we have had in training for many years. As you know, my admiration for your ability has been very evident. However, no matter how I feel personally, I cannot break the rules. Part of the requirements for the prize relate to classroom achievement. The winner must maintain a certain average in her grades in order to be eligible. This year, your average fell below the required level. I had no choice but to omit your name from the list. I did so with a heavy heart, but I want you to understand that in order to preserve the meaning of the Gold Medal Award, our recipients must live up to all of the requirements. We cannot allow the standards to be bent to fit the recipient. Miss Bayuk, if you think that I have treated you unfairly, please feel free to say so."

"Miss Frances," I replied, "you were kind enough to call me in and warn me when you realized that my marks were slipping. I truly appreciated your interest. I should have listened to you then. Losing the medal was my own fault. I allowed personal problems to interfere with my training. You often told me that this is inexcusable in a nurse. I don't deserve the gold medal. But I hope that in the future I will live up to your good opinion of me. You have been more than fair. I have learned a great deal about integrity and devotion from your example."

The doctors left, after wishing me well. Miss Frances remained at her desk. We looked at each other. For a moment I thought that I saw tears in my supervisor's eyes. She turned away before I could be sure. I know that I must have been mistaken. The very strict and capable administrator would never allow sentiment to mix with duty. We shook hands solemnly and said "Goodbye."

In the evening, we attended our graduation dinner in one of the hotels. Afterward, there was a gala dance in our honor. When I came out of the dining room Dr. Meyerhoff was waiting to present me with a corsage. As I pinned on the flowers, he whispered in my ear, "Your fiancé is here, waiting to see you."

"Since you are my escort," I replied, "let's go together. Please dance me over to David so that I can introduce you to him."

After I introduced the two men, my partner and I left for the dance floor again. My card was filled and I proceeded to have a wonderful time. Robert Meyerhoff proved to be a delightful companion and a gentleman. As for David, I had told him to feel free to leave because I already had a date for the evening. However, he remained, sitting dejectedly by the punch bowl. Occasionally, one of my friends would stop to talk to him. I did not come near him again all evening.

When the dance ended, Robert said, "Bluma, thank you for a lovely evening. Now, I'll leave you with your fiancé. I think that he should escort you home."

I thanked the good doctor for his kindness. On the way back in the cab, I told David how I felt about the way he had treated me.

"You're right. Bluma. When I got to Vineland, my father was surprised to see me. He said, 'Isn't Bluma graduating today?' I said 'yes.' Dad was angry with me. He said, 'You belong with

Bluma today. Go back there immediately.' Bluma, I'm ashamed of myself. I should have been at your graduation."

"Didn't you realize how much you were hurting me by not coming?"

"I just didn't think. I seem to go my own way without realizing that other people have feelings too. You know I love you, Bluma, but I just don't relate to your feelings too well. I have no social finesse at all. You are in for a hard time if you marry a thoughtless person like me."

"I know that, David," I said. "If I had any sense at all, I would throw you over and fall in love with someone like Robert. He is so thoughtful and understanding. I know your temper and I have already suffered from your stubbornness. We don't think alike and we probably never will."

That night, I thought long and hard. Life with David as a husband would mean a very rocky road. He would never be an easy person to get along with or to understand. He was poor and likely to stay that way because he lacked a good "bedside manner." Wasn't I foolish to continue this long and thankless relationship? After a sleepless night, I was still not able to make a clear-cut decision. It seemed that although I could not get along with David, unfortunately, I was not ready to face a future without him.

Private Duty

I STARTED my freelance duties with a memorable assignment. At the end of the summer of 1912, as I was finishing my tour at the Home for the Incurables, my supervisor asked if I would like to represent the hospital on a volunteer mission. When I learned the details, I was excited, for I would take part in an historical event. The Civil War veterans of the Battle of Gettysburg were returning to the battlefield for their fiftieth reunion. Our government was going "all-out" for the occasion: erecting special barracks, providing food, entertainment and personnel to attend to the old veterans. The Red Cross had been asked to select a group of nurses to be on hand for the ex-soldiers in case of illness or accident. I was thrilled to be included.

In early fall, I left for Gettysburg from the North Philadelphia station, with eight other nurses. As we alighted from the train, we found the area bustling with activity. To our astonishment, a group of young soldiers was engaged in a strange task at the station. They were unloading empty coffins from the train and placing them on army trucks.

"Where are you taking these coffins?" I asked a young sergeant who was directing the operations.

"To the reunion," he said.

"Whatever for?"

The sergeant laughed, "Everything is figgered out ahead of time. Fifty old men are gonna be raisin' Hell for a week, some of them gotta cash in their chips. So we gotta be prepared."

"Well," I said, "I hope that you keep those things out of sight. It won't be good for morale if the veterans see coffins waiting to turn them into statistics."

A distinguished looking man about seventy-five was standing behind me. He was tall and spare, with an erect carriage that spoke of discipline and integrity. The medals on his lapel glistened.

"Don't worry about us, young lady," he advised. "If we survived all we've been through, a pile of caskets isn't going to stop us now."

When we reached the field, we were amazed at the magnitude of the advance preparations. We saw comfortable sleeping barracks, a large diet kitchen containing all cooking facilities, a roomy tent outfitted as a dispensary and a large enclosure for dining, meeting and partying.

The veterans were well-preserved oldsters who quickly got together to sing old songs and to tell their stories—tales that had probably grown and changed through the years, but were fascinating nevertheless.

The officer in charge of operations came to visit us in the dispensary. "Ladies, we have a problem. We have too many nurses and not enough supervision in the kitchen. Would one of you women like to take over the management of the kitchen? We have plenty of food, cooks and servers, but no one to oversee and to expedite the meal service."

I volunteered. For the remainder of our stay, I was in charge of the diet kitchen, making sure that meals were served hot, and on time. Later on, this experience was helpful to me when I set up my own business. What a strange contrast for me! I had just finished working at the Incurable Home where old, forgotten people lived like vegetables, with no activity, and little hope. Now, I was at a place where eager oldsters were rushing through the battlefield, from spot to spot, with cries of recognition. Whenever I could spare time, I would walk out to the battlefield to listen to the old soldiers.

"Here," one man said, "Here in this very spot, my best friend fell, mortally wounded. I dragged him back to the hospital tent, through mud and smoke, his blood all over me. I never noticed that I had caught it in the shoulder myself, till after I had turned him over to the medics."

"And over here . . ." another man was saying. . . .

"This tree, I hid behind it when. . . ."

"A Reb came up to me right here and turned himself in. He was just a scared kid—and so was I. We been writin' to each other through the years."

The tales went on and on. This field, once a living Hell, had evolved through the years into a storage house of wistful memories. The old men rooted around in the stones and grass, searching for their lost youth and strength, and for the bright promise of peace and brotherhood for which they had fought. For a brief time, they resurrected a Yesterday, buried, like their dreams, in layers of crumbled time.

At the end of the week, the men were still hale and hearty. They had reveled, remembered and were content. On the last evening, the cooks had found a gallon of unused ice cream, beginning to melt. They wanted to know what to do with it. The gallant old gentlemen decided to give the nurses a treat. We sat down in their mess tent while they served us the last vestiges of their party fare. We women enjoyed our ice cream orgy, served by the veterans. We kissed them all and thanked them for our treat. Then we packed for the trip home. Everyone, nurses and veterans, were leaving on the same train, which made stops along the way and ended in Philadelphia. From there, some would be leaving for longer trips.

At the station, I observed the soldiers loading the coffins back on to the train.

"I am happy that you're returning with the same amount of caskets that you brought," I remarked to the sergeant.

The young man grinned, "I guess this is one time that we're all glad that the U.S. Army goofed. I hear that no one even got sick at the reunion."

"You're right, I replied, "The nurses had it easy. There were no battlefield disasters this time."

Unfortunately, disaster struck during the train ride home! One by one, some of the passengers became extremely ill. Soon there were nine people writhing in agony on the floor of the train. The well passengers took care of the sick ones with tenderness. Ironically, the sick ones were all nurses; the old veterans ministered to us, bringing us whiskey to ease our misery. A few of the nurses were so ill that they had to be taken off at the next station and placed in ambulances. Although I was in severe pain and discomfort, I insisted on continuing onto Philadelphia where David was waiting for me at the station. He took me to his home and treated me. I was extremely ill for weeks with ptomaine poisoning. Evidently, the ice cream, our treat, was tainted. I was so thankful, even in my misery, that we nurses had eaten the dessert, instead of the men; for surely the veterans would have been unable to survive such an ordeal.

In appreciation for our services, the Red Cross gave each one of the nurses a special number—one that would be ours for life. The number indicated our place in the history of service to the organization. I hold No. 3,779. Since 1912, the numbers have reached the hundreds of thousands. I still cherish the number and the medal which I received from the Red Cross to commemorate the historic event.

After recovering from my illness, I realized that I was at a crossroad in my life. A momentous choice confronted me: I had completed training and I had acquired a fiancé. Which way should I go? Although I had a woman's normal desire for marriage and children, I still yearned to gain more knowledge and to continue my service to fellow human beings. As Mrs. David Rappoport I knew that I would have to accept the role of housewife only. Was I ready to give up a fledgling career for marriage? Probing my innermost thoughts, I unearthed my true feelings. My heart spoke honestly: "David! But not yet! Let me be me for a little while longer." When he heard my decision, David raged and threatened. I stood up to him, refusing to change my mind. At last, my fiancé grudgingly accepted the situation. We could continue to be engaged. I would go into private practice.

My first priority was to find a place to live. Although I would be going out on assignments, I still needed a home base. Once again my brother Sam offered me a room in his household.

My brothers' lives had changed radically since my first arrival in Philadelphia. Jake had died of pneumonia. Then Esther, Max's wife, passed away. Next, Max, my fun-loving, adorable brother, became ill with a strange malady. David sent him to Dr. Cushing, a specialist in Boston, to no avail. Max died shortly after Esther, leaving three young children. Sam, newly-married, had taken the orphans into his home on North Broad Street, near the Jewish hospital.

Sam's life had been difficult since his divorce. Sending the children to a convent boarding school had not worked out well. The school had been unable to cope with Harry. The five-year-old boy needed a mother, not a teacher. Finally, Sam realized that he should marry again to give his children a real home. This time he was resolved to select a warm, motherly person. As he searched, he noticed a young girl who worked in the factory as a cigar maker. Sadie Cohen, an apple cheeked, bosomy young girl, had caught his attention with her pleasant manners. She seemed strong, healthy and kindhearted. It occurred to my brother that a woman from the lower working class might be a better mate than a society woman. She would not feel above supervising a home and children. Besides, she would be so grateful for the chance to marry a rich man that she would not question his "outside" activities. Sam was a "ladies' man" who had no intentions of allowing marriage to interfere with his amours.

Sadie proved to be an excellent wife. Her greatest problem was Harry, who was uncontrollable. When Sam and Sadie invited me to live with them, they hoped that I would be able to reach Harry and to help him, for Sam's children considered me as a second mother ever since I had cared for them years before.

When I re-entered the household, there were five children: Max's three—Eleanor about sixteen, Beatrice, fourteen, and Eddie, thirteen—Harry was ten and Anna Fay, twelve. In addition, Sadie was pregnant. Not long after I moved in, I helped to deliver her first child, Bernice.

The Bayuk home was gorgeously arranged by an interior decorator. Although Sadie was a plain person, she was able to fulfill her social obligations with the help of servants. She was hostess at many dinner parties with the elite of Philadelphia Jewry in attendance, including the Jacob Lits and the Gimbel family. The erstwhile cigar maker had learned to mingle with society and to be accepted. Sam grumbled that Sadie never dressed up to greet him when there was no company, and that she smelled more of onions than perfume; but nonetheless, he admitted that he had chosen well. Sadie and I learned to love each other dearly, remaining friends throughout her lifetime.

Although I tried my best to give Harry the extra mothering that he needed, it was too late. Harry had been deprived of his own mother's love at the age of five. The early years are the most important ones in forming a person's self-image. David and I knew that only professional treatment could help the boy. When we advised Sam to take his son to a child psychiatrist, he laughed at us.

"Nonsense," he scoffed. "I was a bad kid too. Harry will outgrow it."

This attitude of Sam's was formed by ignorance and stinginess. He should not have refused to consult a doctor at that crucial time. Sam paid the price for his neglect. His only son continued to be a source of trouble and anxiety for many years. (Fortunately, now, Harry has become a wonderful man, helped, no doubt, by the understanding love of his wife, Mary.)

Anna Fay soon learned to get along well with her stepmother. However, Harry felt abused and discriminated against. Edith, the children's mother, had kept in touch with them once a week. Every Saturday Anna Fay and Harry were put on a trolley car. They went to Lit's where their mother met them and took them to lunch at Horne and Hardart's. Eventually, Edith married a non-Jewish doctor. The children never met Dr. Paul . . . Edith warned them never to visit her or to call her at her home.

Several months after I arrived at Sam's home, I received a telephone call from Edith.

"Bluma, tell the children that I won't be able to meet them for lunch for a while. Make sure that they don't try to get in touch with me at any time. I'll contact them when I can."

She refused to answer any of my questions and rang off abruptly. After I told the children, I discussed the situation with Sadie.

"How can a mother do this to her children?" Sadie asked, shocked.

"She must be pregnant," I answered.

At first, Anna Fay and Harry seemed to accept their Mother's absence. As time went on, Anna Fay became upset and melancholy. Sadie and I were worried by her moodiness. Finally, after several months had passed, I came upon the child, sobbing hysterically.

"What's wrong, honey?"

"I want my mother," she wailed. "Something terrible must have happened to her. She doesn't call or anything."

I told the children to dress and to come with me. We went to Erie Avenue, where Dr. Paul maintained his home and offices. There, we discovered that the Pauls had moved away. Neighbors did not know where they had gone. The children were heartbroken. Then, I called David, asking him to find out the doctor's new address. We soon learned that Edith and her husband had moved to an address in South Philadelphia.

On the following Saturday, I accompanied the children to their mother's new home. I left them at the door and watched from across the street as they rang the bell. Edith came to the door. When she saw the children, her face turned red. She pushed them to the side and closed the door. Without a coat, she marched the children down the street, away from her house. Instead of a loving greeting, she screamed at them, "I told you never to come here!"

"But Mama," Anna Fay sobbed, "we were worried about you!"

Edith walked them up and down, agitated. Then she caught sight of me. Hurriedly she marched the children across the street and pushed them at me.

"Don't you ever bring them here again! I have a new baby to take care of now. We live here with my mother-in-law. She doesn't know about my past. You take the children," she said, "They're all Sam's now."

She left without a backward look.

Anna Fay and Harry were pale and shivering. They were still in a daze as I helped them onto the trolley car. On the way home, the trembling girl clung to me tightly. Harry refused to let me touch him. He sat aloof, a ten-year-old reject, staring at the floor.

After settling in the Bayuk household, I did not lack for private assignments. Several doctors regularly called me for their cases. In addition, the Nurses' Registry gave me work. Whenever I was called, I would dress, take my suitcase and venture forth, taking public transportation, day or night, without fear or hesitation.

Between assignments I kept busy in a special way: I used my fees to take private lessons from competent tutors to improve my general education, studying English, writing skills and literature, science and history. Although my studies were interrupted by nursing duties, I continued them whenever possible, absorbing eagerly. Other women might have spent their salaries on clothing or jewelry. My adornment was education. I never regretted those expenditures. My Mother had guided me to this lasting system of values. Today, I am still eager for new knowledge, knowing that it is the most exciting and rewarding activity.

David too was pursuing new avenues of information. He had entered a post graduate course at the University of Pennsylvania. I had encouraged him to study Public Health and Preventative Medicine because he was already ahead of his time in his interest in those fields. In his practice, he always advised his patients that many illnesses could be prevented by good personal hygiene, exercise and proper nutrition. Often, he became furious with people whose illnesses could have been avoided. Naturally, his patients did not appreciate lectures about their negligence when they were sick. Sometimes, he lost their business. What an enigmatic situation! Because he was so good at his work, David was no good for himself. Because his intense feelings about human suffering came out in the form of anger, he was often misunderstood and disliked. He wished, with all his heart, to preserve human beings from pain and misery; yet, he could not communicate his concern to his patients in an acceptable manner.

One of my greatest joys as a private duty nurse was to get an assignment for a maternity case. When Dr. Karp, an obstetrician from the Jewish Hospital, called to ask me to attend a new mother and her child at their home, I was delighted. The baby was a strapping seven-pound boy and the young couple was thrilled with their first child. Mr. Shore, the father, brought his wife extravagant gifts whenever he returned home from his frequent overnight business trips.

By the time I left the family, after two weeks, the baby was well-regulated in feeding and nighttime awakening; the house was tidy and serene. Mr. Shore insisted on giving me a bonus when I left. My heart was filled with joy to see a new family so happy and thriving. What a lucky baby to be born into such a home! I promised to visit the Shores again soon.

Several weeks later, I received a call from Dr. Kahn, a surgeon, asking me to attend a post operative gallbladder case at home. The patient was leaving the hospital the next day; since her husband was a traveling salesman, the doctor thought she should have a nurse for a few weeks. This case was in Strawberry Mansion. I headed out in the opposite direction from my last case to meet my patient Marie Shaw, a plump, cheerful young woman. Her apartment was tastefully furnished. A small guest room off the kitchen proved adequate for my own quarters. Mrs. Shaw confided to me that her husband was a wonderful man. As they had no children, Marie worked for a stationery firm. Although Mr. Shaw was on a trip, he thoughtfully sent his wife a bouquet of flowers with a tender message to welcome her home.

How nice, I thought, two lovely marriages in a row. What a fine omen! I needed reassurance, because I was in love with such a difficult person. David was a stubborn, moody man and our off-again-on-again engagement had left me confused and uncertain about marriage.

When Dr. Kahn visited Mrs. Shaw, pleased with her progress, he took me aside to assure me that my patient was happy with my services. Since my patient had a slight heart condition, the surgeon also emphasized the importance of her mental attitude—she must not become upset.

The next day Mrs. Shaw was pleasantly excited about her husband's imminent return. She asked me to help her with her hair and makeup. I also fixed a nice dinner so that the couple could eat together in her bedroom. While I was in the kitchen making dinner, Mr. Shaw returned and headed straight for the bedroom to greet his wife. I heard their loving greeting and waited until Marie rang the bell before I intruded. Then I carried in the dinner tray. As I placed the tray on the table next to the bed, I looked up to greet Mr. Shaw. As I stared at the man, the smile left my face. For what seemed like an age, I was numb. I continued to stare, unable to comprehend what my eyes were telling me. Then, still the nurse, I realized that I could not in any way betray my agitation to my patient. I managed to stammer an acknowledgment of the introduction and quickly left the room. Mr. Shaw did not follow me. He stayed with his wife for the rest of the evening. I entered the room only to administer medicine and to remove the dinner tray. When I finally had to enter the bedroom later to prepare Marie for sleeping, her husband discreetly left the room, and did not return until I had left for my quarters. I cannot imagine what he was feeling. I only know that I was trembling and miserable. The next morning, when I entered Marie's room in response to her bell, Mr. Shaw had already left for work. When Dr. Kahn arrived for his daily visit, I asked him if I could speak with him privately before he left. Out in the hallway, I asked him to get a replacement for me as soon as possible.

Dr. Kahn was annoyed, "Bayuk," he said, "I don't understand your unprofessional actions. You know that I warned you about this patient's need for serenity. It would upset her if a nurse she liked were to leave at this point. When a nurse takes on an assignment, she is obligated to carry it through unless there are very unusual circumstances. This action of yours could seriously affect your whole nursing career. It is not good to get a reputation for leaving a job. You are just starting out on your career—think of the consequences!"

"You don't understand," I answered. "There is a very real reason why I must leave. You'll have to take my word for it. I just can't tell you."

Dr. Kahn was not impressed. "I'm a doctor, I know how to keep a confidence. I have to know your real reasons for leaving or else I'll have to assume that they are not valid ones."

I took a deep breath, "All right doctor, I'll tell you. But whether you consider my reason adequate or not, I am leaving! You see, I'm not a very good actress, and if I stay, I'm afraid I will hurt my patient a great deal."

"For God's sake, Bayuk, what is this all about?"

"Well, doctor," I said, "I just came from a maternity case on the other side of town. A Mr. and Mrs. Shore had a fine little boy. They were a very loving couple. Mr. and Mrs. Shaw too seem especially compatible. The only problem is—Mr. Shaw is Mr. Shore!"

Dr. Kahn looked at me to make sure that I was serious. The stricken look on my face confirmed it.

"Bayuk, pack your bags. I'll have a replacement for you by four o'clock!"

I never saw either of the couples again.

My routine continued in a pattern of private duty nursing, evening tutoring and dates with David. My fiancé's practice was still not improving. David seemed to be at a standstill both in his career and in his social life. He no longer urged me toward marriage, knowing that I was leading a full and enjoyable life.

My sister-in-law Sadie and I had become very good friends. Sam had tried to get Sadie interested in joining me in my studies. She was not interested in acquiring an education. Instead, she had an absorbing passion, spending her days and evenings playing cards or gambling in any manner that presented itself. In those days, Atlantic City was wide open as a gambling mecca. In the summer, Sadie took the children and her retinue of servants to the shore. She rented a large home on S. Vermont Avenue, where the children enjoyed the beach. Sadie devoted her leisure time to games of chance, both legal and illegal. Often, I would join the family for a weekend, or during an interval between cases. When Sam closed up the Broad St. home for the summer, I stayed with the Rappoports in South Philadelphia. Sam remained in town during the week, staying either at his Club or at one of his lady friend's apartments. Sadie seemed totally unaware of Sam's "extra-curricular activities."

David often came down to the shore to visit me when I was at the Bayuks'. On one memorable occasion, David made a spectacular "entrance"—one that I will never forget.

In July of 1913, I decided to take a week's vacation from work. David promised to join me at the Bayuk home for part of that week. He and two of his friends, a doctor and a rabbi, decided to hike to Atlantic City. A daredevil myself, I was pleased to see my boyfriend showing some signs of activity and spirit. I took some of his clothing with me when I left for Vermont Avenue earlier, so that he would not have to lug too much with him. David carried only his medical bag, with some toilet articles and a few changes of underwear, shirts and socks, figuring that the trip would take about two or three days with stops along the way. By the time the trio arrived in Camden (via the ferry) the other two men had decided against hiking and urged David to join them on the train. My "swain" was too proud to quit. He insisted on continuing alone. Later, I received a post-card from him, saying that he was on his way. The next day I received another, telling me of his progress. On the third day I received nothing. I wasn't worried, because I figured that he would be arriving that evening. At nighttime, there was no sign of David. During the next day, I waited in vain for some word, not knowing whether to be angry or worried. Very late, the next evening, after bedtime, there was a knock on the door. I looked out of the window to see a seedy looking bum in the dim light of the porch. He wore ragged clothing, a hat brim with no crown. His shoes were scuffy and curled up at the tips. He looked for all the world like Sad Willie, circus hobo. Frightened, I shouted, "Go Away!"

A familiar voice called, "Bluma, let me in—it's me—David."

I could not fathom this situation. The voice sounded like David's but in no way could he ever look like that!

"Go Away—whoever you are!" I cried.

Sadie, who had come downstairs, stared intently. "Bluma, let him in. It is David."

I opened the door. In walked David in a truly outlandish getup. Although the rest of him was filthy and ragged, he was clean-shaven and wore a clean white shirt.

"What kind of a joke is this, David?" I shouted.

He was so exhausted that he could scarcely speak. We gave him some supper which he wolfed greedily. After bathing and getting rid of the offensive rags, David was ready to explain. As he was traveling along the road on the second day, a young derelict insisted on joining him. The man was ragged and unkempt. David tried to shake him, but the man kept dogging his heels, acting friendly and pretending that they were two equal bums of the road. David, torn between sympathy and fear, treated the hungry hobo to a good meal and continued on his way with him. During the trip, the good doctor tried to switch the conversation to religion and morality, endeavoring to find the man's better nature, for he feared what the man would do. And yet, since the hobo did nothing threatening, he could not call for help. As they continued on, the bum became belligerent and wild-eyed. Seeing a nearby tavern, my fiancé directed his companion to the bar and bought him a stiff drink—hoping that the shot might make him too sleepy or groggy to cause trouble. The liquor, far from subduing the creature, made him wilder than ever. As twilight approached, the thug pulled David into the woods, threatening him with a knife. Making him strip, he took all of David's good clothing and money. . . . My fiancé was helpless. He begged the young man to leave him his medical bag, some identification and fifteen cents for a shave; for he feared that the authorities would never let him get into the city in rags, unshaven and with no identification. Before the robber left, he warned David to stay where he was for a half hour, and never to tell the authorities about the robbery, or "I will find you wherever you are and your life will not be worth anything."

    David gave the thief his solemn promise. He remained where he was, donning the filthy clothes that the robber had left behind. With only fifteen cents to his name, and with such unkempt clothing, David was not able to hitch a ride. Hiking in the ruined shoes was painful. At last my fiancé reached Pleasantville, where he headed for a barber shop. He was afraid to explain his predicament to the barber because of his oath. The barber, however, realized that David was not a bum. He insisted on giving him an old clean shirt so that he would not have difficulty in entering town. He also shaved him and refused to take the money. David waited until dark to enter town and to head toward Vermont Avenue.

    The next day, his two friends visited us at the shore. We told them what had happened. I urged David to go to the police station and to describe the thief. The criminal was heading for the shore and would probably be found easily. David refused, saying that he had given his word. I asked the rabbi whether a promise, given under duress was still bona fide. Would it be ethical for my boyfriend to break such an oath? The rabbi thought that it would be permissible, since the good of the majority would be served by getting such an evil man into custody before he could harm anyone else.

    David refused to report the incident. "The man was the type to carry a grudge," he said. "His threats were very real. Even if he went to jail, he would get out some day. Suppose he decided to take his revenge? He knows my name, and it would be simple to find me, as a doctor. Suppose we were married and had children? What would happen if he took his revenge then?"

It was an unanswerable moral dilemma. I am not sure that David did the right thing. Nor am I sure that he was wrong.

Back in Philadelphia several weeks later, I was called upon to take care of Mamie S., a ravaged-looking woman about sixty years old, with straw-colored hair and a raspy voice. She had suffered a nervous breakdown and was resting at a hospital while waiting for a bed in a private mental institution in Paoli.

The patient had been putting up a fuss at the hospital, insisting that she wanted to go home to her apartment until she was able to be transferred to Paoli. Dr. Blank, her physician, finally decided to engage a nurse and to allow Mamie to stay at her own apartment. One would not have suspected that the physician's decision was prompted by a scheme of his own, and was not necessarily in the best interest of his patient.

When the Nurses' Registry called to inform me that Dr. Blank had specifically requested me for Mamie's nurse, I was surprised. The prominent doctor and I were not on good terms. In fact, he had ignored me completely for the past few years. He was the same Dr. Blank who, during my early nursing school days, had taken me out on a date and had acted in a lewd manner. I had rebuffed his advances in a very painful physical way, and he was left with a sore reminder of my displeasure. I was skeptical about taking the assignment. Why had he requested my services? I finally decided that on a professional level, the doctor had realized that I was a competent person and that personal animosity should be forgotten.

I was further reassured by the impersonal and completely professional manner in which the physician discussed his patient with me when I met with him at the hospital the next day. After my briefing, I decided to take the case. Mamie and I left the hospital for her home that same afternoon.

Mamie's apartment was on the first floor of a private home in a very fashionable section of Center City, Philadelphia. When we arrived at her quarters, I was appalled at the surroundings. The furniture was large and garishly ugly. The apartment was not equipped with electricity. Light was provided by gas jets, which we had to turn on and light with a match when we came in. The effect of the gas flames in the apartment was eerie. Mamie's bedroom was just behind the living room. My bed was a cot, in a little alcove next to the kitchen. When we got settled, I noticed three strong locks on the inside of the apartment door, which I immediately fastened. For some reason I felt extremely uncomfortable and uneasy in the apartment.

I put my patient to bed and immediately began to search the premises for liquor, destroying all that I found. Dr. Blank had informed me that Mamie was an alcoholic and that I should remove every drop of spirits. When Mamie awoke from her nap, she got out of her bed and started to rummage through drawers and closets.

"Where are my bottles?"

"What bottles?" I asked.

Mamie did not reply. She kept searching frantically, becoming more and more agitated. When I finally attempted to guide her back to bed, she cursed me, struggling to reach the door. I forced her back into bed and gave her sedation.

After my patient again went to sleep, I extinguished the lights and lay down on my cot to rest. The house, which had been so quiet, suddenly came to life. Outside of our rooms I could hear loud voices, laughter, music, and the incessant banging of a door. The noise grew louder and more raucous as the evening advanced. I found it difficult to go back to sleep. What was going on out there? Should I investigate?

Somehow, I could not bring myself to open the three locks to confront the noise makers. I climbed back on my cot and fell into an uneasy sleep. This respite did not last long. I awoke with a strange foreboding, just in time to see a tottering figure, leaning over my bed. I sat up quickly.

"Mamie, what are you doing?"

"None of your business, Bayuk go back to sleep."

"What is that hissing noise?"

"I just turned on the gas jet. I don't want to live anymore."

"Mamie," I screamed, jumping up and closing the open jet above my cot, "I'm young. I want to live!"

"I'm old. I want to die."

I gave myself a few minutes to calm down before I took her by the hand and guided her back to her bed.

"Mamie, you haven't the right to decide when you are going to die. You didn't plan your beginning, and only God has the right to plan your ending. Now, go to sleep and behave yourself!"

I dared not sleep after that frightening episode. The noises continued all night long in the outer rooms. As I lay, sleepless, I finally figured out just what was going on and why I had been selected to accompany Mamie to her home. I was furious. At six o'clock in the morning, I put in an emergency call to Dr. Blank, instructing him to come out to the apartment at once.

Dr. Blank arrived at about 7:00 a.m.

"What's the matter, Bayuk," he sneered, as he walked in the door. "Can't you handle my patient?"

"Oh, yes," I said airily. "She's an easy case. After I kept her from murdering me, we got along just fine. You are the one I am having trouble with, doctor."

My accusing voice startled the doctor. Nurses never dared talk to doctors that way.

"What are you talking about, Bayuk?"

"I am talking about an arrogant doctor who saw a chance for revenge, and forgot about the dignity of his profession. Ever since I discouraged your advances in a rather humiliating way, you have been waiting for an opportunity to pay me back. Well, you had your revenge, but it will boomerang. I'm not a meek nurse who is afraid of tangling with the great doctor image. Right is right, no matter who's involved."

Dr. Blank took one look at my blazing eyes and did not say a word as I continued with my tirade.

"You know very well that you were sending me to a house of prostitution to take care of the Madam. You know no nurse should ever be put in that position. I can report you to the Nurse's Registry and to the Medical Board. You are in serious trouble."

I suppose that the doctor began to realize at that point that his petty spite had backfired and that he had jeopardized his whole career for a moment of revenge.

"Please, Bayuk," he begged, "don't report me. It was a stupid thing to do. I'll do anything to make it up to you. But don't spoil my reputation this way."

"What reputation?" I asked. "All the nurses know what a sex maniac you are. Now everybody will also know that you are not even responsible about your profession. I became a nurse solely to take care of sick people. I have no time for nonsense or petty spite. I take my profession seriously. Why don't you?"

No one had ever dared to talk to the arrogant doctor like this before. I was young and relatively inexperienced, but I had a strong background of morality and faith to bolster me. I have never been afraid to speak up honestly and openly about any problem. When I know that I am right, I am never afraid of the outcome.

"What can I do to make it up to you, Bayuk," he asked, chastened.

"I am still a professional," I said. "Right now we have a patient to consider. However, I will not stay with her in this house. You just see to it that she is taken into the hospital in Paoli today. I'll accompany her there to make sure that she is settled and comfortable. To me she is just a sick human being, and as long as I am not involved in her lifestyle, it is not my business. But you had better mend your ways or you will be blackballed by the Nurse's Registry and by your fellow physicians too."

Dr. Blank made the necessary arrangements so that we were able to leave the apartment right after lunch. The house was extremely quiet in the afternoon. Not a person was seen or heard in the dwelling. The occupants were evidently sleeping soundly. It had been a long night.

Well, I did not report Dr. Blank, because he had married my friend several months before, and I did not want her to suffer because of his actions. I wish I could report that Dr. Blank became a better individual as a result of this incident, but I am afraid that life does not always provide such happy endings to true stories.

As I continued to live at my brother's home between assignments, I grew closer to Sadie, a rare human being who was equally at home in all social situations. With her servants she was friend as well as employer. Her humble beginnings had made her aware of the dignity in working for a living. Whether she played cards with Mrs. Gimbel or with her chauffeur, she acted the same. No wonder the household employees adored her. Whenever they left, for reasons of health or infirmity, Sadie insisted that Sam arrange pensions for each one. In addition, she continued to keep in touch with her former help, because she genuinely cared for them.

During the summer, the entire staff enjoyed going to the shore where the routine was informal and relaxed. In the summer of 1914, Sadie, pregnant again, rented a large home on Atlantic Avenue in Margate, a country-like suburb of Atlantic City, on the ocean. Sam engaged me to stay with his wife as her nurse so that I could be on hand for the delivery.

I was paid twenty-five dollars a week, working every day, all day. In addition to supervising the household, I had charge of Bernice and the older children. I also planned the meals with the cook, and generally worked to keep Sadie comfortable and healthy. My sister-in-law wanted David to deliver the baby. Since my fiancé was going to graduate school at the time, he was able to visit us every weekend, to examine Sadie and to see me.

One weekend in July, when David arrived, he checked the expectant mother immediately.

"Now Sadie," he advised, "this is the perfect time to have your baby. I'm here and ready, so please cooperate."

Sadie laughed and promised to do her best. Later that evening, Sam entered my bedroom, "Bluma, wake up! I think Sadie is having labor pains. You'd better stay with her. I'll stay here."

With complete unconcern, Sam pushed me out of bed and rolled in, going back to sleep. I pattered out to Sadie's bedroom, climbing into bed with her. Suddenly, she groaned as the baby started to come.

"David! In!" I screamed.

David rushed in just in time to help me finish the job of bringing my niece Violet into the world on July 20, 1914. As we cut the cord and prepared to wash the infant, I was still in a happy glow, thrilled as always to participate in the miracle of birth.

Suddenly, David turned white. He shouted at me, "Quick! Go wash your hands thoroughly and put on gloves!"

I obeyed instantly. It was then that I noticed the baby's eyes. They were puffed and swollen shut. We removed Violet to the nursery room which had previously been prepared. I stayed up for the rest of the night, continually applying cold compresses to the infant's eye area. In the morning, David called Sam into the nursery.

"There's something wrong with the baby's eyes. We're not sure what it is. I want you to get the best eye specialist immediately."

Sam went into action. By that evening, the best eye man in Philadelphia was examining Violet. After a long session, the specialist emerged.

"Mr. Bayuk, your baby was born with a severe eye infection. I am sorry to tell you, she is blind!"

At first, Sam refused to accept the diagnosis. David and I had already realized the situation. We finally made him understand that the doctor was telling the truth.

"How can I tell Sadie," he moaned. "What shall I say to her? David, Bluma, please, you go and tell her."

"All right Sam," David said, "we'll tell her. Don't worry, we'll be careful of what we say."

David proved that he could be gentle. He took Sadie in his arms and told her. After the first shock, Sadie sobbing, asked, "How could this happen? What went wrong?"

David replied carefully, "No one really knows. All we can say is that it was unavoidable. When one is pregnant, sometimes things go wrong. Remember that rainy weekend when you went to New York to see Sam off to Europe? You were already pregnant, although you didn't know it. Then you came home with pneumonia and were very sick for a while. I suspect that the baby's eyes may have been forming at that time. If an infection set in, that is what caused the problem."

When we finally left the room, I kissed David gratefully. He had handled his part very well. For once my blunt sweetheart had softened the blow.

My sister-in-law remained in shock for many days. She could not face the reality. The baby, Violet, was a sweet cherub. I cared for her with great devotion. Excitement and joy seemed to have disappeared from the household. Sadie never recovered completely from the tragedy. The family returned to Philadelphia a few week's afterward, so that they could consult the best specialists everywhere. It soon became apparent that nothing could be done to give Violet the precious gift of sight.

One evening, while I, too, was trying to deal with my own feelings about the fate of that innocent child, Sadie's devoted maid came into my room.

"Miz Bluma," she said, "it just ain't right. That sweet sweet Miz Sadie, she don't deserve it! Men! They all the same—white, colored—they does what they wants and we women—we gotta pay."

I knew what she was driving at. "Althea," I said, "I know that you love Sadie as I do. So you must never speak like this again. We don't really know for sure what caused the infection. Anyway, it's too late. The damage has been done. We mustn't make things worse for Sadie by suspecting things. Let well enough alone. Promise that you will not speak like this again."

Althea and I cried together as she gave me her hand and her oath.

After the tragedy, I realized that I could no longer stay in the Bayuk household. My heart was too heavy over the circumstances of the baby's affliction. I found it difficult not to feel bitter against my brother. My thoughts kept turning to David, contrasting the characters of the two men. Sam was rich and successful; David was poor and struggling; Sam was a charm-boy, especially with the ladies; David had a knack for saying and doing hurtful things. Yet, how dear and honorable my fiancé was! I would never have to worry about his faithfulness or his moral integrity. Although he was thorny on the outside, he was a man of deep feeling and principle. There were more important aspects to life than monetary success! I knew that I had to be proud of the man that I married. David was such a man!

Circumstances in the Rappoport household had altered quite a bit in the past year. David's oldest sister, the "spinster," had surprised everyone by getting married. She had moved to Rosenhayn with her husband. Mordecai had then gone to live with his oldest daughter, Rivka, in Vineland. Now, David was alone in his home and offices at 6th and Dickenson, a poor neighborhood with too many doctors.

Late in August, Dr. Greenwood, David's brother-in-law, paid me a surprise visit.

"The family sent me here to talk to you Bluma. We're all concerned about David. He is just floundering around and not getting anywhere. Why don't you two get married. You two are in love. There's nothing to hold you back now. Maybe if David has a wife like you to help him, he will settle down and make something of himself."

The next morning, I arose and went to David's office.

"How is your schedule of appointments for today?"

"Very slow, as usual," David replied, gloomy. "Why do you ask?"

"Oh, I thought that we might get married, as long as you're not busy."

David looked at me in surprise. Then he smiled broadly.

"Good idea. How do we go about it?"

We called a rabbi and made arrangements. Then we went downtown to procure a license. Afterwards, we stopped into Wanamakers where we selected a simple ring. Next, I went to the dress department and bought a stunning black taffeta outfit. Black for my wedding? Why not? Black was the chic choice for all dressy occasions. I was too practical to buy a dress that I could use only once.

Later that afternoon, August 28, 1914, we walked into the rabbi's study where we were joined by Lou Rappoport, David's brother, and Mamie Bayuk, Jake's daughter, who stood up for us. After eight years of stormy courtship, Bluma and David were joined in holy matrimony, in a ceremony of less than five minutes. Afterwards, we took the train to Vineland, where we spent our wedding night in a hotel. The next morning, we continued on to Alliance. My parents welcomed us with open arms.

"Mama, Dad," I announced, "David and I came to get your blessings. We were married yesterday!"

My parents hugged and kissed us, uttering many heartfelt blessings.

At last Mama exclaimed, "I am so surprised! I can't believe it!"

"But Mama, we've been going together for years."

"I know," Mama replied, "That's why I'm so surprised. I thought that you were married a long time ago."

Early Marriage

WHEN I CAME to pick up my belongings at Broad Street so that I could move into the house at 6th and Dickinson, Sadie clung to my arm. "Bluma, I can't bear to see you leave. What will I ever do without you? I know I'm being selfish. Really I am glad that you and David have finally married. But just remember, we are still friends. I want you to be a part of my set now that you are a doctor's wife. We can go to luncheons together, play cards."

"Sadie," I said, "you are very dear to me and we will see each other as sisters. But you must understand. I can't lead the life that you do. I'm the wife of a poor doctor. I could never run with your crowd. I couldn't afford to entertain them."

"But that won't matter. I'll pay for everything. You can charge the luncheons to me when it's your turn to take the ladies."

"No, I pay my own way, or I don't go. That's the way I am. Besides, I expect to be too busy with the housework and my other obligations to spend time with lunches and cards. I knew what I was taking on when I married, and I'm content to live this way."

Sadie understood, reluctantly. We managed to see each other from time to time because I knew that she needed a friend to turn to as she struggled with her sorrows. However, my life was completely changed. Bluma, student and nurse, had taken a back seat to Bluma, housewife.

When I moved into the old four-story, creaky building on Sixth Street, I was appalled at its size and general decay. What a contrast from my former residence, the glamorous house on Broad Street! Immediately, I began to wage war with the dust and dirt. However, one problem was almost too much to handle. The worst aspect of our house was the presence of enormous rats who lived in the basement and socialized all over the place. One day as I sat on the toilet, an enormous rat leaped out of the wall to join me. I screamed and jumped off the seat just in time. The rat landed inside of the toilet. I hurriedly pulled the chain, hoping to drown him and wash him down the sewer. However, the rodent was so big that he stuck in the bowl. How does one fish a drowned animal out of a commode? Helpless, I called a plumber telling him that something was clogging my toilet. When the plumber arrived he was startled to find out what the something was!

"I guess," he remarked, "that I shouldn't ask how the rat got there in the first place."

"Perhaps he was thirsty?" I suggested.

Now that the rat's fate was out of my hands, I was feeling a bit giddy. With the animal disposed of, I was relieved. After all, now I had one less rat to worry about.

I spent my days scrubbing the house from top to bottom and washing our clothing. One day, as I was hanging out the clean laundry, I overheard two neighbor ladies discussing someone. They were speaking in Yiddish and did not think I could understand them. Soon I realized that they were talking about the "dumb" doctor's wife. They said that I must be a "Shiksah" (gentile) because I didn't realize that doctor's wives don't do their own housework. I pretended that I did not understand them. They went right on, discussing me in disparaging terms. They said that my husband had married a servant, not a wife.

That evening, while David was out on a call, I finished scrubbing the marble steps in front of the house. Bathed and dressed, I then sat outside on a cushion on my steps. The same neighbors too were sitting outdoors. They greeted me in English. I answered them in fluent Yiddish. The ladies were flustered.

I minced no words.

"Ladies, this afternoon you spent a lot of time criticizing me because I had the nerve to do my own work. Well, I'm young and healthy! Hard work never hurt anyone, Jew or Gentile. My husband is a struggling doctor. Your husbands are bakers. When they sell a roll or cake, they get paid for it. My husband is the first to be called and the last to be paid. I don't mind doing housework, but I do mind being discussed and criticized."

The neighbors, chastened, never discussed me again, at least not in my hearing. I did not bother with them at all. However, I found another neighbor across the street who was in trouble. Mrs. Crane was so seriously ill that she could not get up from bed to send her little girl to school. When I found out about her predicament, I went to work. For several months, I gave the child breakfast every morning, sending her off to school. Then I would take care of the mother making her comfortable for the day. When the daughter returned home from school, I returned to their house to prepare the family's dinner. Afterwards, an older child arrived home from work and took over the household chores. In addition, I also helped out when David needed a nurse to care for a poor patient.

Money was a scarce commodity in the Rappoport household. Our living quarters were on the first floor with the offices. We rented the second floor as an apartment to defray the rental costs. Although I tried to be loving and understanding, David's disposition did not improve after our marriage. Still morose and withdrawn, he seemed powerless to control his flaring temper. His outbursts continued. I tried my best not to give him any cause, but soon found that his temper would surge no matter what I did. My next problem was to find a way to protect myself from an emotional response to his moods. With time, I learned to put up a wall of silence as a defense, and to go about my duties, ignoring the situation as well as I could. Afterwards, he could always beg my forgiveness and blame it on his "adrenalin."

I was appalled at the way my husband treated his patients. He often drove the rich ones away by his gruff manner. The poor ones only stayed with him because he did not ask for money. Yet, they all knew that he was an excellent doctor. I continued to be puzzled by the fact that the doctor would be very busy;

yet, at the end of the day, he would have very little money to show for it. I began to observe his methods and soon discovered the reason. On a typical day, I saw a poor old lady come in for examination. Because she had a terrible cough, David prescribed an expectorant. When it became evident that the woman had no money for a prescription, David gave me money to go to the drug store to buy his patient the needed medicine. The woman left, not even thanking David because she was angry at him for his lecture about her negligence. Next, a well-dressed woman appeared in the waiting room. I knew her. She was a friend of Sadie's and a patient.

"What are you doing here?" David asked.

"I had a terrible migraine headache yesterday," Florence answered.

"Do you have it today?"

"No, Doctor, it's better today, but I thought—"

"Never mind what you thought. You don't need me today. Next time you get a headache, come at the time that it hurts."

Florence left, dissatisfied. David, of course, received no fee for the visit. I was furious.

"David, Florence is the only patient you had all morning who could afford to pay for her visit. Why did you turn her away?"

"She didn't need a doctor. I couldn't take her money," he said gruffly. Then he went back into his office to read, hoping that he would not be disturbed for the rest of the morning.

This was the last straw. I finally realized that my husband would never do well in private practice. He could not bear to ask his patients for money; he was too impatient with the neurotic women who came to him with their imaginary ills. On the other hand, I knew that he suffered deeply with the patients who were truly afflicted. The only solution for David was to take a position with civil service where he would receive a regular salary and would not have to worry about collecting individual fees.

David listened to my suggestion and applied to civil service. World War I was rearing its ugly head. Soon David received an appointment to work on Hog Island, in the government dispensary there. The employees who were working for the war effort were treated there by David and several other doctors, under the direction of a skilled surgeon. Now that my husband's career was settled, I wanted to use my talents in the service of my country. However, before I could apply, I found out that I was pregnant. Then all thoughts of a job were forgotten. Instead, I continued to be a good Samaritan, working wherever I was needed as a volunteer. News of my availability spread so quickly that I was continually called upon to help in many needed areas. David never knew where I would be when he returned home from work. Most of the time, he would find a note from me on his desk, telling him of my whereabouts.

During the early months of my pregnancy, I received a frantic call from Doctor Greenwood in Vineland.

"Come at once. Your sister and her children are seriously ill."

I packed and left for Alliance immediately, leaving a note for David in the usual place. Poor Lena! When I arrived I found that my oldest sister, eight months pregnant, had contracted diphtheria, along with her four children. Since her husband William had to do all of the farm work, he could give little time to help his family. Immediately, I sent my brother-in-law out to cut fine little twigs from the trees. We shaved the twigs, sterilizing them in the oven, wrapped sterile cotton around them and used them to swab the throats and noses of the sick ones. During my stay, I bathed all of my patients every day, cooked for them, fed them, cleaned the house and did the laundry. At first, they were all so ill that I got no sleep day or night. Gradually, all of my charges improved. After two weeks, they were all on their way to full recovery. Exhausted, I returned home to David to rest.

I did not have long to recuperate from the grueling routine at Lena's. A week after my return home, I received another emergency call from the farm area. "Your mother is very sick. Come at once!" Mother! She was the one who took care of others. It was unthinkable that she could be ill. I got my clothing together and prepared to leave home. David was upset. "You're pregnant, and still worn out from your last ordeal. I won't let you shoulder this responsibility alone. I'll send out a nurse to help you."

I could not wait for the nurse. Arriving in Alliance, I was dismayed to find Mother gravely ill with pneumonia. I worked frantically for the first few days, just to keep her alive. By the time the nurse arrived, I was worn out with anxiety and work. However, when I opened the door to greet my relief, I was horrified! The registry had sent a woman whom I knew only too well. This so-called nurse had been a senior when I went into training. She was one of the worst nurses in the hospital. I don't know how the authorities had ever allowed her to graduate. In addition to her lack of skill, she was also a thief. During my first year, when I missed a Christmas gift and money, all of the nurses' rooms had been searched. Our supervisor had found articles of my clothing, marked with my name, in this nurse's bureau. Although my gifts were not found, I knew that the woman had been the only one with access to my room at the time.

When she recognized me, the nurse acted in an arrogant and offensive manner. I calmed her immediately, realizing that I had to rely on her for some help because of my weakened condition. My Mother's crisis was nearing, and I could go on no longer without a little rest. I immediately put the woman on night duty, begging her to stay alert.

Before I left the sick room, I prepared everything that my Mother might need if she should go through her crisis that night. I told the nurse, "I'm going to lie down at the foot of my father's bed. Be sure to call me if there is any change."

She promised. I went off to the bedroom, falling into an uneasy sleep. Several hours later, I awoke with a start. I had dreamed that I was falling off a horse. Jumping out of bed I rushed to my Mother's side. She lay alone in a cold sweat, looking like death. Terrified, I grabbed the hypodermic that I had prepared and injected it immediately. Then, I ran downstairs, filling hot water bags to surround Mother with heat. Afterwards, I searched for the nurse, discovering her fast asleep on a rocking chair. I shook her.

"Wake up! Run across the street to my sister's. Quick! Call the doctor. Tell him to come immediately. Tell him I gave Mom first aid, Hurry!"

She left immediately. Meanwhile, I discovered a glass of whiskey and water on the nightstand. I tried to revive Mother by patiently feeding her drops of whiskey and hot water.

After an agonizing wait, Mother passed her crisis and began to respond slowly. The next morning, I faced the nurse with blazing anger. I told her that she was just short of a murderer.

"As far as I am concerned, you are the lowest of the low. You don't deserve to be called a nurse. I shall let the registry know what happened here. Here is your week's pay. Get Out!" She left quickly, knowing that what she had done was unforgivable.

I stayed with Mother for three more weeks, taking care of her, Dad and the home. Finally, when the doctor said I could leave, I gladly returned to David. Lena was well enough to take over for me at my parents' home.

The work and the worry of that last ordeal had taken a toll of me. When I returned home, I became ill. Fortunately, there were no more emergencies. I was able to rest and recuperate before the end of my term. On October 19, 1916, I gave birth to a beautiful son, Irving.

Motherhood is one of the most important and demanding careers available to a woman; yet, we are usually not sufficiently prepared for the scope and the depth of this awesome responsibility. My duty in the Children's wing of the hospital was not enough to train me for taking sole responsibility for the little life that I had brought into the world. Yet, I approached my task with delightful anticipation. It had always been my dream to have a baby and to devote all of my time to him. I am aware that some women feel tied down by motherhood; I felt privileged to care for my son. We lived in a good neighborhood in West Philadelphia. David was earning a regular paycheck with the government. I was content with my role of housewife and mother.

Our idyllic situation did not last long. Nothing ever seemed to work out easily for David. After being at Hog Island for less than a year, my husband ran into difficulty. David's superior, a fine surgeon, had run into some political opposition in his job. In a fit of pique, the older man had quit the service. Dear loyal David, feeling that his superior had been ill-treated, followed his boss and quit his post. Leaving the government service in time of war is a very serious act. I was terribly upset. Finally, I persuaded my husband to apply for reinstatement in another area. Luckily, he was able to do so. David then began to work at the Veterans' Administration in Philadelphia. He was really pleased with his duties, helping deserving veterans to get pensions because of injury or disability. I prayed that my husband would curb his impulsiveness and retain that wonderful position.

We continued to keep in close touch with Sadie and Sam. Their household had changed a great deal since I had lived there. They suffered greatly since the birth of Violet. As the child grew, it was apparent that she had other problems. Her coordination was poor. Instead of teaching the child basic skills, the family treated her like an invalid. The little girl could not tie her shoes or feed herself. There was always a sympathetic parent, sibling or servant hovering over her to take away her initiative. I knew that this was not a healthy way to bring up a child.

"You are destroying your daughter with misplaced kindness," I told Sadie. "Violet needs to be taught. She must learn to do things by herself. How can you let her remain helpless? It's cruel. Please, please, Sadie, if you can't do it at home, send Violet to a school where she can be trained to become self-sufficient. You owe it to her."

Although my sister-in-law was reluctant to send her baby away from the protective atmosphere of their home, David and I finally persuaded the Bayuks to send Violet to a local school for the blind. Today this institution is modern, dedicated to turning out responsible self-sufficient students. In those days the school care proved to be more custodial than helpful. Because Violet was one of the few paying pupils, the faculty and administration bent over backwards to make her happy there. Unfortunately, in doing so, they continued the preferential treatment that had been so detrimental to Violet's development at home. The "poor little rich girl" was a victim of her own affluence. Fortunately, in later years, Violet learned the necessary social skills. Today, with a devoted companion, Addie McKinney Booker, she leads a productive and happy life.

Meanwhile, I was finding that in spite of my vigilance and care, Irving was a sickly child. He was constantly ill with childhood infections. David was an unusually concerned father. Whenever Irving became ill, David blamed it on me. Finally, at the age of three, Irving was operated on for mastoids.

His recovery was slow. My husband became extremely worried, deciding that the Philadelphia climate was the cause of his son's troubles.

"I want you to take our son to the seashore. The salt air may be good for him. Let's try living there with him for a year and see if he improves. I'll commute as often as I can."

I left for Atlantic City, at first staying with relatives of my sister Lena, and then, as Irving seemed to be healthier, I decided to find a place of my own. Even with David's steady paycheck, I could not afford to maintain two homes. The solution was obvious. I must do something to earn money to stay in the resort. Fortunately, the way to maintain a home was evident. If I could rent a large home, I could take in boarders just as my mother did in Alliance. The money from the boarders could pay for the rental of the home, and for a nursemaid to take Irving out on the beach and boardwalk.

Although I had no real experience in business, I knew that my plan was a good one. Only one small obstacle presented itself. I had no money to pay for the rental of a house in advance. Where should I go to get the needed amount? I would not think of asking my rich brothers for a loan. When it came to money, they were unapproachable. However, Abe Levin, my host, was a warm individual, with a keen business sense. He owned the Levin Dairy in Atlantic City.

"Abe," I said, "I know that I can make money operating a boarding house, but I need 'seed' money. What should I do?"

Abe laughed, "You should come to me, Bluma, and ask me to co-sign a note for you at the local bank!"

This kind man solved my problem. I received the loan and set up a boarding house in the Inlet section of Atlantic City, on Vermont Avenue, near the beach and boardwalk.

Comfortable middle-class Jewish families from Philadelphia regularly spent a few weeks of the summer at the shore. When the news spread among my friends in Philadelphia about my new business venture, my calendar was soon filled with reservations for the whole season. With a minimum of employees I ran a very successful operation, playing cook and hostess to my guests. Irving thrived in the sunshine, the ocean and the fresh air; David commuted from Philadelphia by train every day. Things worked out beautifully during my first summer as a business woman. I paid back my loan at the end of the season, and showed a profit. In the winter, after the guests departed, I decided to remain at the shore to see if the climate would continue to benefit Irving.

Business World

AT THIS TIME, David had again fallen upon hard times. The government tried to transfer him to Pittsburgh to work at the Veterans' hospital there. David refused to go because he felt that the climate of an industrial city would be harmful to Irving. When one rejects a transfer in government service, it is very serious. David left the civil service with a mark against his name. Once more, necessity forced my husband into private practice. He opened an office in Atlantic City so that we could remain there with Irving.

During that first winter, I realized that David could not support us on his medical practice alone. I knew that I would have to supplement our income if our little family was to stay above the poverty level. Besides, it was time to save for our son's college education. As Irving grew, it was clear that he was an exceptionally gifted child. After he entered school in Atlantic City, his progress was remarkable in spite of frequent absences. Whenever our boy was ill, which was practically all winter, I would keep him at home, collecting his lessons from his teacher and supervising his learning. This tutoring proved extremely effective. When Irving returned to the classroom in the spring, he made the highest mark in his finals.

During that winter, I found a suitable boarding house in the exclusive Chelsea section of Atlantic City. The spacious home, on California Avenue, a few doors from the beach, was for sale at a reasonable price. It certainly seemed wiser to me to buy a house than to keep paying rent. Not having enough money for the down payment, I went to Abe Levin once more.

This gracious gentleman approved of my plan. "You are a good business woman, Bluma. Whatever you decide to do, you will prosper. I'll back you for the loan again!"

How does one adequately thank the Abe Levins of this world? This man was my guardian angel. He was more understanding and generous than my own brothers. I will never forget his kindness and his belief in my abilities. He gave me the courage and help needed to make my entry into the business world.

My future was certainly developing in a strange pattern. Every few years I seemed to be entering a new way of life. After being a farm girl, a tobacco worker, an office secretary, a nurse and a housewife, I was now launching a career as a boarding house operator. I hope that someday someone will write a history of the women who operated boarding homes in Atlantic City. They were a strong, versatile breed. These women were raising families while catering to others and directing the operation of a complicated business; yet they retained their status as wives or widows with integrity and refinement. I am proud to have been one of their number.

After I bought the house, I found another obstacle. I could not get possession of our place until after the summer. Because I could not afford to lose the season's business, I rented a smaller home on the same street. After giving the proprietor a down payment, I arranged to move in within a few weeks. In the spring, when I took possession, I paid Mr. Schmidt the remaining $500.00 and proceeded to get the house in shape. The following morning a stranger knocked at the door. The gentleman asked for Mr. Schmidt. I told him that Mr. Schmidt had left and that I was the new proprietor. The man was surprised at the news.

"I own this house. Mr. Schmidt rented it from me for the summer. He owes me $500.00 balance. Evidently, he went off with your money, because he didn't pay it to me and he's gone. I'm sorry, but you will have to pay me $500.00 if you want to remain."

I was heartsick! I begged the owner to wait for a few days so that I could see what to do. That afternoon I consulted with

Joseph Perskie, a former classmate from Alliance, now a lawyer in Atlantic City.

"Do I have to pay the $500.00?"

Joe reluctantly admitted that I would have to pay the balance if I wanted to stay in that house for the summer.

"But it's not fair. Why should I have to pay?"

"Why didn't you consult with me before you entered the proposition?" Joe countered.

Of course Joe was right, I was a novice, and a trusting person. I would have to develop a tougher outlook if I wanted to exist in the market place. Fortunately, the lesson was not a disastrous one. After paying the extra $500.00 I still made a profit during the summer's operation. By the fall I had paid back all of my debts with enough left over to furnish my new home beautifully.

The move proved to be a good one. I attracted a wealthy clientele who were willing to pay large sums for the privilege of being in a lovely home at the shore, near the beach and boardwalk. Besides, Bluma's delicious dinners quickly became known. In addition to my regular guests, out-of-towners made reservations for dinner when they came down for the day. My Mother's recipes were making me famous.

At the end of the summer, having outgrown my building, I decided to look for a larger house in a more exclusive area. When a gentleman offered me a handsome profit for my California Avenue home, I sold. Once again I was moving.

The real estate agency showed me a mini-mansion in Ventnor, a posh neighboring shore community. Although the location was not zoned for boarding house operation, the agent informed me that the present zoning had only two more years to run. If I could manage to stave off the authorities for two years, I would have a wonderful spot. I decided to take a chance.

My first summer at Dorset Avenue was a huge success. My boarders were delighted with the luxurious surroundings. It was a difficult summer for me. I was in and out of the Ventnor courts, as the neighbors tried to stop my operations. Somehow, I managed to thwart eviction for the season, using every kind of ruse I and my lawyer could think of. After the summer ended, the agent advised me to re-rent the property for the following year, using someone else's name. I did so, but the authorities were smarter than I. They served me with a notice that I could not operate a business there, and my rental was returned.

I rented another house near the beach at Little Rock Avenue in Ventnor, an unrestricted neighborhood. However, the strain of fighting the authorities and frequent moving proved too much for me. I became too ill to manage the business that summer. In addition, to my surprise, I found out that I was pregnant. My second pregnancy was a difficult one. I was so ill that I could not keep food on my stomach. I lost weight and developed fainting spells. My husband, extremely alarmed, insisted that I consult a professor of obstetrics in Philadelphia, a former teacher of David's. In his office, the distinguished physician examined me thoroughly, then asked me to dress and to return for his verdict.

"Mrs. Rappoport, I have made arrangements to have you admitted to the hospital at once. You are in a very serious condition. If you continue this pregnancy, you will be damaged for life. I am going to take the baby from you immediately."

I was aghast. "But Doctor, I'm in my eighth month. You know that the baby will probably die."

"So much the better for you," he said matter-of-factly. "It is probably just a blob of jelly anyway. Your lack of food and calcium is sure to produce an abnormal fetus."

I could not believe this man's attitude. He was discussing the fate of a living creature. How could he speak in such a callous manner? Although I was weak and nervous, I refused to allow the professor to do what he planned. Much to his anger, I left the office and returned to the shore.

David could not believe his mentor's actions. He took me to a kindly obstetrician in Atlantic City. Together we made the decision to continue with my pregnancy. I was frightened. Suppose the child was abnormal. Suppose I became an invalid! Was

I wrong in not taking an expert's opinion? Dr. Barbash, my new obstetrician, gave me courage. He told me that there was every chance that things would turn out well for me.

"And what about the baby?"

"There is an element of chance with every birth, a statistical probability that anyone can give birth to an abnormal baby. However, the odds are always in favor of normalcy. Just do your part and leave the rest to God."

I made a supreme effort to rest and to take nourishment for the rest of my pregnancy. At last, on a March day, my labor pains began. Dr. Barbash came to the house to deliver me in my own bed. As the infant emerged I cried, "Doctor is it whole?"

He nodded and smiled. As he whacked the baby, I heard the sweet music of my daughter's lusty wails. Relieved, I fell back on the bed in a dead faint. The strain had been so great that I was very ill for several weeks. I kept fainting. Fortunately, the doctor had arranged for a competent nurse. My daughter and I were well taken care of.

As I held my perfect little one in my arms, I thought back on the ordeal. If I had listened to the so-called "authority," I would have been denied the joy of holding my lovely baby in my arms. How many women had been cheated of their babies because of an arbitrary decision made by a doctor? There is no such thing as an infallible specialist. One should always get a second opinion before agreeing to any drastic decision in medicine.

Our daughter Jacqueline was born on March 4, 1925, at our home on Little Rock Avenue.

Again the summer was approaching. This time with the help of two other men, David had bought an old hotel, the Avoca in the center of Atlantic City on S. Kentucky Ave. Our intentions were to tear down the hotel after one or two successful seasons and to build a modern structure in its place. I moved to the hotel with the baby and her nurse. Irving, a bright eight-year-old, enjoyed the excitement of living in the center of a thriving resort town, in a hotel.

I supervised the entire hotel operations, especially the kitchen. After becoming used to the middle-class Jewish boarders, I was faced with a contrast in patrons. Our boarders were nuns and priests from nearby seminaries. They took turns in coming to the shore for a few weeks' vacation. Providing menus for the group proved to be my first dilemma. Finally, I decided to continue the same menus that I had used in the boarding houses. Most of the seminarians had never before tasted blintzes, chopped liver, chicken soup or other ethnic dishes. They tried my creations gingerly, then came back for more and more. In fact, the mother superiors and the heads of the seminaries insisted that I write down some of my recipes. From that summer on, I understand that there were many Catholic institutions in Philadelphia who served gefilte fish, prokas, borscht and blintzes in their dining rooms. The nuns and priests used to joke with me about "proselytizing." In truth, good cooking cuts across all ethnic lines.

One of their favorite dishes was prokas, also known as sweet-and-sour cabbage. Here is the recipe that went the rounds of the Philadelphia Catholic institutions:

Ingredients:
One firm head of cabbage
1 ½ lbs of chopped beef
1 can cream of tomato soup
¼ cup uncooked rice
¼ cup brown sugar
½ cup white sugar
½ cup raisins
1 tsp sour salt, ginger snaps.

Remove a few of the outer leaves of the cabbage and core. Put cabbage into a pot and pour boiling water to cover. Let stand for five minutes. Drain. Take each leaf off the head carefully. Prepare meat by mixing it with a teaspoon of salt, uncooked rice and (optional) two tablespoons full of milk. Mix the meat and form into loose balls. Roll each ball into one leaf, turning edges of cabbage so that meat cannot fall out. Lay each roll in a large pot. Add one can cream of tomato soup, pouring it over stuffed leaves. Add one teaspoon of sour salt, the sugar, and bring mixture to a boil. Add raisins and bring to a boil again. Then cook slowly for about three hours, checking to make sure that it does not stick to pan. One-half hour before serving, crumble ginger snaps over mixture and adjust seasoning to taste by adding more sour salt or sugar.

When I wrote to my parents about my activities, Mother enjoyed the description of Catholic fathers and sisters relishing her Jewish recipes. Although I missed my parents, I rarely visited them. I was occupied with the children and the business; Mother and Dad were becoming feeble and could not make trips away from their home any longer. In spite of Sam's urgings, they refused to leave the old farmhouse. Dad did little farming now, growing just enough for their own food. Mother was still pumping water at the well and dreaming her special dream.

"If only I could have indoor plumbing for one year, I could die happy," Mama said.

Somehow, the money never seemed to materialize for Mama's luxury. Sam had been sending the old folks $50.00 a month to pay for their expenses, besides paying for their fuel. This allowance was enough for their daily needs but not sufficient to do any renovating. Finally, shortly after Jackie's birth, I received a letter from my parents, containing great news. Sadie had accompanied Sam to the farm several months before. She was appalled at the primitive condition in which my parents were living.

She scolded Sam, "How can you let your parents fetch and carry water at their age? How can you allow them to use an outhouse in the cold winter months? You and I live in luxury. Where is your heart?" Sam felt ashamed. He had never given these matters a thought. The farmhouse had always been that way and he could never picture it any other way. However, he realized that Sadie was right. Galvanized into action, Sam went all of the way. He installed a regular heating system, hot and cold running water in the kitchen and a complete bathroom inside of the house, with a toilet that flushed beautifully. Mama was beside herself with joy. Her greatest dream had come true!

Everything seemed to be going well for us at the hotel. We had a very successful and enjoyable season, thanks to our Catholic clientele. David and I were encouraged to go ahead with our building plans. The whole town was excited at the prospect of a new hotel. The local newspaper devoted a large article to our project right on the front page. However, Fate stepped in with a new obstacle. Our two investors had fallen into financial trouble and needed their money. David felt morally bound to return their money immediately. We had no idea how to raise the amount. Fortunately, the proprietor of the hotel next door offered to buy the Avoca in order to expand his operations. He offered us enough money to pay off our partners and to have a nice profit for ourselves. This transaction ended our dream of building a large hotel in Atlantic City. The Hotel Jefferson now stands where our hotel once catered to the clerics with blintzes, borscht and sour cream.

After we sold the Avoca, I brought the family to Camden, N.J., where David had started a new practice. The winter of 1926 brought a terrible shock. My dear Mother died suddenly of a heart attack. All of us were numb. True to her prophetic words, Mama had lived to enjoy her indoor plumbing for only one year. My misery was unbounded. Somehow it was unthinkable that Mama would no longer be puttering around the house, receiving our letters as always. Through this tragedy I managed to find solace in remembering all of the wonderful years on the farm with a beautiful, loving Mother. Today my mother is still with me in spirit. I can recall her voice, her advice and the warmth of enfolding arms. Even in the midst of my sorrow, I rejoiced at the privilege of being her daughter.

Life goes on. I plunged myself in work to keep from brooding. That summer, I rented another house at the shore, on Little Rock

Avenue in Ventnor, an unrestricted neighborhood. This home was up for sheriff's sale. The owner urged us to buy it as she could not keep up the payments. David agreed that we should buy it and we did. However, my husband could not trade on another person's misfortune. After we bought the place, David insisted on presenting the former owner with a check for $1,000.00, telling the woman, "I don't want you to walk out of your home without any money."

Such was the moral caliber of my husband. The woman was overwhelmed by his generosity. She remained our friend throughout her life. I ran the boarding house for two years, closing it in the winter and returning to Camden to be with David after the season.

Naturally, David was still having the same trouble with his practice. Once, some of his patients presented a skit about my husband. They portrayed his reluctance to ask for money, showing how they had to slip a dollar into his pocket when he wasn't looking as they left, because he was so diffident about his fee. Yet, David was far ahead of his time in his ideas on medicine. He instituted a family plan of preventative medicine in which, for a set yearly fee, he would see the family on a regular basis to keep them well. Had his manner been more gracious, my husband could have gone far. Unfortunately he could not change his dour personality.

My mind was always teeming with new ideas on how to make money, since our situation was so precarious. Finally I hit upon a marvelous idea—one that seemed natural and inevitable for me. The shore was a perfect location for a nursing home. As a nurse and business woman, I knew that I could run an excellent establishment. My wide acquaintance with doctors in Philadelphia would help. The house on Little Rock Avenue could be turned into a viable nursing center if we made certain changes. I set to work to draw out my ideas for the new operation, measuring and figuring for several weeks. At last I turned my plans over to an Atlantic City architect to put into acceptable form. The architect was amazed at the practicability of my drawings.

"You have utilized every inch of space to its maximum efficiency," he told me.

While the architect completed his work, I returned to Camden. In the spring, I came down to the shore to visit with the architect and to assess his progress. It was a beautiful day. I brought Jackie and the nursemaid with me so that they could enjoy a stroll on the boardwalk while I attended to my business. After visiting the architect's office, I met the baby and her nurse at California Avenue. We decided to take a trolley car to the house on Little Rock Avenue to see how it had fared during the winter months. At Little Rock Avenue, we prepared to alight from the trolley. The nurse went out first, carrying the baby's little stroller. I started out the middle doors with the baby in my arms.

As I waited to alight from the trolley, pleasant thoughts occupied my mind. The future looked great. Plans for our nursing home were proceeding well; we had a small fortune in the bank and owed no bills. I would soon be embarking on a business venture that looked very promising. The spring day was heady and full of hope. When the car stopped, the nurse went out first, carrying the baby's carriage. I began to step down with Jackie in my arms. Suddenly, the motorman started up again, hurling me and my baby out into the street. Instinctively, as I hurtled out, I protected Jackie by holding up my arms. Fortunately, the nurse darted forward and was able to grab Jackie from me. I continued to fall, landing at a contorted angle; my body jerked back against the moving vehicle. Hearing a commotion, the motorman finally stopped. A passing motorist rendered assistance, taking me into her car. I motioned for her to drive us up Little Rock Avenue to a neighbor's house.

At my neighbor's I became violently ill. She called a doctor who examined me, finding that the nerve endings on my spine had been severely damaged. For three weeks I lay in a stupor, unable to move or to communicate. Afterwards, I was moved, bed and all, to my home next door, where I needed nurses around the clock for many months. My ears buzzed continuously; I could not eat; I couldn't write my name, and my speech was garbled. In addition to the physical damage, the shock had affected me emotionally. I suffered a complete nervous breakdown.

The sudden accident had broken up our lives and our plans. Our savings were being used up for my care. Irving stayed with David in Camden, I remained at the shore with Jackie and the nurses. Finally, after almost two years, I began to regain strength. One day the nurse took me on the boardwalk for my first outing since the accident. It was a lovely summer day. I felt shaky on my initial venture away from home. As we sat, sunning on a bench, a priest sat down beside me. After making some observations about the lovely weather, he proceeded, "This is such a beautiful area. Isn't it a shame that the Jews are ruining it?"

My nurse stood up, agitated, trying to change the subject. Too late! The harm had been done. I started to shake all over begging to be taken back home. As we left, the nurse, a Catholic, gave the priest a scolding.

"Father, you are a disgrace to your collar. How can you talk like that? This sweet lady is Jewish and she's just getting over a terrible sickness. You have hurt her!"

The priest left quickly. I went back to my own porch, completely demoralized. Was this the outside world? When my doctor heard about my setback, he spoke to me very seriously.

"You are too strong to allow vicious people to hurt you, Bluma. You've always been able to deal with problems. It is a learning process. If you want to get well, you will just have to keep going and take your experiences as they come. I know that you can handle it."

The doctor spoke wisely. I had never before allowed any situation to keep me down. I would have to stop hiding from life. I had taken bad experiences before. It was a question of relearning what I already knew.

During the time that I was struggling to regain my physical and emotional strength, my brother Sam and his wife came to visit me. My brother never asked whether I had enough money to take care of my bills. Instead, he moaned and groaned about his own troubles. Sam seemed to be on the verge of a severe depression.

"I want to kill myself," he wailed. "I just lost four million dollars."

"I never had four million dollars to lose," I said, "and I managed to live fairly well. Believe me, health is the most important thing. It is a sin to think about ending your life over money!"

Sam was not ready to listen to philosophy. He had indeed lost an enormous sum. His predicament had developed because of a noble gesture on his part. When the Depression hit, Sam had bought back every bit of Bayuk stock that was owned by his employees, in order to keep them from suffering financially. In doing so, my brother had almost ruined himself. To save his business, he had consulted efficiency experts who set up a strict budget for the factory and the home in order to weather the crisis. Sam had counted on Sadie's cooperation.

"Sadie, for years I've been giving you a generous allowance," he told her, "$30,000 a year is not 'peanuts.' But I had it and I wanted to give it to you. Now things are not so good. So, I'm going to ask you to take out some of the money that you've saved and use it for a while to tide you over, because I'm going to have to cut your allowance to only $5,000 a year. You'll have to use your savings to make up the difference until things get better."

Sadie had looked at Sam in astonishment. "What savings? I have no savings! I spent it all. I don't even have enough money to meet next month's bills. I spent every cent!" Sam was speechless. Then he screamed at her. Sadie shut him up immediately.

"You gave me the money with no strings. You didn't tell me to save any of it. So I spent it!"

In order for Sam to arrange matters so that they could avoid bankruptcy, the Bayuks were forced to cut their expenditures drastically. Sadie dismissed all of her servants. Their social life was curtailed. My brother did not mind; he really preferred the simple life. However, Sadie loved to live life "on the run." She struggled with the housework and cooking. As she tried to cope, she was often reduced to tears. One day, when she answered the doorbell, she found her former maid and butler at the door, dressed in their uniforms. They entered and prepared to work. Sadie stopped them.

"I can't hire you. We have no money."

"Who asked you for money?" Tom said gruffly.

"'Miz' Sadie," Althea continued, "now, you just go sit down and leave us alone. You bin mighty good to us when you had it. Now it's our turn."

The wonderful couple remained to help Sadie through her trying days. She was touched and relieved by their kindness.

While visiting me, my sister-in-law spoke about her altered status wistfully.

"I guess if you had it to do over again, you would save some of your money," I remarked.

Sadie answered with spirit, "Hell, no Bluma! Not me! I loved spending all that money. I had a great time! If I had it to do all over again, I would do the same thing!"

I was amazed at Sadie's answer. Her money had been spent on a variety of shallow amusements; yet, she would be content to do the same thing all over again. Poor Sam! He, too, had a narrow sense of values. He was allowing a loss of money to spoil his desire to live. I, on the other hand, would have given any amount of money, just to be well enough to take care of my children and to be able to function normally.

Finally, I became well enough to dismiss my nurses and to move back with David, so that we could be a family again. My husband had moved his practice to Fairview, a lovely community outside of Camden. Fairview is a unique town, with charming homes built around circular driveways. David had rented a duplex, using the downstairs for his office and the upstairs for living quarters. Once again the future seemed bright. The residents were anxious to have David remain because their only doctor had died several months before. Although we had a housekeeper, the doctor had urged me to take on as many household duties as I could handle, in order to strengthen my will. One bright day, I decided to walk to a nearby hardware store to purchase a tin so that I could bake a cake for the family. As I entered the store, I overheard the proprietress discussing the "new doctor" with a customer.

"He won't stay here long," she vowed. "He had some nerve charging me $5.00 for a visit. The old doctor only charged $1.00. It just shows you. When a Jew moves into the neighborhood, he takes advantage of the Christian. Well, you can be sure, I won't give that Jew any more of my Christian money!" My heart began to pound. Gritting my teeth, I forced myself to stay where I was. If I were to become well, I had to learn to face the traumas of the world and to fight back! Knowing David, I could not believe that he had overcharged the woman. I approached her.

"Did the doctor give you anything for that $5.00?"

"Well, no, but he made me get a prescription from the drugstore, and a syringe for my ear."

"Oh," I said, "so the money that you spent was for drugs and the syringe, not just for the doctor."

"Well," she sputtered, "the old doctor wouldn't have made me buy a syringe, and he would have given me the medicine."

"Then, actually, you only paid the doctor $1.00," I persisted.

"Yes, but he . . . "

"Did the medication cure your condition?" "Yes, but . . ."

I held up a cake pan, "Do you ever have Jewish customers in this store?"

"Of course," she replied.

"Then you can take Jewish money?"

"Naturally, why not?"

"Well," I spoke very loud and clear, "you will not get my Jewish money ever in this store. I am the doctor's wife. My husband is a dedicated man. He took only one dollar from you and he cured you. You lied about his fee. You included your expenses at the Christian drugstore, for which my husband received nothing."

I stalked out of the store with my head held high. I came home without the cake pan, but with my fighting spirit restored.

All of the time that I was ill I had wanted only one thing—to get well enough to be able to be a mother to my children. Now I was ready. Although the doctor had warned me that my endurance was limited, I felt that I must go back to work. Even though David appeared to be doing well in Fairview, I knew that he would not be able to meet all of the needs of our children as they grew older. We wanted them to have a college education so that they would take their place in the world with confidence and skills.

Irving was considered a gifted child. He had been skipped in school several times. In addition to his regular work, our son was always creating interesting and unusual extracurricular activities. At the age of nine, he published a newspaper, acting as editor, printer, salesman and distributor. Our son's teachers advised us to send him to a fine college where his potential could be realized. Since our savings had been so depleted by my illness, I knew that I would have to work very hard to achieve our goal. Our son was thirteen when I went back into business at Little Rock Avenue.

Although I was unable to go through with our building plans, I decided to run a nursing home within the existing layout. Although the physical amenities were lacking, I soon attracted a following because I ran the business well. As chief nurse and dietician, I worked long and hard, every day. It was difficult for me to take care of patients and to find time to spend with my children as well. Irving was able to adapt to his new way of life easily; Jackie did not enjoy living in a house full of sick and incapacitated people, some of whom were old and senile. I was constantly torn between the needs of my guests and my family. However, I coped as well as I could. It proved to be fortunate that I had decided to return to business, because David left his practice again. He came to live in Ventnor with us, spending his time walking, reading or sleeping. He went into a "shell," and seemed to be lost in another world, scarcely speaking to me. He spent a little time with the children; otherwise he remained within himself. I knew that my husband was a brilliant man and that his gifts in medicine were unusual. He was mainly interested in preventative medicine but the public was not ready for this advanced notion. Today, we are just beginning to go into this aspect of medicine. Indeed, the majority of physicians are too busy or too greedy to instruct well people how to remain that way. The Chinese people have the right idea; when they are well, they pay their doctors for keeping them that way. When the Chinese become ill, the doctors pay the patients, for then they have not fulfilled their obligations.

I knew that David was not capable of doing well in private practice. His personality was too abrasive. Yet, he kept coming back to this mode of practicing. Each time, he failed. At that point in his career, there were no other avenues of employment open to him, since he had left civil service with prejudice.

My husband was too proud to become "second fiddle" by helping with nursing and medical duties at our home. The result was a tragic waste of years in the life of a gifted, capable human being, who vegetated and vacillated in limbo. Not until much later did my husband resume his medical practice. Who would have dreamed that he would become successful in a strange, unusual capacity. It would take twelve long years before David took up the practice of medicine again, having at last a successful career in an unlikely setting!

Meanwhile, back at the nursing home, I was struggling to meet my financial goals. In spite of the success of the business, the college fund was not growing. Money that I had been counting on had not come in. Our real estate dealer had withheld $1,000.00 of our money after we made settlement on our hotel. Although I repeatedly asked for our funds, he kept making excuses for not having it. Finally, I called his bluff, warning him that I would start court proceedings to get our money. Then the man confessed to me that he had used our funds for himself and that he could not pay us back right away. He begged me not to sue him, promising to make good as soon as possible. Not wishing to cause him and his family any trouble, I agreed to take a note from him. We discounted the note at the bank, but when it came due, Mr. "Wendkos" could not pay. We had to pay back the money ourselves. The man kept evading my calls and did not answer my letters. Finally, one day I met him on a trolley car. Although he tried to avoid me, I marched up to him and spoke my mind.

"Mr. Wendkos, I need the money you owe us to send my son to college."

"But my son has to go to college too!" he replied indignantly. "Why don't you just send Irving to a state school, they're not expensive."

I was astonished by his answer, "Where are you sending your son?"

"The University of Pennsylvania!" he said proudly. "He's going to be a lawyer."

"Well, he'd better graduate soon, because you are going to be his first case. How dare you send your son to school on the money you embezzled from us?"

The man turned his back on me and did not reply. When I returned home, I could not decide how to treat this matter. I hated to expose Mr. "Wendkos'" actions to the public; yet, he was arrogant and unrepentant for his crime and my son was going to suffer as a result. Before I could make up my mind on what action to take, I read that Mr. "Wendkos" had dropped dead. Although I had the man's note in my possession, I could not bring myself to inform his widow of her husband's dishonesty. I would have to find another source for the college fund.

While I was trying to find other avenues of income, I received a distinguished-looking visitor. He was a retired lawyer, Mr. Dyer informed me. He wanted to rent living quarters for his sister, a former school teacher. Miss Dyer needed a permanent home and daily nursing care. I showed Mr. Dyer my finest front room. He was pleased with it.

"Do you have an adjoining room for rent too?" he asked. "My sister requires a private sitting room."

I showed the lawyer an adjoining room praying that he would approve. The gentleman smiled, "How much will you charge for the suite by the year?"

My heart leaped with hope. This could be Irving's schooling.

Mr. Dyer took the suite. He paid and left to fetch his sister. I ran through the house like a delighted child. What a wonderful break! The solution to our problem had walked in the door at precisely the right time. Miss Dyer came and stayed with us for five years, as if it had been planned. Her rental paid for Irving's entire college education. At the age of fifteen and a half, my son entered Ursinus College thanks to my new patient and her brother.

Elsie Dyer was a dedicated elementary school teacher. She had never married, but her pupils were "her children." At the age of thirty-five, she had become ill. The diagnosis was cancer of the eye. Elsie was forced to resign from school and to take drastic treatment to prevent the cancer from spreading. The treatment at that time was radium therapy. Unfortunately, the treatment itself did great damage to her face. Elsie was hideously disfigured with burns and scar tissue. She wore a heavy black veil at all times, and had retreated completely from all social contacts, except for her brother. Mr. Dyer had finally persuaded his sister to move to Ventnor, near his residence. The poor woman needed to have her wounds dressed twice a day, an agonizing procedure because of the tenderness of the area and the extreme pain that it caused. At first, I was the only person allowed in her presence. The maid would leave her food tray outside of her door. Then I would bring the food in and take the tray out when she was through. I alone did her dressings, every day, taking one hour each time. Although the tedious, delicate work was most difficult, it was a burden I willingly shouldered to give my son his schooling.

Miss Dyer and I gradually became friends. I admired her for her great courage and resignation in the face of her tragic existence. Her only diversion was a visit to her brother's home once a week. On those occasions I accompanied her. She went, heavily veiled, into a waiting taxi for the short trip to her brother's house. There we would spend an interesting afternoon with Mr. Dyer, who had a host of amusing stories to relate. He had been the attorney for Thomas Edison. Most of his anecdotes were about his former employer. It was good to hear Miss Dyer chuckle during her brother's conversation.

I remember how she laughed over the story of Mr. Edison's eating habits. The great inventor never took the time to eat or to sleep on a regular schedule like most people do. Instead, he would work around the clock, snatching short catnaps and bits of nourishment at will. He never ate a regular meal. Instead, he carried food around in his pockets, nibbling whenever he thought about it. His favorite snack was dried fish. All of Edison's pockets were filled with little dried smoked smelts which Edison would pop into his mouth whenever he wished. As a result, the inventor smelled like a fish market. Since he was not aware of the odor, the great inventor went his way, meeting kings and commoners alike, in his rumpled, smelly suits.

Since Edison had no regular sleeping time, he was oblivious to others' schedules. He believed that his employees lived the same kind of life that he did. Therefore he would summon them at any time of day or night if he wished to talk with them. This habit sometimes made things very difficult for Mr. Dyer. However, he was proud of his association with the "Wizard of Menlo Park."

In the course of time, the gentle Miss Dyer admitted one other person to her "sanctum." My little Jackie, who was timid with most people, came to Miss Dyer's room every Friday, after school. She took tea with the former teacher, answering questions about her activities in school. These sessions made Jackie feel very important. She knew that Miss Dyer really wanted to hear about what she was doing in class. My sensitive child enjoyed these visits. She was never afraid of the strange, veiled lady who lived in lonely isolation on our second floor.

During the busy years when I managed my nursing home, I was forced into a never-ending routine of work, service and supervision. In my limited "spare time," I tried to fulfill my duties as wife and mother. Often, unfortunately, the needs of desperately ill patients took precedence over the ordinary needs of my family. This situation caused me a great deal of distress because my children and I were deprived of a most important segment of our relationship.

Irving, fortunately, seemed to enjoy his freedom from close parental supervision. He maintained a full schedule of activities outside of the home, remaining cheerful and sociable. Jackie, much younger, resented the atmosphere of a home filled with old and sick people. How difficult for a child to accept the idea that strangers seemed to have first priority on her mother's attention! I did try to spend as much time with my daughter as I could, often depleting my own limited strength to ease her unhappiness. However, the situation was not a healthy one.

Ironically, in spite of my training in nursing and business, I was never interested in being a career woman. All I really wanted was to be a wife and mother, without any outside interruptions. However, I was forced by circumstances to continue working in order to sustain my family. At this point my brother Meyer saved my business by arranging a loan to pay off my mortgage. I paid him back as soon as I was able. His help has always been remembered with gratitude.

David, still out of practice, had plunged into a deeper depression. Although he lived with us, he was unable to help me in any way. His morale had been completely shattered by a disastrous business venture in Camden. A trusted friend, Sam Miller, had embezzled our investment money. When David learned of Sam's treachery, he had suffered a complete breakdown. I tried, but could not help him. In order to keep going, I was forced to view David's trauma as one more tragedy among the many that played themselves out in the setting of my business on Little Rock Avenue.

Elsie Dyer had a life of tragic dimensions. Loving children, she could have none of her own. Craving human companionship, she was forced to become a recluse. Enjoying her teaching career, she had to give up her vocation for a life of pain and isolation. Her days were full of torture, especially when I dressed her lesions twice a day. Each session, which took one hour, was extremely traumatic for both of us. Elsie was a stoic most of the time. However, occasionally, the poor woman could not bear even the lightest touch. Then she would slap my hands until I pulled away. On such days, I would quietly withdraw, advising her that I would return later. After such outbursts, Miss Dyer would often send me an apology and a lovely gift as a "peace offering."

After Elsie had been with me for a year, she arranged for me to go on a cruise, paying for my ticket. When I tried to protest, she assured me that she was being very selfish.

"I need you to stay well for my sake. You're at the breaking point. I couldn't go on without you."

I trained my best nurse to take my place for two weeks.

The cruise was a life-giving respite from my grueling daily routine.

In spite of her limited environment and her constant pain, Elsie really loved life. She conducted herself with great dignity and gentle resignation throughout the years that she lived with me. Toward the end of her five-year stay, she became so weak that it was necessary for her to engage her own private nurse. I continued my visits as usual. The lady especially enjoyed seeing me all dressed up whenever I was planning to go out for an evening. One Friday evening, I was preparing to go to synagogue. I stopped in to show Elsie my new outfit. When she saw me she said, "Bluma, when you pray tonight, ask God to take me. I am ready to die."

I was surprised to hear those words. Saying nothing, I left Elsie's room to tend to a few last-minute details. Then I returned.

"Elsie, do you really want me to do what you asked? The decision is yours. I will do what you really want. What is your wish?"

Elsie looked at me for a long moment. Then she smiled gently.

"You are right Bluma, forget my request. Don't ask that favor—not yet!"

Several years later, Elsie succumbed, peacefully and quietly, in the same suite that had become her home five years before.

My patients were not always old or terminally ill. Sometimes I treated young people whose physical symptoms were caused by emotional problems. Often, the basic problem was sexual. Ever since I had studied the works of Sigmund Freud, I had respected the strong influence that sexual pressure has on the normal human condition. In the era of my nursing home days, most people were ashamed to discuss their personal problems openly. Because I had been raised on a farm in a very open and honest fashion, I had no such inhibitions. Often I was able to reach the core of a problem by talking with my patients, opening up avenues of communication long repressed.

I recall the case of one beautiful woman, Collette, a teacher, who was sent to me by a New York doctor. The woman had complained of severe stomach cramps. Her doctor had prescribed a diet and a rest cure at my nursing home. After interviewing Collette, I realized that she had more than a simple stomach disorder. After winning her confidence, I set about to discover what was really bothering this lady.

At last, the young matron began to talk. A few years before, she had married a wonderful man whom she loved. However, she had married reluctantly because she feared her own secret nature. Collette was over-sexed. She had led an extremely promiscuous life before her marriage.

Soon, as she had feared, she found that one partner was not capable of satisfying her sexual appetite. Yet she did not want to cheat on her husband. Therefore, she had sent her husband away, without telling him the truth. Now she was planning to divorce him so that she could go back to her former wild life. Her decision had precipitated the painful stomach symptoms.

As we began to talk, we explored various aspects of her nature and possible solutions to her predicament. We also tried to project her lifestyle into the future, assessing what the result would be. Finally, she realized that eventually, she would become physically and emotionally drained from the frantic lifestyle she was contemplating. Then she would end up in "skid-row" or a mental institution. Collette decided to stay on with me and to take a leave of absence from her teaching job while we continued therapy.

After a few weeks, we decided to invite her husband down for a week. First, I spoke to him alone. Although Jack was deeply in love with his wife, he knew nothing about her basic sexual nature. He was bewildered by her "sudden" change. I asked him if they had ever discussed their relationship frankly and openly. He had never thought it necessary to do so.

After explaining various aspects of women's sexuality, I gave Jack some advise. "Stay here, now that you are going to be together for a period of time, try to talk to each other openly and frankly. Come to terms with your relationship, terms that will accommodate each of you and still leave room for individual growth. Adjust your actions to each other's needs. Each one can learn to give in a little so that at last you can find a common way to please each other. By honest experimentation and a will to please, you will develop a new relationship, save your marriage and enrich your lives."

The young couple listened, talked earnestly, spent long hours together and finally departed, well along in their new relationship.

I did not hear from them for several months after they left. One morning, I received a package, a book by Lin Yutang, *The Art of Living*. The card read, "To the only woman who truly understands the art of living from the happy couple whose marriage you saved." It was signed by Collette and Jack.

At the time that I was working with an over-sexed woman, a Philadelphia doctor sent me a patient with the reverse problem. Anne, my new patient, was a woman in her thirties. She seemed to be in great distress, nervous and depressed.

She told me, "I have a wonderful husband, two lovely children and every material comfort I need. But somehow, I feel restless, empty, unable to function. Something is wrong with my life."

I soon found, upon further questioning, that she was troubled by her lack of sexual desire. When her friends talked about their sexual relationships with their husbands, she was unable to relate to their enjoyment. Anne always dreaded her husband's approach.

I asked the younger woman to describe the routine of her home life. She told me that her husband came home, read the paper, ate dinner, listened to the radio and retired early. Then he wanted sex. There was no preliminary courtship.

"I am usually tired at night, so I just lie back to give him what he wants, hating every minute of it. After he relieves himself, he turns over and goes to sleep."

"And you?"

"Well, I guess I just feel used and I toss and turn the rest of the night."

"Did you ever tell your husband how you feel?"

"No, of course not! He's such a good, hard-working man. I wouldn't want to hurt his feelings."

"But," I reminded her, "he is hurting you!"

"It's not his fault that I can't respond. There's something wrong with me—not him."

"There's nothing wrong with you, Anne, you just don't know your own nature. Do you know that women have sexual needs that can and should be met by their husbands, as well as vice versa? Your husband is taking what he wants, but he is not living up to his marital responsibilities."

This was a new idea to Anne. She knew of a husband's right to sexual satisfaction with his wife; she did not know of her own need for sexual fulfillment. I asked her to stay with me for one week while we discussed women's physiology, and what married love should be. At the end of the week, I asked her to invite her husband for the weekend. I set him up in a separate room. Then I invited him into my office for a private conversation.

"Roger," I began, "do you really love your wife?"

"Of course," he said. "Don't I prove it? I work hard. I don't cheat on her."

"But you do cheat her of her rights."

Roger did not know what I was talking about. I reviewed the routine of his marital relationships, then I gave him an insight to a woman's sexual nature. Roger was amazed. He did not know that normal women had erogenous zones. He had never been taught that "nice" women had sexual desires. Finally, I was able to convince him that a truly loving relationship was a mutual sharing of delight and that the ultimate marital experience was reciprocal. Understanding at last, Roger caught fire. He was eager to enjoy the kind of relationship that I had described. He vowed to make up to his wife for his former ignorance. He asked me to help him. I advised him to start courting his wife all over again.

"Take her out on a date tonight. Make her feel desirable and loved for all of her attributes. Don't go to bed with her after your first date. Just kiss, hug and pet. Tomorrow night, do the same. Then, when you bring her home, ask if you can stay with her all night. If she is willing, make love to her slowly and tenderly. Remember to use words and lots of touching. Try to concentrate on giving her all of the pleasurable sensations you can. You will soon find that this method of lovemaking builds up into an exciting longer-lasting ecstasy for both of you. After you both have reached a climax, do not turn your back on Anne. Make her feel that you appreciate the wonderful relationship that exists between you at all times. Continue to pet her and to use tender words. Fall asleep in each other's arms."

Roger did as he was told. On the following night, he dated his wife and retired to his own room. On the next night, he stayed in her room. On the third day, the couple did not stir from their room at all. They did not even come out for meals. However, on the fourth morning when I arose early and came into my office, I was surprised to find Roger sitting there.

"Roger, what went wrong? Why are you up so early in the morning?"

Roger smiled sheepishly, "Nothing is wrong, Bluma. I just had to get up for a while because I needed the rest. For the first time in our married life, my wife just won't let me alone! She wore me out!"

After Roger and Anne left, I heard from them often. On every one of their anniversaries, they sent me a special card, thanking me for making each of their successive anniversaries more wonderful than the last. Needless to say, Anne regained her health completely.

It is a curious human phenomenon that people in need of help often become so self-absorbed that they are not aware of other's needs. At the time that I was counseling the two distraught women, I was suffering from a severe gallbladder condition. In addition to my regular duties in the nursing home, I was forced to become my own patient twice a week. On these painful occasions, I swallowed a tube so that I could inject Epsom salts into my stomach. Even during my tortured episodes, I was not allowed to be alone in my misery. I can vividly recall one day when I was in terrible pain, lying in bed, draining the bile from my system. During the ordeal, both Collette and Anne were in my bedroom, one on either side of me, crying about their own troubles. Although I could not do much talking with a tube in my mouth, I nodded and grunted as I listened through my own pain. After I removed the tube, I assured them that they would triumph over their problems. Finally, they left, still intent on their own affairs, and seemingly oblivious to my own sickness and to the selfishness of their continuous demands on my vitality.

These young women were weak and obsessed with themselves at that particular time. I do not feel bitter about their indifference to my own problems. To mend broken lives is a gift and a reward in itself. Looking back, I am proud that, even flat on my back, I was strong enough to help others.

I know that on many occasions I was taken advantage of by unscrupulous people. Yet, in the final analysis, one has to develop a philosophy that encompasses all aspects of giving. I feel that one must try to help all those who ask for aid. It is wiser to accept the risk of being taken advantage of, than to miss the one who truly needs and deserves help.

Often I rendered help even when I was aware that the person who imposed his needs on me did not deserve any good from my hands. In one particular instance, I knowingly became a victim of a man who had already victimized our family cruelly. Yet, I was forced to help because innocent people were involved.

One day, while I was drinking my breakfast coffee at the nursing home, early in the morning, I saw a strange sight from my window. Two tiny bedraggled children were walking up the street, dragging a heavy suitcase between them. The boy could not have been more than six years old; the girl, about ten. To my surprise, they turned into my house and rang the bell. The little boy silently handed me a note. "Please take care of my children until I find a place for them. They have no place to go. Sam Miller."

I was astonished! Sam Miller was the real estate dealer who had embezzled David's money. Now, divorced, he had the nerve to send his children to me! Although I was furious, I could not turn my back on the pitiful tykes. I settled them in a spare room and gave them breakfast.

Later, I phoned Sam at his office. "Come and get your children. A nursing home is no place for them. I can't take a mother's place, I hardly have time to spare for my own children. And, I need my rooms for sick patients."

Sam refused to listen to my arguments. He promised to pay for their keep as soon as he got the money. Of course I knew that he would not pay. I insisted that he come to take back his children. He said he would get back to me in a few days and rang off. Subsequent efforts to reach him failed. The children stayed on with me. Sam never sent enough money either to pay for their personal needs or for their room and board. I was forced to clothe them, send them to school, and to do my best to give them some human tenderness and love in my limited time. Somehow, I managed to sustain my "extra" family through one long winter. At last, in the spring, I sent a telegram to Sam. "Come for your children at once, or I will turn them over to Juvenile Court."

A few days later, Sam sent someone to pick up his children. He did not dare to confront me because he feared he might have to pay for their keep. The family left. I never heard from Sam again. He never sent me a card of thanks.

Many years later, long after I had forgotten all about Sam Miller and his family, a young, handsome man walked into my home. He put his arms around me and kissed me. I did not recognize him. He had tears in his eyes.

"Aunt Bluma, many years ago you were very kind to a little boy and his sister. I have never forgotten the winter we spent in your home. Many times I wanted to write or to call you and tell you of our gratitude. I have always felt too embarrassed to approach you. Now, I made up my mind to come to see you and to let you know how very much you did for us during that lonely, frightening time when my sister and I needed someone to care."

All the difficulties of my struggle to maintain those children had long since vanished. My resentment of their father had abated. What remained and will always remain is the glow that I experience every time I think that in my limited way, with so much going on, I was still able to give some comfort and sustenance to two abused innocents.

In truth, each patient presented another unique and fascinating life story. However, I must get back to my own saga. After David had been out of work for about eleven years, he became restless and eager to find a suitable position again. We had decided that private practice was not for my husband. David's best opportunity lay in government work. Finally, after much effort, David was accepted back into civil service. However, he had to start at the bottom rung again, taking a job that few doctors wanted. David accepted a position as physician to federal prisoners at Leavenworth, Kansas. A year later, he was transferred to Maxwell Fields in Montgomery, Alabama. These positions entailed another separation for our family. I could not afford to give up the nursing home because David's salary was not adequate to support our family and the children's future educational needs.

Although I was delighted with David's return to good health and activity, the separation was difficult. Jackie, especially, was devastated to be away from her father. We made up our minds to visit each other at every opportunity. I began to train my staff to function without me for periods of time so that I could take Jackie to visit her father whenever feasible.

Irv graduated from college at nineteen and joined his father in Montgomery. I took Jackie at Christmastime on our first visit to Montgomery. What a complete change in David! He was happy and full of spirit. My husband loved his job. The other doctors in the hospital were much younger men who admired David for his skill and devotion to his work. He was soon put in charge of the entire operation. The prisoners, too, recognized David's integrity and essential fairness. Although he was tough, he was kind in his gruff way. Imagine, after all the years of being a misfit, my husband found his true vocation in a federal prison hospital!

Jackie and I were amused at the accommodations which were given to us on our visit. We stayed in a barracks-like building in the prison compound. The large public bathroom was on the other side of the building, down a chilly, dismal corridor. The bathroom was also used as a laundry room by the prisoners. In the middle of the night when I found I had to use the bathroom facilities, I girded my strength for the freezing trek through the long corridor. Upon arriving at my destination, I was greeted by a strange sight. A long row of headless figures stood at attention like sentries, guarding the entire front of the bathroom. After my first initial shock, I realized what had happened. The prisoners had done their laundry and had strung it across the room to dry. It was so cold that their uniforms had frozen and were standing stiffly on the line, blocking my way. I punched them aside and pushed through the cold, erect row to reach my destination.

Our sporadic visits were not satisfactory. Jackie, aged thirteen, was anxious to leave the nursing home. She wrote to her father, begging him to bring us together again. At last, David and I decided to live together in Montgomery and to be a family again.

Jackie was elated. I left a trusted nurse in charge of the business, determining to fly back often to keep tabs on the operation.

David had rented a place for us near the prison. When we arrived I examined the old home he had rented. Appalled, I saw that it was dilapidated and without any heat. I cautioned Jackie not to unpack. We sat in the house that night without adequate electric or plumbing facilities, and with little furniture except for a few broken-down pieces. I just sat on a rickety rocker and cried and cried.

Jackie hugged me and whispered, "Mother, I'm sorry. It's all my fault."

I looked up at her unhappy face. "No, Jackie, you did the right thing. We all belong together. Don't worry, tomorrow I will fix everything up again."

The next morning I went to a real estate agent who found us a suitable home. In the afternoon, I went down town and ordered a complete houseful of new furniture. The store promised to deliver everything the next day. By the next evening, the house was completely furnished and in order. We slept in our own beds that night. We stayed in our rented house for three years. From there, we moved to the prison camp where they had built us a home right on the grounds. For twelve years, we lived on the grounds at Maxwell Fields.

Although our quarters were next door to the prison compound, the neighborhood posed no security problem. The federal penitentiary, a one-story barracks, was surrounded by a high fence. I suppose that a desperately unhappy inmate could have scaled the fence. However, none did. Why should they? The whole unit was run like a fancy hotel. The kitchen had the finest equipment available, and was spotless at all times. A blackboard across one wall detailed the menu for the day. Food was plentiful and well prepared. The institution had a social service director and a well-stocked library where the prisoners were free to read whatever they desired. Classes were also given on a variety of subjects. It was an ideal place for poor young people to receive fine accommodations plus an excellent education at government expense.

The inmates were either white collar criminals or prisoners of war. There were no dangerous men in custody. The operation was expected to maintain the highest standards. In fact, the Bureau of Prisoners once called the warden to Washington for a thorough interrogation because the German prisoners had complained about their food. It seems that the Nazis were unhappy because they were receiving too much meat and not enough potatoes. The warden quickly rectified the situation.

Several of the prisoners were constant repeaters. As soon as the weather got cold, the men would throw bricks through government property windows so that they could be arrested and sent to Montgomery for a warm, carefree winter, at the taxpayers' expense.

Whenever I arranged a party at my home, a few prisoners were dispatched to help in the setup. On Sundays, David often invited some of the "boys" to our home for a musical concert.

At the end of our twelve-year stay, David was transferred to a new job in the Veteran's Hospital in Montgomery. At this point we purchased a beautiful home in a lovely area of town. My grounds became the showplace of the community. I prepared and planted a delightful flower bed, which I called the Friendship Garden, naming each plant after a friend. Full of clay and hard soil, the Montgomery soil was no better than the stubborn sand of Alliance. A great deal of loving care and attention coaxed my flowers and shrubs to brilliant beauty. My grass became soft, even and beautiful. I spend a great deal of money on my growing things and could not bear to see them not living up to their potential. Just as I had nursed my sick people, I nursed my sick plants, shifting them from one location to another to give them the best environment. Then I would loosen the earth around the plant and inject the ground with castor oil or mix the dirt with Epsom salts to strengthen it. The technique seemed to work. My plants were magnificent.

One day, I noticed that my beautiful pine trees were in trouble. The needles were dropping off. David sent a biologist to examine the trees. He was baffled by the problem. The scientist sent specimens to Auburn University for analysis and suggestions for treatment. Impatient for an answer, I embarked upon a course of action which stemmed from my farm experience. I took a bar of Fels Naptha soap and shred it into a pail of water. Then I gathered rolls of cotton, a kitchen stool and a ladder. With these implements, I washed down every needle on every pine tree on my property. Then I dug up the soil around each tree, put fertilizer and water into the cavity, being careful not to touch the bark of the tree. On the next day, when the soap was dried on the branches, I took my hose and sprayed the soap off; using plenty of water. My pine trees recovered, and grew beautifully from then on. Three weeks later, I received my answer from Auburn University. They were sorry, but they did not know what was wrong with my trees.

My remedy had worked so well on my trees that I subsequently tried the same formula on my azaleas and other plants whenever they seemed to be ailing. Later, I wrote to Auburn, telling them what I had done and advising them about how well my cure had performed. I never heard from the college again. I have since studied biology, botany and other related sciences, without learning why the remedy worked.

Life in Montgomery was idyllic. I functioned as "just plain housewife," Mrs. Rappoport. I made friends; joined in social and philanthropic activities; gave dinner parties and luncheons, so I felt myself to be a true part of this warm, friendly southern community.

On one occasion, I invited an orthodox rabbi to my home for dinner. The young man was a visitor in town. Although I did not keep a kosher kitchen, I was careful to use special dishes and cutlery and to feed him appropriately. While I was clearing the dishes after the dairy dinner, David drove my daughter to the nearby club for a party. Meanwhile, the young rabbi browsed among our books in the library. Suddenly, he burst into the kitchen, waving a familiar-looking book. "What are these books doing on your shelf?"

"Why," I began, "they were written by Moses Bayuk..."

"I know," he said, "I studied these very books in Jerusalem, where I took my training for the rabbinate. Only the deepest scholars are able to read these wonderful books. Moses Bayuk is one of the great thinkers of our times. I have been looking forward to learning more about him and perhaps meeting with him some day."

"Well," I said proudly, "I am his daughter. These books were written by my father in the evenings after he had farmed our land all day long. But you are fortunate to be able to read them. They are in Hebrew and I can't understand a word!"

The rabbi was overjoyed to meet the daughter of the "Great Rev. Bayuk." I, too, was delighted to know that my father's works were considered so valuable. In my mind's eye, I could see him writing at the kitchen table, by candlelight far into the night, after a day of physical toil and before another long day of the same. I still bask in the reflected light of that small candle which illuminated such shining words.

During our stay in Montgomery, the children were growing up beautifully. Jackie came to Alabama when she was fourteen years old. When she first entered high school in the south, her marks dropped alarmingly. The teacher called me in for a conference.

"Mrs. Rappoport," she began, "I know there is something very strange here. Up north your daughter was an outstanding student. Here she is barely passing. There must be a reason for her change. Is she so unhappy here?"

"No!" I said, shocked at the news. "In fact, Jackie begged me to come here to Montgomery."

We finally got to the root of the problem. Jackie just didn't understand the southern dialect. It was like hearing a foreign language to her "northern ears." She could not follow her teachers' lectures. After a while, my daughter grew accustomed to the

Alabama drawl, and developed a bit of it herself. Then, once again her marks became good and she was graduated with honors and afterwards accepted at Cornell University, which she attended for four years.

Irving, who had graduated from college at the age of nineteen, was already making a name for himself as a radio announcer in Montgomery. David was thriving in his job. I loved my new way of life. During the summer, I returned to Ventnor to run my nursing home; otherwise I was a happy housewife in the South.

However, nothing can last forever. Soon the ominous portents of World War II loomed on the horizon. Irving was aware of his role in the future.

"Mother, I'm going to enlist in the Air Force. We're going to be at war very soon and I would like to prepare myself as a cadet."

Like every mother, I was fearful, yet I knew that Irving would do what he felt was right. He enlisted and was sent to Florida for his training. In what seemed like a very short time, Irving was graduated and commissioned as a second lieutenant, a navigator in the Air Force. Immediately, he received his orders to report for duty in Guatemala. Unfortunately, our son was sent away immediately, without a leave of absence to say goodbye to any of us. I was heartbroken. I wrote to Irving asking him if there was any way that I could go to Guatemala to see him. Then I wrote to Washington for a visa.

At that point, I had a little problem. When I was born, in Alliance most women were attended by midwives. No one bothered to register her children's birth. I had no birth certificate! The school had burned down and all my records had been destroyed.

Finally, through the efforts of my nephew, Judge Harry Levin, I was able to find two old settlers, his father and Mr. Bailey, who signed for me saying that I was born. I sent these affidavits to Washington, also mentioning that I was registered as a Red Cross nurse, and giving them the special number that I had received when I attended the Civil War reunion many years before. To my surprise, I received a visa, listing my occupation as a Red Cross nurse. With the visa in hand, I wrote to Irving, telling him that I would be coming to Guatemala as a Red Cross nurse.

Irving advised me to be careful when I was traveling, not to talk to anyone about my mission. He asked me to give him the date of my flight so that he could alert the American Embassy to smooth my way in crossing the borders. It was fortunate that Irving had taken these precautions. When I reached the Mexican border at Brownsville, Texas, customs was not satisfied with my visa. They wanted to know my business. I said, "Either contact Washington or the American Embassy in Guatemala."

I was forced to remain in Brownsville overnight until the border officers made their investigation. Finally, on the following morning, I was awakened and put on a plane to Mexico. From there, I was flown to Guatemala. Irving was on hand to greet me when I arrived and to settle me in a comfortable hotel. During the day, I would sightsee this beautiful area. At night I would meet my son after his work day. I, being the only American mother at the hotel, became "Mom" to all the boys. They were ready and eager to do anything for me.

During my month's stay in Guatemala, I was able to take a few exciting trips. One in particular is memorable. We were traveling by bus to a small town called Chichicastenango. The road was narrow, winding around a steep mountain. A sheer drop of thousands of feet was visible at the edge. Although the bus was old and wobbly, the driver seemed to be indifferent to the danger below. However, the mountain view was breathtaking. The stones were the color of emeralds and the majestic trees were a sight to behold! About fifty miles from our destination, the bus broke down. No one seemed to know what to do about it. Were we facing the prospect of sleeping out in the woods all night? Since all kinds of snakes and other reptiles kept slithering out across the road, the prospect of remaining there was not pleasant.

Finally, the bus driver took off his belt and wound it around something in the engine. Then he asked a passenger to give him his belt. This, too, was wrapped around the engine. At last, with a shudder, the engine started up again. The road was so full of lime that we passengers kept our handkerchiefs over our noses and mouths to keep the harmful dust from blowing into our throats. When we arrived at our destination, the trip suddenly seemed worthwhile. The Mayan Inn was charming. A lovely church stood on one side of our hotel—the Guatemala Indians had been converted to Christianity years before.

In the early morning on one certain holiday, Indians carrying their goods on their backs hiked through the narrow paths in the mountains, setting up their wares in front of the hotel. After selling their merchandise, they took part in the holiday celebration. Climbing the steep steps of the church, they made a procession into the building. We followed them. The immaculate church was decorated with pictures of saints all over the interior. At the far end lay a glass casket with a black figure simulating the body of Christ, lying in full state. It was disturbing to me to see the casket with its contents. In the evening, the worshipers marched with the casket, carrying it around the square in a large procession. Afterwards, the coffin was brought into the home of an outstanding member of their church. Unfortunately, the home was next door to the hotel, and just outside my window. When I retired, conscious of the coffin next door, I could not go to sleep. Finally, I dressed and knocked on the door of another woman guest in the inn. She asked me what was wrong. I told her of my uneasiness. The woman was kind enough to join me, to keep me company in my lovely room. I had a large suite with plenty of room for a guest. With someone else nearby, I was able to sleep.

I ran into many adventures, seeing parts of the country that are usually not visited by tourists. I bought many interesting handmade rugs and blankets. The natives' yards were a riot of color as they dried their yarns on strings outside. While I was doing my sightseeing, Irving and his crew were fighting a war. Later, I found out their mission: to find enemy ships and bomb them. On one mission, Irving, the navigator, spotted two Japanese ships which had been eluding the scouts. His plane scored direct hits. Later, Irving and his crew received medals because of this action.

I was included in many of the affairs at the Officers' Club and the Embassy while I was in Guatemala. In fact, the wife of the President of Guatemala invited me and many officers' wives to a party at the presidential residence. I carried a Spanish dictionary with me so that I could form a few sentences. The President's lady was most gracious. Even after I left, she continued to ask Irving about my welfare.

On one memorable occasion, I was planning to be at a party at the lake. Irving was supposed to meet me there after completing his mission. When he did not arrive at the usual time, I tried to find out what had happened. No one could tell me anything.

At 5 o'clock, two women from the Embassy called for me and asked if they could take me to the lake. I refused, saying that I would wait for Irving. The women said, "Irving will be there later."

The women were from the decoding section. They had received word that my son's plane had developed trouble and was trying to make it home on one engine. Of course, they were not permitted to tell me; however, they felt that I should stay with them until such time as they could tell me. I stayed at the hotel, waiting, and at midnight, I went to my room. I sat, trembling and crying because I knew that something terrible had happened. After midnight, I heard a knock at the door. Irving rushed in and hugged me.

"Mom, I couldn't get in touch with you. As soon as I got in I went down to the lake, but you weren't there. I was delayed."

I could get nothing more out of him. Irving tried to dismiss the whole episode. A few days later, as I sat with my son at the Officer's Club, the major of his squadron walked over to our table. The officer put his arm around me and said, "Mother, I want you to know that we are here today because of your son's skill. We had trouble with the plane. We couldn't maintain our altitude, so we jettisoned all of the ammunition into the ocean, and came back on a wing and a prayer. Your son's navigational skills brought us home."

It was during our comfortable days of sightseeing and parties that Irving and his crew were going off to perform dangerous acts of war. How strange it was for these brave young men to leave comfortable, luxurious and peaceful surroundings to plunge themselves into hellish dangers and then to fly back to the same plush environment all in the space of a few hours.

At the end of my month's visit, I said a reluctant farewell to my son, not knowing whether I would ever see him again. When Irving took me to the airport, he actually pushed me onto the plane so that I would not see his tears. When I handed in my ticket, the attendant accidentally clipped my ticket from Mexico to the United States. I was not aware of what he had done because I was crying. When the plane landed in Mexico City, I had reservations for a three-day stay there. At the station, I arranged to leave my baggage, taking only a small valise with me for the short stay. As I was leaving the station, my name was called over the loud speaker. A pilot approached me when I answered the call.

"Mrs. Rappoport, you don't have a ticket from Mexico to the United States. You had better come back with me."

I refused, saying, "No, I am going to continue just as I planned. It will straighten out."

When I arrived at the hotel, I called the ticket office and told them what had happened. They said, "Don't worry, we'll cable Guatemala and see if they have your ticket." When they phoned Guatemala, they were told to allow me to continue on, because they had clipped my ticket by mistake. I continued my sightseeing in Mexico City, unperturbed.

After I returned to Maxwell Fields, I made it my business to write Irving every single day, never knowing whether or not he would receive my letters. I would sit at my typewriter, speaking to my son through my letters, while my white cat perched at my desk, trying to grab my fingers with her paw. Although Irving could not always write, he tried to use the news media to get through a message.

The reporters would quote an unnamed officer, and we would understand by his words that the officer was Irving. One evening, when we were having dinner with friends, I heard an announcement over the radio. All I heard was Irving Rapp . . . and "hit." I dropped my platter and collapsed in panic. My friend called the press office immediately. They said Yes—Irv Rappoport had made a hit, sinking a ship.

Another time, when I was in our Temple, our rabbi was reading bits of letters from boys who had written to him from the service. As I listened to excerpts from one letter, I knew that it was Irving's because of some of the references he made to places where I had been while in Guatemala.

One day, we got a letter from Irving, saying that he was planting watermelon but did not expect to be there to eat them. Excited, I told my husband that Irving must have been grounded, and that he would be home soon. David warned me not to be so optimistic, but I continued to live in hope. Meanwhile, I spent my days in Montgomery making life easier for the young men who were training at Maxwell Fields before going off to war.

One Passover night, I entertained thirty-six soldiers, officers and enlisted men, ranking from private to colonel. When they entered, I said, "During this evening, there will be no salutes. We all are one, no matter what your official standing."

I was used to cooking for a large group. The only help I had was from the prisoners who were allowed to come in to move my furniture so that I could put out long tables and benches to accommodate the crowd.

After dinner, my cocktail bar was open and dessert and coffee were served. Many extra people came in for dessert and for the evening. Every week, I entertained the soldiers and their families.

One Mother's Day, I was entertaining a few friends. I said sadly, "If only I could have heard from my son today. God only knows where he is."

At about three o'clock the next morning, I awoke with a start. I seemed to hear someone calling, "Mother!" It was so real that I ran to the door. No one was there. I could not get back to sleep. I awoke David and told him what had happened.

"Bluma, you are always thinking of Irving. It is just another dream."

The following day the phone rang. California was calling. When I answered, I heard my son's voice. He had been trying to get me on the telephone. I asked him if he had arrived in the states about 3:00 a.m., our time.

"How did you know?" he asked.

I said, "I heard your voice calling me, and I ran to the door. I didn't sleep for the rest of the night, waiting for your call."

I have had this sort of intuition many times in my life. I simply accept the fact that my senses are often so keen that I can pick up the thoughts and feelings of others.

My son was sent to the west coast of Florida for a physical examination. He had been grounded because of a back injury which had occurred while he was flying in a plane which had experienced a severe shaking during an attack. He had a slipped disc and was in excruciating pain. Irving had been in an Australian hospital, where they worked on his back, telling him that he would never again be able to fly. He argued that his crew needed him and insisted on going back. His bombardier also became ill with appendicitis. The two of them had to be rushed to the hospital. While they were being treated, a new navigator and bombardier were assigned to their pilot. They went out on a mission and did not return. Irving and the bombardier were the only original crew members to survive. When Irving was sent to Florida for a physical checkup, he knew that his active days in combat were over. He had time to think about the future now. He was footloose and fancy-free, but anxious to get on with his life.

Although there had been many girls in my son's life, his most serious romance with a young French-Canadian woman had ended in a heartbreak. Laurette Bouret had broken off with Irving before he went into combat. My son, on the rebound, met a young girl in Miami. Soon he brought her home and informed me that he and Gloria Dauman wished to marry. I was delighted, of course. After the wedding, Irving and Gloria came to live in Montgomery.

Jobs after the war were difficult to get. Irving was forced to sell shoes for a while, in order to support his wife. Soon a child, Annette, was born.

David and I were delighted to be grandparents of such an adorable baby. However, our joy was short-lived. Gloria began acting strangely. She told Irving that she was not well, and wished to go to New York to her parents' home to consult a doctor. Irving got her a ticket, and she went off, taking the baby with her.

I visited my son after his wife left. He was upset about Gloria's illness. As I looked around the apartment, I realized that something was amiss. I did not know whether or not to voice my suspicions to my son. What I had noticed was that Gloria had taken all of her clothing and all of the baby's clothing and paraphernalia as well. I feared that my daughter-in-law was not planning to return.

A few hours later, Irving received a telegram. "Annette arrived safely." Irving was puzzled. I gently explained what was going on.

"Irving, I'm afraid your wife has left you and has no intentions of returning."

Irving jumped to the phone and called his wife. She refused to talk to him at first. Finally, her father brought Gloria to the phone.

Irving said, "Gloria, what the heck is going on?"

Gloria answered, "I want a divorce. I'm not coming back!"

After the initial shock, Irving agreed to the divorce without further negotiations, providing that he could see his child and keep her with him during the summer. Gloria agreed to the terms. Irving and Gloria were divorced.

Strangely, Irving received a visit from his old flame, Laurette, shortly after his divorce. Six months later, Irving married the spirited redhead from Canada. They have been together ever since, leading an interesting and happy life, blessed with their daughter, Michele.

Unfortunately, after twenty wonderful years in Montgomery, David had to take retirement at sixty-five because of illness. His records affirmed that he had performed outstandingly during his government service. The veterans had no greater friend and champion.

By this time, Jackie had also married, right after graduating from Cornell University. So it was just David and I.

David, refusing to stay retired, had taken another position at Jackson, Mississippi, much against my will. Being a good wife, I prepared to follow him after I wound things up in Montgomery, and left my beloved home.

When I arrived in Jackson, I was bewildered to find that David had not come out to meet me. Finally, a woman approached me as I stood with my baggage, not knowing which way to turn.

"Are you Mrs. Rappoport?" she said.

"What has happened to David?" I asked. "What's wrong?"

She told me as gently as she could. "Your husband has suffered a heart attack. He is in the hospital."

The woman, who was my neighbor at the barracks, took me straight to the hospital. David was lying in bed, pale and thin, under oxygen. He smiled wanly when he saw me.

"I'll be all right now, Bluma, now that you're with me."

I spent the night at David's side. The head nurse said, "I want you to go to a room on the same floor and get some rest. I promise, if there is any change, I will call you."

The next day, my neighbor called to say that the movers had arrived with my furniture. Knowing that David was in excellent hands, I crossed the fields to the barracks and started placing furniture in my new home. There was a pouring rain outside, my husband was seriously ill, and I had just left a home that I adored for an area that was not at all attractive or promising. I set up all of the essentials for immediate living, but I did not unpack the rest of our belongings.

In a week I brought David back from the hospital. Then I pleaded with him to retire and move back either to Montgomery or to Atlantic City with me. David was stubborn, "No, I'm going back to work!"

Each day he crossed the fields and went to work. In order to keep myself occupied, I followed David and donated my services to caring for the mental patients.

There were large groups of soldiers who had come back from war in a very bad state of emotional illness. Our purpose was to help these fractured human beings to get back to normal living.

It was extremely difficult for some of the young men to recover. I worked in a special occupational therapy department, which was carefully guarded. I tried my best to help each young man to become normal again. It was heartbreaking to see how broken in spirit some of the boys had become because of the horrors they had been through. Some recovered; some were beyond reach.

After a few months in Jackson, David had another heart attack. This time he had no choice. He had to quit. I had already rented out my home in Atlantic City. Therefore, we rented an apartment in Philadelphia for five months until we could get possession of our home. David was lost without any work to do. A friend asked him whether he would like to be a camp doctor for the summer. David went to interview the owners of a camp in the Poconos.

The site was lovely—the surroundings magnificent. I told the owners that I would have to go with David in order to feed him his special diet. They agreed, saying that I would have accommodations next to the area where the children would stay if they became ill. They also mentioned that very few children ever became ill in their camp.

That was my first experience in a camp. David was paid very little and I was not paid anything. We lived in the same house with the owners. It was set up so that ill children could also be housed there. Contrary to the owners' words, I never saw so many sick children. Every night my sleep was disturbed when children were brought in with elevated temperatures. Because there was no nurse to take care of them, my conscience would not allow me to sleep. I became the nurse.

Dr. Rappoport was concerned with the set up of the camp. He was always ahead of his time in his interest in preventative medicine.

"You are going to have some very severe accident some night if you don't put a gate at the head of the stairs."

The owner laughed and said, "Nothing will happen here."

David and I did not like the owner's attitude. He was very careless.

As the summer went on, I was night nurse on a regular basis, while David attempted to keep the camp as accident free as possible. One day, one of the students was bitten by a yellow bug. His whole body swelled up and he could barely swallow. I sat up with him all night, with a small dropper, feeding him with sugar water, dropped into his mouth. My ministrations may have saved his life.

David told the owners that they would have to find someone else to take over for the night. I could not work both shifts. The people ignored the request. Many times David and I were so disgusted that we wanted to leave. However, we were afraid for the lives of the children there. The owners plainly did not have the correct responsible attitude.

Toward the end of the summer, in late August, I had finally reached the breaking point. I just had to have some rest. I told David to give me a sleeping tablet and to watch over things. While I slept, there was a terrible storm. When I awoke, everything was in total darkness. I saw the owner walking around and asked her to guide me to the bathroom with her flashlight. I came out of the dark bathroom without a flashlight, as the owner had not bothered to answer. Walking into the black corridor, I made a misstep and stumbled down twelve steps, hitting my chin on every step. I tried to keep my head up as I fell. Dr. Rappoport heard the clatter. He, the owner and a friend came running down the stairs. I could not get up. I asked for a drink of whiskey. They lifted me up and carried me back to bed. I could not move. There was no one to take care of me except David. He did his best. We could get no help and could not leave the camp because the bridge had washed out and we were stranded.

I lay in my bed for three days, helpless. Finally, the owner came to my room. The bridge had been repaired and she knew that we would be leaving.

"Bluma, will you please tell your husband not to say anything about what happened at this camp?"

I was furious. "Whatever he says about this camp will be true. You are irresponsible people and should not be allowed to have so many innocent children in your care. David warned you that those stairs would cause a serious accident. It could have happened to a child. You are the most negligent people I have ever seen. I am going to say plenty about you and you can't stop me. You took children with all kinds of diseases and illnesses without screening them first. As long as they could pay, you weren't interested in anything else. You took children that wet their beds and made them a laughing stock with the other children, instead of trying to help them. You gave them the worst food and never even put sheets on their beds except for parents' visiting day."

This experience taught me a lot about camps. It is ridiculous for parents to get rid of their children for the summer without carefully examining the place where they send their offspring. They pay a high price to send their kids away, believing they will be taken care of adequately. Unfortunately, many camp owners, counselors and teachers are not so competent or concerned as parents. Camp may be a traumatic experience for a child unless the parent makes sure that the camp he chooses is the right one.

After the bridge was repaired, my daughter and son-in-law came for us. I was taken to the Orthopedic Hospital in Philadelphia, where it was ascertained that I had injured my back. I was put in traction and had to have nurses around the clock. I remained in the hospital for three weeks. On returning home, I continued a series of exercises to strengthen and repair my back. It has never ceased to pain me since that injury.

When our house in Ventnor was vacated, we settled down, living a private life. I rented some of my rooms and baths in the summertime, but I did not go back to the nursing business.

David lived on for five years extremely ill and morose. Toward the end, he developed a morbid fear of death. He spent most of his time reading.

Finally, when David had his last severe attack, he also developed uremia. When he went to the hospital, I knew that the end was near. We engaged nurses around the clock because his doctor made me go home to rest for a few hours every day. David's day nurse was very kind to him. He did not like his nurse on the four to eleven shift and made me get another one.

A black woman who had worked for me several years before came in answer to our call. Susie Parker, an undergraduate nurse, stayed with David for a week. As the hours were closing in on my husband's life, the doctor told my children, "I want your mother to lie down for a few hours or she will go before her husband." My daughter took me to a motel near the hospital and engaged a room.

As I tried to rest, the telephone rang. The nurse said, "Mrs. Rappoport, come back to the hospital." When I arrived, Susie, the nurse on duty, told me gently that my husband had passed away very peacefully.

He had awakened suddenly and said to her, "Hurry, get me a cold, cold drink!" He was running a high fever. The nurse took him in her arms and held a glass of water to his lips. He drank all of it, kissed her hand and said, "Thank you for being with me." Then, David closed his eyes and passed away in peace.

I grieved for my companion of 47 years. Together we had weathered many ups and downs. He was selfless; throughout our marriage, his first concern was his wife and children. To his dying day he never compromised his high standards. Even his final act of gratitude to his nurse shows his extraordinary feelings for his fellow human beings.

I shall always remember with gratitude the kindness and gentleness of Susie Parker, who eased my husband's last moments.

I gave her my own nurse's cape, which she still wears proudly. Susie told me, "Bluma, you have always kept my soul warm, and now your cape warms my body as well."

We must be grateful to the good nurses in this world who are true "angels of mercy," sent to ease our worst moments.

Miles to Go

After David died, I tried to pick up the pieces of my life and to go on as well as I could without him. I had determined never to interfere with the lives of my children or to be a burden to them in any way. I had my home and the inner strength which had been built up by many years of good and bad times and by the lessons that I had learned from my parents so many years ago.

I decided to do a lot of traveling. David did not enjoy going to distant places. He liked to stay home to read or to study in his free hours. I, on the other hand, had always had a great curiosity about other lands and people. After David's death, I visited London, Holland, Israel, Greece, Italy and France, fixing all that I saw in my mind's eye. I needed no camera because my powers of observation have remained keen. When one has true interest, one retains what she sees or learns. Today, my paint brush reviews the memories of the many countries I have visited.

I was seventy-three years old when David died. Aside from my back, I was strong and healthy and as much in love with life as ever, even though I was saddened by the loss of my husband. My great desire to learn more about so many subjects kept me from brooding or wasting time in useless self-pity. Besides, my children have been a great comfort to me.

Jackie is married to a fine man, Herbert Siegel. They have two delightful children, Carol and Donald. The Siegels live in a beautiful home in Philadelphia and have always been most attentive and concerned toward their parents.

Irving and Laurette, after living in Japan, came to settle nearby in Northfield, New Jersey. Their daughter, Michele, born in 1952, has been a great joy as a close friend as well as a granddaughter to me.

However, I am a very independent person. I do not believe in leaning on anyone else. I belong to myself. No one owes me any of their precious time. My dear family has a right to live their own lives without worrying about me. Fortunately, I have been strong and healthy enough to be able to get around and to do everything for myself. This is the greatest blessing one can have in advanced age.

After David died, I still felt that I had "miles to go before I sleep." Life offers so many interesting challenges and new experiences. I did not intend to waste any of my precious moments.

For five years after David died, I was a very busy woman. After traveling, I decided to alter my nursing home to make several apartments so that I could rent them out for the summer for added income.

After the apartments were built, I advertised for tenants. Soon, a nice-looking gentleman appeared, asking to see the rental unit. His name was David Purmell. His wife was seriously ill in a nearby nursing home.

Mr. Purmell wanted a small apartment to stay in so that he could visit his wife every day. He moved in and faithfully visited his critically ill wife every day. When he arrived home after his day's visit, he was often distraught. I used to speak to him to calm him down and to answer his medical questions about the condition of his wife. It was evident that Mr. Purmell was a well-educated, fine family man.

After his wife died, David remained in the apartment, lonely and depressed. I tried to talk to him to ease his trying moments. We began to take long walks together. As a widow, I could understand everything that the recent widower was going through.

David was a most interesting person. He had been a professor of Agronomy at Doylestown Agricultural College. My own interest in farming led to many spirited and delightful conversations between us.

After a few months, David told me that he would be going into the hospital in Atlantic City for tests for a few days. He asked me to visit him there and to bring his mail.

When I visited Mr. Purmell in the hospital, we had a pleasant chat. As I rose to leave, David Purmell got out of bed, put his arms around me and said, "Bluma, I love you."

I was astonished. "You don't mean me?"

"Yes," he said, "I do mean you."

I left the hospital in a daze. When I returned home, I telephoned my daughter-in-law. "Laurette, I think your mother-in-law has a romantic lover!"

My children were not surprised.

My son said, "I was beginning to suspect that Mr. Purmell was paying a lot of attention to you."

The prospect of a new romance at my age was startling and frightening. However, I could not see any objection to a new experience.

David Purmell was an exceptionally fine person. We were both active, healthy and self-sufficient. We had many common interests. Too, we were both lonely.

David and I continued to see each other. Then he left town to visit his son, who was a doctor in Michigan. Two days after David's departure, as I was entertaining friends at dinner, the doorbell rang. David was at the door.

"What are you doing here?" I asked. "You are supposed to be in Michigan."

David put his arms around me and kissed me. "Bluma, dear, I can't stay away from you."

My dinner guests were wondering what was going on. I invited David to join us. As I served cocktails, David lifted his glass and proposed a toast, "To Bluma, my wife-to-be!"

My friends were excited. They congratulated us. "Bluma, why didn't you tell us before?"

"I didn't know myself," I answered, dazed.

David assured the ladies that he knew what he was saying.

"David, are you asking me to marry you?" I asked.

"No!" David told me, "I'm not asking. I'm telling you."

A few weeks later, on October 29, 1966, at a lovely, quiet ceremony, I became a bride again, at the age of seventy-eight. By that time, I knew the whole story of David Purmell.

My new husband had been a native of Russia, son of a well-to-do merchant. At the age of sixteen he had migrated to America with a scholarship to attend the famous Baron de Hirsch Agricultural School in Woodbine, New Jersey. That town is not far from my own Alliance. After graduating from the University of Michigan, he became a teacher of agronomy at Woodbine, staying until the school closed its doors. Later, David transferred to Doylestown to teach at the Delaware Valley College where he remained for many years. In addition, he worked a farm and ran his own summer camps for young people. He had been married to a lovely woman and had three fine children.

David's hobby was the language and history of Russia. He is a respected Russian scholar and is often called upon by members of our community to translate letters written in Russian. When I met him, he was already retired as a college professor.

After our marriage, David and I went to Michigan to visit his family. At a party in our honor, his relatives asked, "Where did you find her?"

I answered, laughing. "Well, all I know is that I opened my door one day and there he was."

Since we both loved to travel, my new husband and I started out on an odyssey that took us to many countries during the early years of our marriage. We visited Japan, Portugal, Spain, England and the Scandinavian countries. Finally, David's greatest dream was realized. In 1973, we took an extended tour to Russia, after the Iron Curtain had been lifted. Since many of David's relatives still live there, it was most exciting and memorable. It was also a sobering and frightening experience.

Life for the Jew in Russia was always difficult. In my father's day, Hebrews were denied the rights to learning and freedom.

Only a privileged few were allowed to attend Russian schools.

Most Jews lived in a segregated area known as the Pale. They were forced to carry yellow tickets marked "JEW." No Jew could travel to a non-Jewish area without a special permit. Christian children were encouraged not to play with the Jewish children. Peasants were allowed to rape and pillage Jewish homes at will.

During my visit in 1973, I observed that life for the Jew in Russia had overtones of the dark days of the "pogroms." Persecution is more sophisticated and subtle today, but the Jew is still afraid and mistreated. Jews still cannot travel from one section to another without a special visa. Most synagogues have been closed, especially in the smaller villages. The younger generation is encouraged to forget religion and to accept the Communist way.

Although David and I were able to meet with his sister, there was an edgy atmosphere in our exchanges. We visited other members of the family, including a niece and cousins, in Leningrad and Moscow. Always, there seemed to be a feeling of constraint—as if they were afraid to express their true feelings. Leningrad is a beautiful city, with impressive statues. The Hermitage Museum is exciting with its marvelous collection of paintings. Yet, with all the beauty that we found, there existed an undercurrent of tension. I detected a strained look in the eyes of most of the Russian people we met. There is no substitute for a free life. Every one there is a prisoner in some way, and they know it.

When we were in Moscow, we visited the old synagogue. It was dilapidated and neglected. A few old men sat praying there. They were friendly and asked us to come back. However, they did not attempt to arrange for special communication with us.

Next, taking a bus, we traveled over three thousand miles into the smaller villages of inner Russia. We saw the contrast between city dwellers and the villagers. Daily life in the small towns was very primitive. We, ourselves, were forced to put up with crude facilities on the bus trips. There were no bathrooms in the bus or along the routes. Every few hours the driver would stop and say. "Ladies one way; men, the other way!" We did what we had to do. After the first day's outing, I always carried a flask of water so that I could wash my hands.

It is amazing what one can become used to. We women had to squat on an open road to do our duty without any privacy.

On one trip, our bus broke down. The driver and guide left to summon help. My husband, who spoke the language, got out of the bus to talk to a farm woman who stood in the fields, grazing her cow.

David asked her about her lifestyle.

The woman told him, "I have a little plot of ground which I take care of, planting enough food for our needs. My son lives with me. When he comes home drunk, he beats me up. Then, I can't get up for a few days. And that's my life," she said.

After the bus was fixed, we continued on and entered Poland, where I felt the same strain. We visited the gruesome places where millions of Jews were exterminated. A few houses remain in the Jewish area. They are riddled with gunshot holes. The ghastly reminders of the horrors of the past gave me an eerie sensation. How could such cruelty exist?

At our hotel in Poland, we felt as if we were being constantly watched. Whenever we left the hotel, we had to turn in our keys to the caretaker. We were not allowed to have visitors. The same restrictions had prevailed in Russia. In fact, one day at the hotel, I thought David had been arrested. Fortunately, the manager had merely detained my husband to help her translate some English sentences into Russian.

Our next stop was East Germany. Then we crossed the famous bridge to "Check Point Charley," where the Allies used to exchange prisoners from West Germany. We waited for hours before being checked out so that we could get into West Germany. Once we arrived at the western section we gazed at the wire wall which separated East and West Germany. Thousands of people had dared to jump over the hot wires or to tunnel their way underground in order to escape from the Communist-dominated eastern half. Many had died in their desperate attempts to leave.

We were happy to leave both parts of Germany with the terrible history of its past. Not until we got out of the plane onto American soil, did I feel free again; I have no desire ever to visit those countries again.

Full Circle

I am no old woman, sitting in her dotage, plucking the threads of memory. My recollections are intact, etched on a vital brain that sorts, sifts and collates the useful data of experience. I am a teeming library of reference. The sounds, sights and tastes of Yesterday are alive in my being. My mission is to represent the value of the elderly; we are primary sources of unique wisdom and history.

Our natural audiences do not heed us, fearing, perhaps, the truth in our wrinkles. The media has done a thorough job of seducing our children from us with a promise of eternal youth. Advertisements hint that old age is the punishment for using the wrong soap. Against such false propaganda, I continue to write and to paint of what I have learned and of where I have been.

Eventually, the years will carve their tell-tale message on today's young faces. Then, when our children become as we are, they shall be ready to accept and to understand the true nature of Time. The Present lingers but a moment; the Future is but a dream; only the Past exists, intact, forever. Eternity is in the keeping of Memory.

Full Circle

David and I no longer travel. We live in Atlantic City in an apartment at the beach and boardwalk, where I can sit on my balcony enjoying the swing of the ocean through its many moods.

We are not idle. I am busy during every waking hour. David enjoys reading and walking outdoors in every kind of weather. Meaningful activity leaves us no time for boredom.

My greatest love is nature—my second love, art. Now I have time to devote myself to my two great loves and to combine them creatively, keeping my mind and heart young, eager to welcome each day. As a self-taught artist, I retain my unique vision to interpret a variety of subjects: landscapes, portraits and still-lifes. Memory makes it possible for me to go back in time and to revive on canvas the wonderful, innocent days of childhood. My paintings of the farm are done in a primitive manner, befitting the era and the state of mind of the child who experienced those times. I have recently completed a large family tree for Bayuk descendants so that they may retain their heritage.

To live for almost an entire century is a great feat; to retain one's mental capacities is a blessing. Surely, I have been granted these gifts for a purpose. I feel obligated to share with others some of the wisdom that I have evolved during my extended sojourn on this planet.

I am aware that my present status is not a usual one for those of my age. Although the general life span has increased, the quality of life at the end of the age line has deteriorated. Our society is backward and cruel in its manner of treating the aged. Too many older human beings find that their added years are a mockery.

Their longevity serves only to embitter their memories of past joys, loving relationships and activities.

I am convinced that most senile behavior is caused by neglect and hopelessness. Most oldsters would retain their faculties if they were allowed to keep exercising their minds in a meaningful way. Unless a senior citizen is extremely resourceful in concealing the cosmetic ravages of time, he is shunted to the background as an embarrassment. Since everyone who lives must eventually become old and look it, there is something very strange about the attitude of most younger people toward aging. They have been led to believe that youth is permanent and that those who age are freaks. Smooth advertising presents myth as truth. Wrinkles represent unacceptable reality. By the time "they" becomes "we" the emotional damage has been done.

When I was proprietor of a nursing home, I saw that a parent, troubled by severe illness, was often treated by his children as a criminal or a source of shame. Yet, this same parent had once been the hub and strength of the entire family. I vowed, then, that I would prepare myself as well as possible for an independent old age, including financial security. Moreover, I sought to establish many interests and activities of my own, freeing my family of the prospect of filling my time. Now, my children feel free to go their own ways, without guilt, because I am self-sufficient.

In addition to retaining reasonably good health, the secret of my successful adjustment to aging lies in the depth of my curiosity. So many facets of living remain to be studied! Science and nature retain fascinating opportunities for learning. Moreover, creativity unfolds in endless layers for the adventurous.

During the busiest days of my earlier life, I used to say, "If only I had more time, I would love to: travel, paint, write, read more, learn more about the mysteries of this world!"

When one is young, there is never enough time. Age gives us this gift, if we recognize its value. Now, I have enough time to pursue my postponed daydreams. No boss interrupts; no children clamor for attention; no deadline looms.

Constantly I set new goals for myself. I finish every project that I begin. Every day presents a new adventure or a continuation of yesterday's absorbing interests. In addition, I take complete charge of my household, including the laundry and cooking. Besides my daily chores and activities, I maintain a large correspondence. I also welcome many visitors to relax with me in my art-filled living room.

My paintings, the family tree and this book are my way of leaving behind a portion of myself and my roots. I believe very strongly that death is not the final word. Just as we can pick up a telephone or mail a letter to communicate with a distant friend, so I believe we can communicate with those who live in another dimension. Memory is our wire to connect us to our absent loved ones.

Long ago, my father told me that the soul does not die. It has a place in the universe. My own experiences have reinforced the truth of my father's beliefs. During my days as a nurse, I witnessed the last moments of many patients and loved ones. The look of serenity on the faces of the dying showed me that death is a gentle closing of one door and the opening of another. I am not concerned about my own mortality. Even at ninety-two I feel that I may have "miles to go before I sleep." All of us have only today. I revel in today, and try to make each precious moment a pleasure.

Having experienced a great deal of upheavals and changes in lifestyles, I have come to the inevitable conclusion that the family is still the most important unit in preserving and enriching the human race. It is important for today's leaders to emphasize the need to strengthen the concept of the family. No other social structure is better for our civilization.

The basic structure of the family is father, mother and child (or children). Because of a woman's biological role in the birth and nursing of the baby, there should be no doubt that women have been structured to devote their time to their children during infancy and early childhood. The renewed interest in breast feeding underscores a woman's role in the family. A woman who elects to have a child should respect the natural order. She should plan to devote her energies to her baby for the first five years of his life. Barring unusual circumstances, the mother is the best person to provide the best environment for her infant. If the woman arbitrarily elects to deprive herself and her child of her primary responsibility during the critical years of her child's formation, there is great danger of emotional scarring to the child.

I am modern enough and woman enough to champion a woman's right not to become a mother. If she wishes to pursue an absorbing career without interruption, a woman's choice should be accepted and respected. Each person has the right to use his talents and energies as he sees fit. However, if a woman chooses to be a mother, she should be admired and aided as one who has undertaken a most demanding and elevated career. Motherhood demands a variety of highly developed skills and great intelligence and resourcefulness.

I am aware that woman's status in our society is far from ideal. Much improvement is needed. However, in their rage, radical feminists often deny the basic facts of biology. While we should overcome denigration and attain equality, we must not deny that we are the sole possessors of wombs.

It is important to remember that we are all in charge of our own destinies. We come into the world one-by-one, and we die alone. Each person's life path is unique. As others come in and out of our orbit, we continue along in our individual ways, in control of our own thoughts as well as our actions. We have the power to discard from our memories whatever events are harmful or unproductive to dwell upon. Unhappy or tragic times, from the vantage point of distance, can be relegated to learning experiences. To brood over what is already past is wasteful and self-indulgent, changing nothing.

I have revived my story for myself with joyful recognition and with a deeper understanding of the past. I present my life now in the hope that my remembrances will be to others a source of history and a guide to creative living.

There is no doubt that each being has a significant place in eternity, far beyond his role on this earth. Each of us has a role in a cosmic master plan. Perhaps one purpose of our stay in this segment is to gain mastery over pain and suffering. Once we have completed our assigned missions, we are ready to go on to the next level.

Science has uncovered many proofs of the resourcefulness of nature. In the universe, all that exists continues in some form throughout conceivable time. The Master Planner, endowing us with a brain, confirms our immortality. Surely this awesome creation of limitless potential was not given to us for just one short lifetime. Nature is not that wasteful!

Therefore, I believe that when our human framework decays, the brain, with all of its stored power, is transferred to another vehicle. Each soul is keeper and protector of its own brain and travels with it to the next level. Then, because I exist, I will always exist in some form. I say to my loved ones what my father said to me long ago. "The soul has a life of its own. In some form, I shall always be with you."

The End

Memory Paintings by Bluma

and

Family Photographs

A Farmer's Daughter: Bluma

Memory Paintings

Life on the Farm

A Farmer's Daughter: Bluma

Planting and Irrigating by Hand

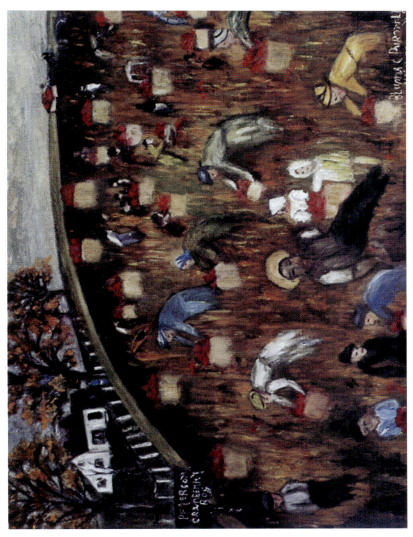

Picking Cranberries at Peterson's Bog

A Farmer's Daughter: Bluma

The Sacredness of Life

Memory Paintings

The Family Bath

A Farmer's Daughter: Bluma

The Blizzard

Memory Paintings

Laundry Day

*Congregation Scheris Israel,
Built in 1889*

Memory Paintings

Girls Fight Insects While Dad Tells Summer Stories

274 A Farmer's Daughter: Bluma

Harvest Time in the Strawberry Patch

Memory Paintings

A Farmer's Daughter: Bluma

A Farmer's Daughter: Bluma

The Old Homestead

Fear: In the Time of Pogroms

The origins of the painting "Fear" are unclear. It may be original to Bluma or perhaps a copy of an artwork that moved her.

A Farmer's Daughter: Bluma

Family Photographs

The Bayuk family c. 1893. Bluma stands in front of her father Moses; Lena (middle) and Bertha stand with their mother, Annette.

Bluma in the corn field at the Alliance farm, 1902. This photograph may be the model for the painting *A Farmer's Daughter: Bluma*.

Bluma as a young nurse.

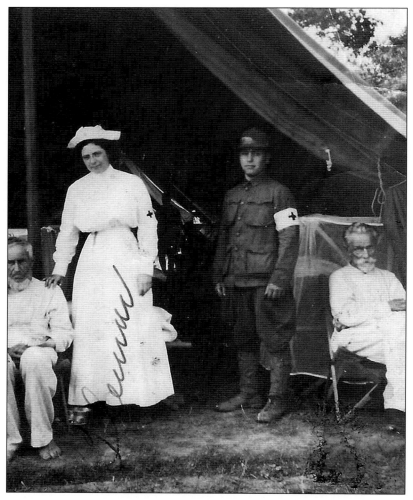

Bluma posing with two Civil War veterans at the 50th anniversary reunion of the Battle of Gettysburg. Bluma's retelling dates the event in the early fall of 1913, but the reunion was held June 29–July 4 of that year.

Bluma with her husband David Rappoport on their 25th wedding anniversary, August 28, 1939, at Bluma's nursing home at 106 S. Little Rock Ave. in Ventnor, New Jersey. The sign behind them reads, "The Ventnor Hotel, Supervised Care and Diets, Bluma C. Rappoport, Reg. Nurse." The woman looking on from the porch is "Aunt Sadie Bayuk." Bluma was 50 at this time.

This photograph carries a note that says it was taken at Ft. Bragg, North Carolina, in June 195[final numeral cut off]. Bluma and David lived in the South in the late 1940s – early 1950s. Bluma would have been in her early 60s at this time.

Bluma and David Purmell, her second husband, at their wedding on October 30, 1966, at the home of Irving and Laurette Rappoport. Bluma was 78.

A Farmer's Daughter: Bluma

Bluma at 94 years old.
© Steven Zerby – USA TODAY NETWORK.

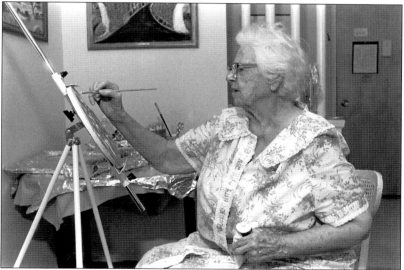

(Top) Bluma painting the Bayuk family tree c. 1982. Photograph by Marilyn Margulis. (Bottom) Bluma at 99, painting in her apartment at the York House South near the Albert Einstein Medical Center in Philadelphia (coincidentally the old "Jewish Hospital" where she trained as a nurse many years previously).

(Top) Bluma with Felice Rovner, her co-author. The photo was taken at the party held for the publication of *A Farmer's Daughter: Bluma* in 1981. Bluma was 93. (Bottom) Bluma's 100th birthday party held in 1988 in Jenkintown, Pennsylvania.

Index

Ackleys, 6
Alexander II, Tsar, 3, 4
Alexander III, Tsar, 4
Allen, Mr., 121
Alliance Cemetery, 37, 44, 57–58, 60, 61, 94, 135
Alliance Colony, ix, xiii–xiv, 101
Alliance Israélite Universelle, 4
Alliance Land Trust, 6
Allivine Canning Factory, 117, 120
Althea, 185–86, 211
Am Olam, 4,
Astle, 6
Auburn University, 230
Avoca Hotel, 203, 206

Bacall, Michael, 4
Bailey, Emma (daughter of Sidney and Esther Bailey), 34
Bailey, Sidney, 4, 232
Barbash, Dr., 203
Baron de Hirsch Agricultural School, 250
Bayuk, Anna (daughter of Jacob and Rose), 28–32
Bayuk, Annette Ethel (né Goroshofsky, Bluma's mother), v, xiv, 9–16, 17, 21–22 (receives sewing machine from Jacob Schiff), 26, 35, 37–42, 42–45 (death of twins), 47, 48, 51–53 (as doctor), 55 (winter chores), 59–61 (ghost of Frank Golder), 71–74 (laundry at river), 75–83 (Golden Boy), 93 (agrees to stay on farm), 104 (receives hat from Max), 124–25 (gives Bluma her blessing to attend nursing school), 187 (learns of Bluma and David's marriage), 193–95 (pneumonia), 205–206 (running water, bathroom installed in Bayuk farmhouse), 206 (death), 279
Bayuk, Annie (daughter of Moses and Annette), 37–38, 42–45 (death), 78

Bayuk, Bernice (daughter of Sam and Sadie), 170, 183
Bayuk, Chana (Moses' mother), 3
Bayuk, Eddie (son of Moses and Annette), 78, 87, 88, 93
Bayuk, Edith (né Adler, first wife to Sam), 96, 99, 104–109, 170–72
Bayuk, Esther (né Caplan, wife to Max), 169 (death), 169 (children mentioned: Eleanore, Beatrice, Edward)
Bayuk, Etta (daughter of Jacob and Rose), 28–32
Bayuk, Fannie (daughter of Moses and Annette), 37–38, 42–45 (death), 78
Bayuk, Fanya (second wife to Moses), 3–4, 5–6 (dies), 103
Bayuk, Harry (son of Sam and Edith), 105, 109, 169, 170–72
Bayuk, Jacob (father of Moses), 3
Bayuk, Jacob (son of Moses and Minna), 3, 5, 15, 28, 103, 109–111, 158 (death)
Bayuk, Julia (né Mann, wife to Meyer), 104
Bayuk, Mamie (daughter of Jacob and Rose), 28–32, 187
Bayuk, Mary (né Hughes; wife to Harry), 170
Bayuk, Max (son of Moses and Fanya), 4, 5, 15, 96, 103–104, 169 (death)
Bayuk, Meyer (son of Moses and Fanya), 4, 5, 15, 96, 103–104, 218
Bayuk, Minna (né Bash, first wife to Moses), 3
Bayuk, J. Moses (Bluma's father), v, xiv, 1, 3–8, 13–16, 17, 25–32 (grape harvest and trip to Philadelphia), 35, 37 (repairing shoes), 39–42, 42–45 (death of twins), 48, 55 (winter chores), 59–61 (ghost of Frank Golder), 71–74 (laundry at river), 88–94 (Rabbi Moses), 92 (berry thief), 93 (decides to stay on farm), 109, 139–40 (visit with Bluma in Philadelphia), 159 (afterlife), 187, 205, 230–31, 259, 279
Bayuk, Rose (né Rothman, wife to Jacob), 28, 31
Bayuk, Sadie (né Cohen, second wife to Sam), 169, 170, 171, 176–77, 183 (described), 183–86 (birth of daughter Violet), 189, 196, 205, 210 (Sadie's allowance), 210–211 (return of house keepers), 283
Bayuk, Sam (son of Moses and Fanya), 4, 5, 15, 82, 94, 96, 97, 99, 103–104, 109 (believes Bluma is taking advantage), 169, 170, 176, 196, 205, 209–211 (financial difficulties)
Bayuk, Shlomo (brother to Moses), 5
Bayuk, Violet (daughter of Sam and Sadie), 183–86, 196–97
Bayuk Brothers Tobacco Company, ix, 103–104

Index

Becker, Isaac, 12, 76–77
Becker, Moishe, 12, 75–83
Berkowitz, Abe, 123
Bialystock, Russia, 3, 4
Blank, Roger, Dr., 129–33, 179–83
Blizzard of 1888, ix
Booker, Addie McKinney, 197
Bradway Station, 5, 6, 7

Cannon, Bridget, 149, 150
Carmel, New Jersey, 119
Castle Garden, 12
Coltun, Aaron, 86, 91, 121
Cornell University, 232, 240
Cushing, Dr., 169

Dearborne Museum, xiii
Deas, 6
Delaware Valley College, 250
Dyer, Mr., 215
Dyer, Elsie, 215–217, 218–20

Edison, Thomas, 217
Evil Eye, 11, 51–52

Fels, Maurice, 117–18, 122–24
Fido (the Bayuk dog), 44, 79–80
Francis, Susan, 134, 138–39, 140, 156–57, 160–62 (Gold Medal award)
Frank, Max, Dr., 147–48
Franklin, Anna Fay (né Bayuk, daughter of Sam and Edith), xv, 105, 109, 169, 170–72
Franklin, Marc Bayuk, xv
Freud, Sigmund, 17, 220

Garrisons, 6
Gartman, Mr., 107–108
Gershal Road, 37, 75
Gettysburg 50th reunion, ix, 165–68, 282

Gimbel family, 170, 183
Golder, Benjamin, 63
Golder, Clara, 113–14
Golder, Frank, 58–63
Golder, Mandis, 63
Golder, Sam, 63
Goldman, Chaim, 67
Goroshofsky, Abraham Isaac (Bluma's maternal grandfather), 9, 10–11
Goroshofsky, Bluma (Bluma's maternal grandmother), 9, 10–11
Granger (Mr. and Mrs., daughter and son-in-law of Mrs. Solomon), 154–56
Greene, Ilene, 130–31, 132,
Greenwood, Dr., 120, 186, 193,
Greenwood, Rivka (né Rappoport, David's sister), 119–20, 186
Grey, Martin, Dr., 149–51

Hanthorns, 6
Hebrew Emigrant Aid Society, 6, 7
Herder, Moses, 4
Herman, Margaret, Dr. (né Bailey, daughter of Sidney and Esther Bailey), 34
Hirsch, Maurice, de, Baron, xiv, 5, 22, 101, 250
Home for Incurables, 153, 156, 265
Horne and Hardart's, 170

Jaffee, Lillian (né Bailey, daughter of Sidney and Esther Bailey), 34
James, Miss, 124, 133–34
Jewish Hospital (Einstein Medical, Northern Division), 123, 125
Jewish Maternity Hospital (Sixth and Pine), 148–51

Kahn, Dr., 173–75
Karp, Joseph, 85–91
Karp, Dr., 173
Kowalski, Mary, 9, 10–12, 77
Kowalski, Wasyl, 9, 10–13, 77
Kraftzow, Israel, 34, 55–56, 95
Krassenstein's store, 38, 87

Larkin, Mr., 36

Index

Leach brothers, 6, 7
Lentz, Mr., 43, 44
Levin, Abe, 198, 199–200
Levin, Bertha (né Bayuk, daughter of Moses and Annette, married to Mendel), 17, 23, 25–32 (grape harvest and trip to Philadelphia), 34–36 (Mr. Wordsworth), 38–40, 42–45 (death of twins), 47–49 (bath), 65, 71–72, 81, 85–87, 94, 97 (shopping with Bluma), 113–14, 120–21, 279
Levin, I. Harry (son of William and Lena), xv, 88, 232
Levin, Lena (né Bayuk, daughter of Moses and Annette, married to William), 17, 23, 33, 34, 38–40, 42–45 (death of twins), 47–49 (bath), 65, 71, 81, 96 (married William Levin), 103, 114, 121, 193 (diphtheria), 195, 197, 279
Levin, William (married to Lena), 96, 193, 232
Lewis, Mollye, xiv
Lin, Yutang (*The Art of Living*), 221
Lit, Jacob, 108, 170
Lit Brothers department store, 170

Magic Curler Company, The, 111, 117
Mamie S., 179–83
Mary (the Bayuk horse), 72, 74, 85
Maurice River, 27, 72, 74, 97–98
Meyerhoff, Robert, Dr., 160, 162, 163
Military service, 9–10 (forced)
Miller, Sam, 218, 225–26
Moore, Miss, 61–62
Mother's cocktail, 39–40, 51–53

New Jersey Central Railroad, 5, 6
Norma post office, 86, 87, 121
Norma train station, 7, 27, 81, 82, 85–86, 97

Odessa, Russia, 9, 10, 75
Ostrow, Sophie, Dr., 148–49

Paintings, Bluma's, xiv, 70, 257, 265–277
Parker, Susie, 244–45
Parvins, 6, 98

Paul, Dr., 170–71
Perskie, David, 24
Perskie, Jacob, 24, 201
Perskie, Joseph, 24, 200–201
Perskie, Lazar, 23–24 (barn burns)
Perskie, Marvin, 24
Perskie, Stephen, 24
Peterson, Mrs., 56–57
Peterson's cranberry bog, 55–57, 267
Pincus, Chasaleigha (né Bayuk, daughter of Moses and Minna), 3
Prokas recipe (sweet-and-sour cabbage), 204
Purmell, Bluma Bayuk Rappoport, ix–xi, 8 (birth), 17–18 (farming at five), 25–32 (grape harvest and trip to Philadelphia), 33–36 (country school), 42–45 (death of twins), 47–49 (bath), 51–53 (mother's cocktail), 65–68 (February blizzard), 69–70 (eclipse), 70 (cataracts), 71–74 (laundry at river), 97–99 (moving to Philadelphia), 105–109 (lives with Sam and Edith), 107–108 (packs tobacco), 109–111 (moves to brother Jake's home), 110 (Wanamakers and classes at Temple Business School), 110-11 (works for Mr. Ross and then Magic Curler), 113–16 (meets David Rappoport), 120–22 (sends David a fake letter), 129–63 (nursing school), 129–32 (date with Roger Blank), 133–34 (run in with Miss James), 136–37 (caring for children with measles), 139 (taming of Bluma), 139–40 (visiting with father in Philadelphia), 144–45 (intolerant patient), 145–51 (inappropriate male advances), 149 (first child delivery), 151 (appreciating David Rappoport), 153–54 (Home for Incurables), 155–56 (dinner with Grangers), 156–57 (advised by Miss Frances), 157–58 (preparing body for morgue), 157, 159 (quarreling with David), 159–63 (graduation), 160–62 (Gold Medal award), 165–68 (Gettysburg reunion), 172 (private nursing and private lessons), 179–83 (nursing care for Mamie S.), 183–86 (birth of Sam and Sadie's daughter Violet), 186–87 (marriage to David R.), 189–91 (move to Sixth St., Philadelphia), 190 (rat in commode), 195 (nursing Lena and children), 193–95 (nursing mother), 195 (birth of Irving), 195–96 (on motherhood), 197–98 (boarders in Atlantic City), 199–208 (boarding house management, Atlantic City), 202–203 (pregnancy), 204 (prokas), 206 (move to Camden), 207 (house on Little Rock Ave, Ventnor), 208–209 (trolley accident),

209 (incident with priest), 211–12 (incident at hardware store), 213–226 (nursing home, Ventnor), 220–24 (marriage counselor), 225–26 (Miller children), 227–28 (Montgomery, Alabama), 232 (no birth certificate), 232–36 (visits Irving in Guatemala), 242–43 (accident at Poconos camp), 247 (travels), 248 (meets David Purmell), 250 (marriage to David Purmell), 250–53 (traveling through Europe), 257 (living in Atlantic City), 257–58 (thoughts on old age), 259 (the soul does not die), 265–77 (memory paintings) 279–88 (family photographs)

Purmell, David (Bluma's second husband), 248 (takes small apartment in Bluma's building), 248–50 (friendship turns into more), 250 (marriage), 250–53 (traveling through Europe), 285

Pogroms, ix, x, 5, 10, 11–12, 75, 91, 251, 277

Raab, Dr., 137

Randolph, Mr., 95

Rappoport, Annette (daughter of Irving and Gloria), 239

Rappoport, Baila (David's mother), 119, 157

Rappoport, David (Bluma's first husband), 113–16, 117, 118–22, 129, 131, 140–42 (shaved head), 151–52, 156–57, 159–63 (Bluma's graduation), 168, 169, 172 (post graduate studies), 175–79 (walks to Atlantic City), 183–86 (birth of Sam and Sadie's daughter Violet), 186–87, 191–92 (bedside manner), 192–93, 196 (civil service), 195, 199 (leaves civil service), 211 (practice in Fairview, NJ), 213–14 (David's character), 226–27 (employment in Leavenworth, Kansas, and Montgomery, Alabama), 240–41 (retires, heart attacks), 241–43 (camp doctor in Poconos), 244–45 (death), 283

Rappoport, Gloria (né Dauman, Irving's first wife), 238–39

Rappoport, Irving (son of David and Bluma), 195 (birth), 197, 199, 203, 213, 218, 227, 232 (enlists in Air Force), 233–39, 238–39 (marriage to Gloria), 239 (marriage to Laurette), 247, 285

Rappoport, Jacqueline. *See* Siegel, Jacqueline.

Rappport, Laurette (né Bouret, Irving's second wife), 238, 239, 247, 285

Rappoport, Lou (David's brother), 187

Rappoport, Michele (daughter of Irving and Laurette), ix–xi, 239, 247

Rappoport, Mordecai (David's father), 119, 186, 157

Rebecca of Sunnybrook Farm, 131

Red Cross, ix, 165, 168, 232–33
Rosenhayn, 120, 186
Ross, Mr., 110–11
Rovner, Felice Lewis, xiv, xv, 288

Schiff, Jacob, 21–22
Schmidt, Mr., 200
Seldes, George, 34
Seldes, Gilbert, 34
Shaw, Mary, 173–75
Shore/Shaw, Mr., 173–75
Siegel, Carol (daughter of Herbert and Jacqueline), 247
Siegel, Don (son of Herbert and Jacqueline), 247
Siegel, Herbert (married to Jacqueline), xv, 243, 247
Siegel, Jacqueline (né Rappoport, daughter of David R. and Bluma), xv, 203 (born), 205, 208, 209, 213, 217, 218, 227–28, 231–32, 240, 243, 247
Solomon, Mrs., 153–55
Stavitsky, Elias, 5

Tiphereth Israel Synagogue (Congregation Scheris Israel), 272
Tolstoy, Leo, ix, 3, 4
Tom, 211

University of Michigan, 250
University of Pennsylvania, 119, 172, 215

Ventnor, New Jersey, x, 61, 201, 202, 207, 213, 216, 232, 244, 283

Wanamaker department store, 110, 146, 187
Wendkos, Mr., 214–15
Wilson, Mr., 106
Wordsworth, Mr., 34–36

Yonkel the fish peddler, 75, 78, 79–80; Yonkel's brother Jacob, 75, 78

Zager, Goldie, 38, 39–42
Zager, Harry, 39
Zager, Joseph, 39–42, 43, 44

Colophon

Editing interns at Stockton University completed the initial layout and proofreading for this second edition of *A Farmer's Daughter: Bluma*. They include Katelyn Comer, Chris Curtin, Jennah Figueroa, Elizabeth Glass, Lea Hawthorne, Daniel Jacoby, Ethan Jardim, Chris Lopez, Cassius Navarro, Makena Olson, Felix Ramos, Katharyn Sagusti and Rose Shaw. Jennah Figueroa assisted Tom Kinsella with final layout, design and proofreading. Patricia Chappine, Rudnick Fellow at the Alliance Heritage Center, assisted with final preparations for publication. Jena Brignola designed the dust jacket. Body text is set in 12-point Minion Pro.

Signature Book Printing, Inc., of Gaithersburg, Maryland, printed this book on 60# House Natural, smooth paper, 420 ppi. The signatures were gathered, Smythe-sewn, and case bound into the finished book by Signature Printing.

In May 1882, forty-three immigrant families arrived in Pittsgrove Township, New Jersey, to begin a new life. Carrying their possessions, they walked two miles from the train platform to hastily constructed barracks. They wore uncouth clothing, spoke strange languages, and exhibited foreign manners. They were mostly ignorant of agricultural pursuits, and yet these families founded the first successful Jewish farming colony in America, the Alliance Colony. The Alliance Heritage Center at Stockton University is preserving the history of Alliance. We are telling the story of the founding generation, and that of their children and their children's children. The details are both inspiring and instructive.

Alliance, N.J.
Carmel, N.J.
Norma, N.J.